Race, Trauma, and Home
in the Novels of Toni Morrison

SOUTHERN LITERARY STUDIES

Fred Hobson, Series Editor

RACE, TRAUMA, AND HOME

IN THE NOVELS OF TONI MORRISON

EVELYN JAFFE SCHREIBER

LOUISIANA STATE UNIVERSITY PRESS

BATON ROUGE

Published by Louisiana State University Press
Copyright © 2010 by Louisiana State University Press
All rights reserved
Manufactured in the United States of America
First printing

Designer: Michelle A. Neustrom
Typefaces: Arno Pro, text; Telegrafico, display
Printer: McNaughton & Gunn, Inc.
Binder: John H. Dekker & Sons

LIBRARY OF CONGRESS CATALOGING-IN-PUBLICATION DATA

Schreiber, Evelyn Jaffe, 1948–
    Race, trauma, and home in the novels of Toni Morrison / Evelyn Jaffe Schreiber.
    p. cm. — (Southern literary studies)
    Includes bibliographical references and index.
    ISBN 978-0-8071-3649-2 (clo : alk. paper) 1. Morrison, Toni—Criticism and
interpretation. 2. Morrison, Toni—Characters—Slaves. 3. Slavery in literature.
4. Home in literature. I. Title.
    PS3563.O8749Z853 2011
    813'.54—dc22

                                                              2009053714

For Scott,
who became my home
when he put his story next to mine

CONTENTS

ACKNOWLEDGMENTS

Books spring from the intersection of thought and life experiences. This project grew out of my previous critical study of Morrison's novels, *Subversive Voices: Eroticizing the Other in the Works of William Faulkner and Toni Morrison,* where I compare Faulkner's use of nostalgia to protect white culture with Morrison's exposure of the black gaze and the black struggle for subjectivity. I turned to consider the moments in Morrison's work when black characters express nostalgia and concluded that uncontrolled nostalgic memory provides psychic relief because treatment for trauma involves helping the ego to feel safe and secure by building self-esteem and social connections. To discover the source of these moments when characters turn to nostalgic memory for psychic support, I explored the psychological uses of nostalgia in subjectivity, and my research on this protective function of nostalgia brought me to the study of trauma and recovery in Morrison's novels. I examine how a concept of "home," retrieved through memory, creates and preserves a sense of self for marginalized and oppressed characters. I conclude that a concept of home is crucial to combating the levels of trauma that Morrison reveals in her novels.

My work took shape over the past few years during my formal study of trauma in classes conducted by the Washington Psychoanalytic Society, the "Psychoanalytic Theory for Scholars Program," in Washington, DC. I thank Dr. Marshall W. Alcorn Jr., who organized these classes and mentored my studies. The course readings and class discussions led me to an analysis of trauma in Morrison's novels. I am grateful to the instructors Christine G. Erskine, Dr. Ernest Wallwork, Dr. Doug Chavis, Dr. Richard Waugaman, and Dr. Arthur S. Blank Jr., as well as to class members, from my four years of coursework at the Washington Psychoanalytic Society.

Most especially, I thank Professor Toni Morrison, not only for her exquisite and inspiring novels, her Louvre exhibition, and her gracious engagement with the Toni Morrison Society but also for her generosity in discussing my project with me at conferences and for her continued validation of my work in its various stages.

Many of my colleagues at the George Washington University provided wise readings and support. In particular, I thank Marshall Alcorn for his tireless, generous, and invaluable readings of my work and his discussions with me, which helped to hone my theoretical grounding and my argument. Jim Miller, Chris Sten, Jeffrey J. Cohen, and Faye Moskowitz gave me guidance and advice.

Another scholar, Jean Wyatt, deserves mention for her inspiring psychoanalytic scholarship on Morrison and for encouraging me to pursue this study. My colleagues in the Toni Morrison Society—Carolyn Denard, Marilyn S. Mobley, Kristine Yohe, Alma Jean Billingslea, Yvonne Atkinson, Marc Conner, Maryemma Graham, Tessa Roynon, and Susan Mayberry—provided useful suggestions and support.

Many thanks go to my research assistant Christina Mueller for her thorough and insightful readings and rereadings of each chapter, as well as her assistance with the index. I also thank Sharon Cummings, Kaitlin Vignali, Nicole Welsh, Jonna Gilbert, Marissa Ciampi, and Sadaf Padder for their feedback and proofing of chapters; my graduate students Gerald Cook and Suzanne Sable for checking quotations; and students in my Morrison classes.

The feedback from Fred Hobson and my two unidentified readers was extremely useful; their conscientious suggestions helped strengthen my argument. John Easterly, at LSU Press, provided unwavering and cheerful support.

I wish to thank members of my family, near and far, for their continued support and inspiration. My gratitude to my parents is boundless, as psychoanalytic study was "written on my body" by both of them: my father, Daniel S. Jaffe, whose dedication to Freudian psychoanalysis molded my interest in psychoanalytic readings of literature, and my mother, Caroline R. Jaffe, a keen observer and interpreter of behavior whose professional career as a clinical psychologist inspired me to complete my doctoral degree. They would have appreciated the insights into children and couples that my work on trauma reveals. Special thanks go to my daughter-in-law, Tera Schreiber, for introducing me to the work of Daniel Siegel and for her lengthy discussions with me about child development. Also, I thank my sister-in-law Selina Morris for her careful and thoughtful readings of all the chapters. I am thankful to my sons, Michael and Eric, for their continuing interest and feedback about my work. Finally, I am most grateful for the "wide open and snug" love of my husband Scott, my main source of inspiration and guidance. He challenges me, sustains me, and makes all things possible.

Race, Trauma, and Home
in the Novels of Toni Morrison

Trauma, Memory, and Subjectivity

The Healing Power of "Home"

One of Toni Morrison's greatest achievements is her ability to depict what it means to be black in American society. In a culture where whiteness is the norm, black identity is marginalized, and the nuances of this marginalization suggest a range of trauma associated with black experience. Blacks in America are continually defined as "other" by mainstream culture; consequently, access to a positive, individual subjectivity unrelated to race is problematic. In her essay "Home" Morrison states,

> I have never lived, nor has any of us, in a world in which race did not matter. [...] I prefer to think of a-world-in-which-race-does-*not*-matter as [...] home. "Home" seems a suitable term because, first, it lets me make a radical distinction between the metaphor of house and the metaphor of home and helps me clarify my thoughts on racial construction. (3)

To eliminate racism from American culture, says Morrison, we need "to convert a racist house into a race-specific yet nonracist home" (5). In such a society, individual and communal racial identities could exist without the psychological burden of hatred, scapegoating, or otherness. In Morrison's fiction characters struggle for self-definition free of racial encumbrances, and time and again they rely on psychic as well as physical aspects of "home" to survive their racial trauma. Home, whether a place or a concept, retrieved through memory, provides protection from trauma. This seemingly simple statement addresses complicated, elusive terms: *self, home, trauma,* and *memory.* Each of Morrison's novels explores manifestations of self and home, building on each other to retell the story of African American trauma. While the core cultural trauma of slavery underlies each work, characters in various generations work through personal and contextual layers in unique ways. Home—the psychic support for the "self" or subjectivity —develops (or fails to do so) in connection with trauma, community, and memory. Psychoanalytic, neurobiological, and cultural and social theories help to explain the almost insurmountable task of recovery from trauma to gain subjectivity. The French psychoanalyst Jacques Lacan claims that subjectivity develops after recognition of the Real or the gaze "of the Other" in the symbolic structure that marks one as lacking (*Four* 104). Such confrontations with the Real, often experienced as trauma, can lead to one's movement from an object position to the position of a subject with agency. Specifically, the body becomes a placeholder for memory and trauma, accounting for personal and cultural behavior (of both blacks and whites) and explaining why trauma persists, transferred from one generation to another.

My analysis of this bodily component of trauma and memory, so evident in Morrison's novels, augments the now familiar aspects of trauma studies, such as the importance of verbalizing trauma and the need for an empathetic witness to hear the trauma story if one is to recover.[1] Another area of trauma research discusses the role of adequate mothering to protect against trauma, and my analysis considers the fundamental impact of attachment.[2] Finally, much has been written about the need for community support for trauma survivors.[3] However, these studies fail to explore what I consider the crucial neurobiological aspects at trauma's core and how they interact with the psychological structures that determine behavior. Trauma, whether initiated by physical abuse, dehumanization, discrimination, exclusion, or abandonment, becomes embedded in both psychic and bodily circuits. Psychoanalytic theory and neurobiological studies explore the difficulty of the recovery process, given the psychological structures and bodily components. My discussion expands prior considerations of trauma by investigating the generational transmission of trauma despite parental or communal attempts to erase it. Attachment theory adds to our understanding of trauma. Morrison's novels depict how these deeply embedded aspects of trauma perpetuate trauma in successive generations, and I enlarge the critical discussions of Morrison's work by analyzing the difficulties involved in recovery, employing theories of attachment, separation anxiety, and neurobiology, in addition to cultural and psychological dynamics, to suggest how societies and individuals experience and work through the trauma of difference in concrete ways. This interdisciplinary approach brings together the social, bodily, psychological, and racial aspects of trauma in a literary analysis of Morrison's novels.

Lacan's work in particular explains how identity stems from social interactions or encounters with an imagined "gaze of the Other" (*Four* 84). Unfortunately, cultural ideology constructs subjectivity, and the positive gaze necessary to establish subjectivity does not exist in the white, patriarchal symbolic structure for black Americans. How can a white racist culture, bodily repeating the ideology that composes its legacy, provide the compassionate and empathetic listener necessary for healing? If aggression and projection to protect the self are almost reflexive responses, how does society move beyond inter- and intraracial violence and strife? Trauma and recovery are complicated, layered processes for all individuals because both personal and cultural memory reactivate past experiences stored in bodily circuits. Hope for agency lies in coming to terms with how the body stores trauma.

Black Americans, as Morrison shows in adept and nuanced ways, suffer from specific historical, contextual, and inherited trauma. She claims that her work functions as "an unblinking witness to the light and shade of the world we live in" ("The Future of Time," qtd. in Denard, *What Moves* 185) and as such presents a study of human weakness and resiliency through characters who experience the crises of black lives from different angles: slaves, former slaves, children, orphans, women, expatriates, fathers, mothers—dark and light-toned, poverty-stricken and affluent, rural and urban.[4] Morrison's Nobel Lecture, like her novels, examines "What it is to have no home in this place. To be set adrift from the one you knew. What it is to live at the edge of towns that cannot bear your company" (*Lecture* 28–29). Specifically, she teases out the lasting effects of slavery's transplantation in the orphaned, abandoned, and othered souls that populate her novels. A more complete description of trauma in black Americans precedes my discussion of trauma's psychoanalytic and bodily components.

SLAVERY'S LEGACY: BLACK AMERICAN TRAUMA

In *Playing in the Dark* Morrison describes how the white imagination creates a "fabrication of an Africanist persona" and states that "in that construction of blackness *and* enslavement could be found not only the not-free but also, with the dramatic polarity created by skin color, the projection of the not-me" (17, 38). According to Morrison, the white construction of black subjectivity produces chronic trauma for black Americans, generated by being defined as other by a racially exclusive larger culture.[5] Specifically, the "legacy of slavery led in the nineteenth century to the institution of Jim Crow laws designed to separate blacks and whites, to segregated housing and schools, to discrimination in the dispensation of justice, to the myths about interracial sex, and to economic and political oppression" (Berry and Blassingame 241). Such exclusion, according to Ron Eyerman, leads to "a dramatic loss of identity and meaning, a tear in the social fabric, affecting a group of people that has achieved some degree of cohesion," such as the collective memory of slavery (61). The rejection by white culture during and after Reconstruction "was traumatic not only because of the crushed expectations, but also because it necessitated a reevaluation of the past and its meaning regarding individual and collective identity" (80). Further, "the meaning and memory of slavery and the failure of emancipation to fully integrate American blacks would remain the point of departure of collective memory and identity formation, as the primal scene of cultural trauma" (98). Rejection through separation perpetuates trauma.[6]

Such cultural trauma, claims Jeffrey Alexander, marks a people's "memories forever and chang[es] their future identity in fundamental and irrevocable ways" (1). For example, J. Brooks Bouson describes the vestiges of slave trauma that carry over to the present:

> Morrison focuses not only on the collective memories of the trauma of slavery in works like *Beloved*, but also on the horrors of the postbellum years and of racist and urban violence [. . .]. She is intent on portraying the trauma of defective or abusive parenting or relationships and also the black-on-black violence that exists within the African-American community. (3)

Persistent social taboos that reinforce separation, especially regarding sexual relations between blacks and whites, perpetuate trauma (J. Jones 149). The experience of slavery and cultural rejection leads to "self definition by negation" (Ferguson 17). Images of black people "reinforce and reinscribe white supremacy" and lead to an "internalized racism" that results in "self-destructive rage, hatred, and paralyzing despair" (hooks, *Black Looks* 1, 4). Saidiya Hartman also examines the difficulty of becoming a subject when all ways to define a human are denied. Babacar M'Baye further argues "that the invention of whiteness as a hegemonic identity that is antithetical to Blackness is the major obstacle to successful cross-racial relationships in the United States" (184). In explaining intraracial problems, Candice Jenkins claims that "early black nationalist figures often covertly (or overtly) embraced aspects of white culture" and thus "ultimately evidenced contempt for the very blackness they worked to preserve" (276). Patterns of cultural behavior toward race relations born in slavery persist.

The impact of the white perspective is evident in many early slave narratives. Although these writings formed initial attempts to articulate the black experience, "to create a counterdiscourse to the official documents of slaveowners and their specious claims about the benevolence of the institution," they failed to confront the horrific core of the slave experience (Peterson 21). By romanticizing personal narratives for acceptance by white culture, the slave narrative forged a literary convention that denied the traumatic aspects of slavery by "downplay[ing] its reality and its effects" (McDowell and Rampersad, Introduction xii). Essentially, by erasing the "witnesses" to slavery's brutality, such slave narratives reinforced white versions of slavery. Morrison's writings in particular subvert this genre to split open slavery's traumatic essence. Keith Byerman describes how Morrison reconstructs a past that is "beyond rationalist discourse(s) of historiography and social analysis," revealing the "psychological and social effects of suffering" (*Remembering* 3). As survival narratives, her novels can be read as "trauma stories [. . .] of both tremendous loss and survival," stories that "replicate black abjection" (3, 5). To counter the silences of slave narratives, "*Beloved* dramatically registers the violence done to motherhood and mothering by the slave system" (Peterson 29). In this novel Morrison represents "that which could not have ever been recorded by the slave in writing" (Simpson 52) and presents "the unhealed psychic wound that America suffers in the wake of slavery" (Sabol 7).[7] Slavery's trauma forms the kernel of collective identity and individual memory, playing out in successive generations. Gwen Bergner describes how in *Beloved*, "[m]emories of slavery bleed into the present to influence the present lives of the former slaves—a process analogous to the way that the legacy of slavery shapes our contemporary culture" (113). Further, the "damage done to an individual subject carries a certain historic force. The physical presence of these memory-images is the cultural work slavery performs, even after abolition" (114).

W. E. B. Du Bois describes this internalization of social structures, saying that an African American is

a sort of seventh son, born with a veil, and gifted with second-sight in this American world,—a world which yields him no true self-consciousness, but only lets him see himself through the revelation of the other world. It is a peculiar sensation, this double-consciousness, this sense of always looking at one's self through the eyes of others [whites] [. . .] two unreconciled strivings [. . . and] longing [. . .] to merge his double self into a better and truer self. In this merging he wishes neither of the older selves to be lost. [. . .] He simply wishes to make it possible for a man to be both a Negro and an American. (3)

The internalization and awareness of social identity in black subjectivity highlights the psychic component of culture in that this double-consciousness presents an ever-present gaze of the Other.[8] Yet this awareness of self as other can sometimes lead those on the margin to differentiate between the master narrative and their own desire. For example, Patricia McKee describes how "Morrison's black American cultures struggle to claim the spaces of their existence, their culture, and their history that whites have seen as empty. [. . .] Given the constructions of meaning available in white culture, they can find their places only by refusing to use those constructions as given" (25). Morrison's fiction presents characters who struggle to escape white constructions of black identity.[9]

Another layer of black trauma incorporates the specific causes and consequences of the black mourning process. In *African American Grief*, Paul Rosenblatt and Beverly Wallace discuss how the persistence of discrimination leads to premature deaths for black Americans. Consequently, the mourning process occurs at a young age, "when one is rather short on experiential, cognitive, emotional, financial, social, spiritual, and other resources for dealing with a loss, understanding one's own grief and the grief of others, facing the mortality of loved ones, and facing personal mortality" (6). Anger and resentment mix with this early grieving process because many deaths are unnecessary, resulting from poverty, poor health care and living conditions, denial of services, or dangerous military or work assignments. Therefore, "emotions associated with racism and discrimination may be entangled in feelings of grief [. . . and] may include anger, rage, moral indignation, despair, and vengefulness" (18). Each grieving process renews the wounds and pain of slave trauma. Verbalization of loss, while necessary for recovery, raises complicated emotional responses. In particular, grieving reactivates the loss of family ties, and these "losses and incomplete knowledge—particularly in terms of origins—are a central part of the legacy of slavery" (Ubois 170).

Echoes of slavery erupt in varying ways. One by-product is the difficulty of developing relationships that require trust and interactions with others because slaves have experienced the "inability to conceive of love dissociated from the paradigm of ownership and a reluctance to love wholeheartedly. [. . .] For slaves, who literally do not own themselves, intermingling of identities is particularly threatening to the sense of self" (Bate 41). In *Beloved* Sethe ponders this dilemma when she says, "Freeing yourself was one thing; claiming ownership of that freed self was another" (95).[10] Indeed, "ownership marks the experience of being a slave [. . .]—the experience of being raced, dehumanized, or made property" (Franco 426). Slave ownership forms a major influence on black identity because "[s]elf-hood is impossible when one does not own oneself" (Raynaud 53). Black men, in their dehumanized role of property, had particular difficulty adopting new roles. Nancy Peterson comments that with "the severe constraints the system of slavery placed upon black men, we might wonder how, or if, they could preserve any sense of themselves as autonomous individuals, as men, as lovers and husbands, as fathers, and as sons" (63). In her work on Morrison's representation of masculine figures, Susan Mayberry concludes that the lack of "the ability to choose and be chosen by loved ones remains an important by-product of slavery for the African American community" (*Can't I Love* 198).

As Genevieve Fabre and Robert O'Meally point out, "The legacy of slavery [, . . .] racism and prejudice have meant that even the most optimistic black Americans are, as the expression goes, 'born knowing' that there is a wide gulf between America's promises and practices" (3). Yet, "[a]dmitting and exploring the reality of slavery is necessarily painful for a black American, but only by doing so can he or she begin to understand himself or herself and American and Afro-American culture in general" (Rampersad 123). Morrison's novels chronicle how each generation processes slavery's traumatic residue. In order to unravel how race complicates slavery's legacy, in the following discussion I consider the psychoanalytic, ideological, and bodily components at work.

PSYCHOANALYSIS AND TRAUMA

In her groundbreaking *Psychoanalysis and Black Novels,* Claudia Tate discusses how "psychoanalysis can tell us much about the complicated social workings of race in the United States and the representations of these workings in the literature of African Americans" (5).[11] She explores the complicated relationship between ideology and identity. Marshall Alcorn Jr. explains that the connection between socially constructed identity and ideology accounts for the blind repetition of communal behavior:

The human subject is an entity *subjected* by discourse to ideology. [...] Something within a subject operates to preserve and maintain a characteristic identity. [...] These modes of discourse serve as symptoms of subjectivity: they work repetitively and defensively to represent identity. [...] Lacanian theory suggests that subjects, in their adhesive attachment to discourse, defend and tenaciously repeat the symptoms of their subjectivity. [...] Subjects would often rather suffer from a bad ideology than suffer from changing their ideology. (9, 17, 18, 28)

People are born into a community discourse that socially constructs their identity, and "'master signifiers' [...] function as bearers of our identity" (Bracher 23). In southern culture, "whiteness" is the defining master signifier that represents the subject. This interconnection between ideology and subjectivity underlies the complicated structure of trauma in Morrison's novels.

Psychoanalytic theory considers trauma in terms of the ego and life experiences. That is, in psychoanalytic terms, a paralysis of the ego results in insecurity from some ego injury that leaves the individual without a way to manage anxiety. Arnold Cooper claims that "a psychic trauma is any psychological event which abruptly overwhelms the ego's capacity to provide a minimal sense of safety and integrative intactness, resulting in overwhelming anxiety or helplessness, or the threat of it, and producing an enduring change in the psychic organization" (44). Similarly, Sidney Furst suggests that "[i]n trauma the ego is overwhelmed and put out of action [...]. Trauma represents a failure of the psychic apparatus to perform what may be considered its basic function—that of mediating between the organism and its needs on the one hand, and [...] stimuli which impinge on it, on the other" (30). Thus, trauma results from a lacking protective function, and treatment for trauma involves helping the ego to feel safe and secure. Further, Judith Herman claims that "traumatic events generally involve threats to life or bodily integrity, or a close personal encounter with violence and death. They confront human beings with the extremities of helplessness and terror, and evoke responses of catastrophe" (33). Traumatic events leave people feeling abandoned, "cast out of the human and divine systems of care and protection that sustain life" (52). Abandonment is a prominent theme in Morrison's novels.

Some psychiatrists "label as 'traumatic' the absence of adequate loving, the failure to support the child's self-esteem efforts, failure to supply adequate sensory and cognitive stimuli, and other failures. The tendency of these researchers is to use the term *trauma* as a reference to a deleterious environment, rather than to a disturbing event" (Cooper 50). In other words, people experience trauma not just from specific traumatic events but also from their physical environment and support systems. These elements form key concepts in Morrison's novels, where the individual, family, and culture intersect. Mental and physical re-creations of home perform a protective function by supplying a sense of adequate loving and self-esteem in the midst of material deprivation.

Cooper elaborates that "secure self-esteem and a solid sense of social ties tend to be protective against the effects of trauma," and "[m]astery requires an active affective reliving of the traumatic event with sustained social support" (49, 55). Thus family and community ties build self-esteem to protect against trauma. For example, research shows that withstanding battle trauma depends on two things: "(1) self-esteem, and (2) a sense of belonging to a group and of well-being in it" (Furst 36). Morrison's work intricately depicts how home, family, and community can moderate trauma and, as a result, self-esteem. Specifically, such trauma surfaces for Sethe, Paul D, Baby Suggs, and Denver in *Beloved;* Pecola, Pauline, and Cholly in *The Bluest Eye;* Violet, Joe, and Dorcas in *Jazz;* Jadine and Son in *Tar Baby;* and Helene, Eva, Hannah, Sula, and Nel in *Sula.*

In addition, according to Furst, "vulnerability to trauma and the effects of trauma will vary depending on the period of life during which the trauma occurs" (35). That is, "[a]dults are less vulnerable to trauma than children because they have a longer path to regress before reaching a state of helplessness. [. . .] In more severe trauma, the greatest danger is that of separation from or loss of parents, which, of course, stems from the child's dependence" (36–37). Thus, the vulnerability of children renders them in greater need of parental and community care or the safety of home. Morrison's characters who are traumatized as children carry their trauma into adulthood, as we see in Nel, her mother, and Sula in *Sula;* Connie and the other women in *Paradise;* Cholly and Pauline in *The Bluest Eye;* Macon, Guitar, and Ruth in *Song of Solomon;* Son and Jadine in *Tar Baby;* Joe, Violet, and Dorcas in *Jazz;* Christine, Heed, and Junior in *Love;* and Florens, Sorrow, and Rebekka in *A Mercy.* As a defense, "traumatized children develop ways of mental functioning designed to prevent the return of the helpless or hopeless state of traumatization" (McDougall 138). Unfortunately, these compensations are often harmful to the individual or the community, as Morrison's novels so aptly capture through such memorable characters as Sula, Guitar, Macon, Cholly, Beloved, Joe, Violet, Christine, Heed, Gigi, Steward, K.D., and Son.

Trauma victims, who feel helpless and unsafe and have low self-esteem, experience trauma after the event and in varying forms. Cathy Caruth describes trauma as "a response, sometimes delayed, to an overwhelming event or events, which takes the form of repeated, intrusive hallucinations, dreams, thoughts or behaviors stemming from the event, along with numbing that may have begun during or after the experience, and possibly also increased arousal to (and avoidance of) stimuli recalling the event" (*Trauma* 4). She pinpoints the conflicting aspects of trauma: its repetitive intrusion and its repressed numbing of the event. That is, trauma gets either reenacted or repressed; "we only know retrospectively whether or not it was shattering" (Cooper 51). Apparently, each person responds to and acts out trauma in his or her own way. The opposing philosophies and actions of Macon and Pilate Dead in *Song of Solomon* attest to this theory, with Macon manifesting greed, hostility, and lack of empathy in contrast to Pilate's generosity, caring, and connectedness.

Like Caruth, Bessel Van der Kolk and Onno Van der Hart find that "traumatic memories of the arousing events may return as physical sensations, horrific images or nightmares, behavioral reenactments, or a combination of these" (164). Uncontrollable repressed trauma surfaces in various ways, often to protect the survivor. Recognition of trauma comes in stages, with each symptom aiding the acknowledgment necessary for recovery. Integrating the brutality of trauma with its incomprehensibility is necessary "both for the sake of testimony and for the sake of cure" (Caruth, *Trauma* 153). Morrison's characters continually vacillate between repressing and revisiting trauma in their attempts to verbalize and move beyond it. Verbalization helps combat trauma, for it is only "by telling stories, narratives that inevitably appropriate the past and help the community learn to live into their future" that people work through trauma (Foster 746).[12]

In writing about survivors of the Holocaust, Dori Laub and Dominick LaCapra discuss the need for empathetic listeners to witness and thus validate a survivor's trauma. Such a witness can heal the erasure of history. Laub explains that the "testimony is, therefore, the process by which the narrator (the survivor) reclaims his position as a witness: reconstitutes the internal 'thou,' and thus the possibility of a witness or listener inside himself" ("An Event" 85). This act of testimony needs to occur "in a dialogic context and with an authentic listener, which allows for a reconciliation with the broken promise, and which makes the resumption of life, in spite of the failed promise, at all possible" (91). Verbalizing trauma allows one "to know one's buried truth in order to live one's life" (78).

Yet like slavery's unspeakable essence, trauma carries "the impossibility of tell-ing" and thus leads to silence (79). "[O]nly when the survivor knows he is being heard, will he stop to hear—and listen to—himself" ("Bearing Witness" 71).[13] Thus, working through trauma results from being able to talk about traumatic events. Such a verbalization can lead to a "mourning [. . .] and a proper burial," which would restore "to victims the dignity denied them by their victimizers" (LaCapra 66).[14] However, on a psychological level, letting go of trauma some-times may feel like a "betray[al] of lost loved ones" (70). Thus, the assistance of a witness is crucial.

Unfortunately, American culture has failed to integrate the slave experience so as to perform the witness function. The erasure of black experience by white culture in essence erases any witnesses to the horrors of slavery. Morrison's nov-els serve the witness function.[15] Herman's work with trauma details the stages of recovery as "establishing safety, reconstructing the trauma story, and restor-ing the connection between survivors and their community" (3). In Morrison's novels community, family, and other connections create the psychic support or home that can allow characters to safely relive trauma and survive it.[16] Baby Suggs's meetings in The Clearing in *Beloved* constitute a striking example of a community's efforts to heal.

ANOTHER LAYER OF TRAUMA: THE BODY SPEAKS

In addition to the psychological contributions to trauma, bodily components store and perpetuate traumatic events and sensations. Caruth concludes that "[w]hat causes trauma, then, is a shock that appears to work very much like a bodily threat" and that "[w]hat is passed on, finally, is not just the meaning of the words but their performance" (*Unclaimed* 61, 111). Her work explains the visceral nature of trauma; embedded in the body, its performance passes from individual to individual and from generation to generation. Researchers have studied this bodily and transferable aspect of trauma and how it creates a troublesome cycle of inherited behavior. For example, the work of Erik Hesse and Mary Main elabo-rates the transfer of trauma unknowingly from otherwise "good" parents who do not maltreat their children:

[A]s a result of [his or her] own traumatic experiences or frightening ideation [. . . a parent] sporadically alarms the infant via the exhibition of frightened, dissociated, or anomalous forms of threatening behavior. We suggest that spurious but ongoing interactions of this kind can occur even when a parent is normally sensitive and responsive to the infant, and can lead in turn to the infant's inability to remain organized under stress. (483)

In other words, good parents who experience trauma place their infants at risk through their behavioral response to trauma. In turn, infants who are frightened by their parents are "in an irresolvable, disorganizing and disorienting paradox in which impulses to approach the parent as the infant's 'haven of safety' will inevitably conflict with impulses to flee from the parent as a source of alarm" (484). This "situation [of] fright without solution [. . . results] in a collapse of behavioral and attentional strategies" (484). Fear of a parent who acts out unresolved frightening experiences jeopardizes the infant's ability to feel safe and regulate fear (485). In *Beloved,* Denver both loves Sethe and fears that what "made it all right for my mother to kill my sister could happen again" (205). If, as current research suggests, "attachment behavior is now viewed as the central mechanism regulating infant safety, and maintenance of proximity to attachment figures is understood to be the *sine qua non* of [. . .] infant survival," children attached to traumatized parents will be overwhelmed with a sense of fear and impending harm (Hesse and Main 493). Thus, attachment theory proposes "the powerful indirect influence of events which occurred in the previous generation and [have] become associated with anomalous fears, fantasies and ideation" (531). Examining attachment theory's interaction with trauma studies provides insight into individual and group suffering and recovery. Cultural and familial circumstances dictate either the continued repetition of trauma or the ability to re-create the self. Morrison's characters provide good examples of how people inherit and pass on trauma, as well as how their early attachment experiences influence behavior and social interaction.

According to Mauricio Cortina and Giovanni Liotti, the "basic function of attachment is to seek protection and care in moments of distress," and "[t]he fundamental developmental task in infancy is the establishment of a secure attachment" (3). When the parenting function suffers due to inconsistency or insensitivity, faulty attachment results, with children suffering the consequences. Joan Woodward reports that children with "'insecure attachments' [. . .] can feel themselves deeply alienated from the rest of society. Such feelings make them highly vulnerable to further abuse, inflicted either by themselves, or by others"

(16). The protective function of a mother's bond necessitates proximity to her children, as shown in the studies of children separated from their parents during wartime. Although the children were sent away for their safety, the children only felt emotionally safe with their mothers. Thus, they suffered trauma in the "safety" of their foster homes. Other studies show the traumatic impact when children in hospitals are separated from their parents (J. Woodward 17).

Separation anxiety also can surface as a result of poor attachment, resulting in a child's concern about "personal safety and injury [. . .], being alone [. . .], and sleeping alone" (Eisen and Schaefer 3). Studies show that youngsters in particular "cling to safe persona, places, transitional objects, or actions during anticipated separations" (13). Forced separations and insecure living arrangements compound this anxiety. Rose Dear and May, in *Jazz,* suffer when their mother, True Belle, unwillingly deserts them to follow her mistress and care for Golden Gray. In turn, Golden Gray clings to True Belle, replaying his attachment to her as he seeks out his father and stays with Wild. Pecola, in *The Bluest Eye,* lacks any safe place or parent, as both her community and her parents reject her. The three factors that contribute to her sense of safety and well-being are "biological (temperament, anxiety sensitivity), psychological (attachment), and environmental (separation-anxious events) vulnerabilities" (Eisen and Schaefer 22). The linking of an individual's self-esteem with inherited traits (biological), familial attachment (psychological), and cultural discrimination and taboos (environmental) explains many of the actions in Morrison's novels.

While Morrison's characters suffer on these multiple levels, the texts explore avenues for social change. She explains that she mines images from her family and community history as a "route to a reconstruction of a world, to an exploration of an interior life that was not written and to the revelation of a kind of truth" and "to fill in the blanks that the slave narratives left—to part the veil that was so frequently drawn" ("Site of Memory" 115, 113). Writing about real lives "is also critical for any person who is black, or who belongs to any marginalized category, for, historically, we were seldom invited to participate in the discourse even when we were its topic" (110–11). Morrison claims to write "village literature, fiction that is really for the village, for the tribe," believing that her works "should clarify the roles that have become obscured; they ought to identify those things in the past that are useful and those things that are not; and they ought to give nourishment" ("The Language Must Not Sweat," qtd. in Denard, *What Moves* xiii). Her novels are imbued with the culture and the life stories of real people at real times in history. It is always some narrative told to her, some value passed down, some event remembered, some person in her community, some newspaper story or artifact revealing an essential truth about the lives of Black people in this country that ignites her imagination. [. . .] each novel is also an artistic commentary on life and history reaching beyond the story told at the center of the text. (Denard, *What Moves* xiii–xiv)

Morrison asserts that literature takes on a political and social role in the altering of future lives when it can present "an informed vision [of optimism] based on harrowing experience that nevertheless gestures toward a redemptive future" and that "the milieu from which this vision rises" is "race inflected, gendered, colonized, displaced, hunted" (Morrison, "The Future of Time" qtd. in Denard, *What Moves* 185).

One of the most disturbing barriers to changing lives is the connection between early trauma, attachment issues, and brain development. Allan Schore finds that "the early social environment, mediated by the primary caregiver, directly influences the final wiring of the circuits in the infant brain that are responsible for the future social and emotional coping capabilities of the individual," concluding that brain development is tied to early interactive experiences with both the mother and the father (112). Daniel Siegel concurs, noting that "communication within attachment relationships is the primary experience that regulates and organizes the development of those circuits in the brain that mediate self-regulation and social relatedness. A sense of self emerges directly from self-other interactions" ("An Interpersonal" 31).[17] Given that "the same system that is shaped by the attachment relationship regulates aggression" as well as empathy, early developmental attachment relationships are crucial to a child's later ability to relate positively to others (Schore 122). Schore reports that "infants who experience abuse and/or neglect and little interactive repair are at high risk for developing aggression dysregulation in later stages of life. [. . .] Children maltreated as toddlers are more angry, hyperactive, distractible, inattentive, noncompliant, and aggressive in preschool and kindergarten" (127, 138). One hopeful finding is that although "the brain is hardwired to take in signals from the social environment to alter its own internal states" and "the mind is created in the interaction between neurophysiological processes and interpersonal relationships" (Siegel, "An Interpersonal" 9), with individual and community nurturing neural hardwiring *can* be reversed later in life (Siegel, "Attachment" 29–30). As Morrison expresses in both her fiction and her nonfiction, the social ramifications of individual and communal caretaking are enormous.

Siegel explains behavior on the biological level, where "experience (the activation of neural firing patterns) can activate genes (thus leading to protein production) and therefore change brain structure. [. . .] When overwhelmingly stressful experiences occur, the brain may respond with excessive cortisol secretion which, if sustained, can lead to neuronal cell death" ("An Interpersonal" 17). The social and personal intersect as individual experiences in a cultural environment influence private development. Accordingly, environment, experience, and interpersonal relationships can seriously impair neuronal development and can lead to problematic social interactions at a future point in time. The damaging system of slavery routinely separated children from their parents, interfering with the process of attachment and mothering. Andrea O'Reilly calls this the severing of the "motherline," including its traditional and cultural properties and ancestral memories (*Toni Morrison* 11).

This separation also interferes with the formation of supportive memories, which can assuage traumatic ones. Van der Kolk's research shows that "[t]he fundamental function of memory is the creation of particular connections between the neuronal groups, which enables people to get around in the world" (244). Further, the "memory of the trauma [. . .] acts like a foreign body which long after its entry must be regarded as an agent that is still at work. [. . .] Some memories seem to become fixed in the mind and remain unaltered by the passage of time. [. . .] traumatic scenes were reexperienced over years and decades, seemingly without modification" (244). According to Allan Young, the neurological traces that are left from these memory experiences develop so that "at the moment of remembrance and reenactment" memory can fuse "the ancestral past and the experienced present" (93). Trauma victims seek to repeat these experiences because the endorphins released in the repetition produce a tranquillizing effect and reduce "feelings of anxiety, depression, and inadequacy. [. . .] Over time people would become addicted both to their endorphins and to the memories that release these chemicals" (95). In this way the body attaches to trauma.

Thus, "bodily memory installs a second narrative and also a second system of accounting—one whose elements are reduced to fear, anger, and pain" (Young 99). To reverse the bodily effects of traumatic experiences, new experiences that counter helplessness are necessary. That is, "[t]raumatized individuals need to have experiences that directly contradict the emotional helplessness and physical paralysis that accompany traumatic experiences" (Van der Kolk 255). Further, such "[m]astery requires an active affective reliving of the traumatic event with sustained social support" (Cooper 55). Therefore, retelling and remembering the trauma within a supportive community enables trauma victims to move forward. Morrison's novels explore how loving relationships with individuals and communities assist in this creation of self.

The vulnerability of both parents and children results in a seemingly endless repetition of trauma, where cultural dynamics compound personal experience. Vamik Volkan's work on large-group dynamics elaborates how "transgenerational transmission of massive trauma [. . .] is the end result of mostly unconscious psychological processes by which survivors *deposit* into their progeny's core identities their own injured self-images" (48). For example, in Morrison's *Paradise* people in Ruby define themselves in connection with their forefathers' traumatic "Disallowing." In doing so they exhibit how "[b]y sharing this image of their ancestors' trauma, a new generation of the group is unconsciously knit together [. . .]; what is essential is this marker's unseen power to link the members of the group together in a persistent sense of sameness through history" (Volkan 49). Parental transmission of trauma leads to a cohesive subgroup identity that can carry insurmountable negative self-images.

Fortunately, later nurturing relationships with individuals and groups can repair early deficits. Siegel's research indicates that "while experience shapes who we are, we are *not* destined to repeat the traumas of our past *if* we make sense of their impact on our lives. [. . .] Becoming the author of one's own life story is the ongoing goal of the making-sense process" ("Attachment" 31–32). Pilate in *Song of Solomon* exemplifies the ability to reshape one's life in this way. A supportive community can aid this process for traumatized adults and, consequently, assist in the attachments and adjustment of trauma in their children. Positive experiences can reverse neuronal damage because "experience leads to neural firing that can activate genes that then lead to the production of proteins that enable the formation of new synaptic connections" (Siegel, "Attachment" 29–30). In *Beloved*, Denver's positive interactions with Lady Jones and Janey Wagon illustrate the power of social connection to build a positive sense of self.

LACAN AND HOME: SUBJECTIVITY

Lacan's theory of subjectivity further explains this process of creating a sense of self. In Morrison's black communities, race relations produce and perpetuate inherited parental trauma stemming from a history of slavery and discrimination. Lacan accounts for the trauma that begins in the mirror stage and continues with the debilitating gaze of the Other. Briefly, Lacan suggests that a subject is born into the Real as a "body in pieces" or a fragmented self (*Seminar* 54). During what Lacan calls the mirror stage, the subject visualizes an imaginary self that reflects a perfect, unified, totalized image. When the mirror stage ends, the subject's apparent wholeness begins to dissolve. The subject's sense of unity crumbles because the imaginary wholeness is a virtual one, always being interrupted by outside forces. Social and cultural forces form the organizing structure outside of the self that Lacan calls the symbolic structure (*Écrits* 2–4). In this structure, language and laws or codes of society divide the self and establish it as a subject of lack that seeks to recapture a sense of wholeness. Lacan states that "[w]hat determines me, at the most profound level [. . .] is the gaze that is outside. [. . .] The Other" (*Four* 106, 130).

This gaze upends the imaginary whole image of the self, and as a result, according to Lacan, the divided subject constantly seeks the fictional unified self of the mirror stage. To encounter the Other's gaze or Lacan's Real is to encounter one's "own nothingness" (92). Therefore, to avoid fragmentation, the subject tries to avoid encounters with the Real and seeks the establishment of a coherent sense of self through recognition from the outside world (Lacan's symbolic structure). Nurturing attachments facilitate such recognition by providing self-esteem and a sense of safety. Concepts of home—the creation of a positive self-image—deflect encounters with Lacan's Real. In his groundbreaking and much-cited work *Black Skins, White Masks,* Frantz Fanon, a psychoanalyst from the Antilles who endorses Lacan, describes by relating his own experiences the black man's objectification by white culture: "The goal of his behavior will be The Other (in the guise of the white man), for The Other alone can give him worth" (154). Identification with whiteness results from the desire to be recognized as an authentic self. Pecola and Pauline in *The Bluest Eye* exemplify this phenomenon.

For Morrison's characters, lack of such recognition from white culture increases trauma or unmanageable anxiety. In essence, the mirror stage is a complicated stage for black identity because blacks must identify with whiteness in order to have a "lovable bodily ego" (Silverman 19). Kaja Silverman explains this paradox, saying that "the mirror stage represents a *méconnaissance* [or misrecognition], because the subject identifies with what he or she is not," even while the subject sees "literally his or her own image" (10–11). The unified self of the imaginary stage is difficult when society values whiteness, because "only certain subjects have access to a flattering image of self, and [. . .] others have imposed upon them an image so deidealizing that no one would willingly identify with it" (29). bell hooks describes the task of self-definition for blacks in white society as complicated by this self-hatred, stemming from the "contradictory longing to possess the reality of the Other, even though that reality is one that wounds and negates" (*Killing* 33).[18] When blacks internalize white "negative perceptions of blackness," self-hatred and deidealization result (32).

Fanon describes this process when he claims that the colonized "becomes whiter as he renounces his blackness, his jungle" (18). In psychoanalytic terms, Fanon claims that "[i]n the man of color there is a constant effort to run away from his own individuality, to annihilate his own presence" (60). According to Fanon, he will "suffer from not being a white man to the degree that the white man imposes discrimination on me, makes me a colonized native, robs me of all worth, all individuality, tells me that I am a parasite on the world" (98). His attempts to be white are efforts to "compel the white man to acknowledge that I am human" (98). In a society that perpetuates racism in order for the white race to feel superior, blacks try to achieve whiteness to gain recognition. Fanon describes the trauma created by white culture when he states that a "normal Negro child, having grown up within a normal family, will become abnormal on the slightest contact with the white world" (143).

Charles Brenner defines this experience of turning hatred against an oppressor onto the self as a "defense mechanism [. . .] called [. . .] *turning against the self*" (103). We see Morrison's characters searching for a coherent self that the mirror and the symbolic structure do not provide. Kalpana Seshadri-Crooks describes this process, claiming that "[w]hiteness, as the inaugural term of difference, is the primary signifier of the symbolic order of race" (25). Lack of whiteness and thus no recognition of a coherent self in the symbolic order leads to the trauma that Lacan describes as taking shape in the gaze of the Other and serves as an encounter with the Real. Subjectivity disintegrates because this gaze reveals a fundamental nothingness, undermining the illusion of control and creating trauma (*Four* 75). Bombardment by ongoing encounters with Lacan's Real—the whiteness of the Other and one's own lack in its presence—perpetuates fragmentation, fear, and trauma for black characters.

Priscilla Wald analyzes how the official stories of a culture—its ideology—shape identity so that our national story limits black identity because it is written from the white perspective. The national narrative distorts reality because "characters' internalization of cultural conventions and imperatives further limit the tales they can tell," resulting in a sense of "alienation" and "self estrangement" (11, 178). Lacan describes how this narrative is defined through history and welded to the past, reinforcing structures of repetition and repression. Characters repeat past patterns of a cultural symbolic order based on southern patriarchy. Lacan suggests that enjoyment comes from the repetition of the past because doing so represses the anxiety of lack.[19] The repression of lack gives rise to desire, which can drive subjects to repeat outmoded and even dangerous behavior or, in more open conditions, lead to changes in signification. Lacan explains the connection between desire and lack as follows:

> Desire is a relation of being to lack. [. . .] It isn't the lack of this or that, but lack of being whereby the being exists. [. . .] Being comes into existence as an exact function of this lack. Being attains a sense of self in relation to being as a function of this lack, in the experience of desire. [. . .] Relations between human beings are really established before one gets to the domain of consciousness. It is desire which achieves the primitive structuration of the human world, desire as unconscious. (*Seminar* 223–24)

Thus, desire—arising from a sense of lack—structures a subject's socially constructed unconscious. Lacan describes the perpetuation of the cultural symbolic structure as "the discourse of the circuit in which I am integrated. I am one of its links. It is the discourse of my father for instance, in so far as my father made mistakes which I am absolutely condemned to reproduce [. . .]. I am condemned to reproduce them because I am obliged to pick up again the discourse he bequeathed me" (*Seminar* 89). Historical past and place produce and maintain one's cultural symbolic structure.

Lacan's Real reveals that the unprotected ego needs support from the symbolic structure to ward off anxiety. When the symbolic structure fails to provide such support, the insecure ego responds on both the communal and the individual level. As already mentioned, discrimination and segregation produce trauma for marginalized groups, and individual members pass trauma on to future generations. The need for a positive self-image in response to the negative gaze of the Other is related not only to racial discrimination but also to generational poverty. Personal trauma reflects specifically deprived family and community situations.

Thus, Lacan's Real surfaces when race, class, and community factors interfere with imaginary wholeness. Slavoj Žižek defines Lacan's Real as "a traumatic place which causes a series of failures," as "the void place of the subject [. . .] a certain limit which is always missed" (*Sublime* 173). James Berger concurs that traumas "mark the place of the Lacanian Real" (208). For black Americans, the inability to attain whiteness blocks an imaginary wholeness that would support a positive sense of self.

The cultural symbolic structure of southern patriarchy accounts for the persistence of an ideology tied to a historical past, whether or not that ideology is currently appropriate or effective. Only when this unconscious desire—the cultural symbolic structure—is understood to be the irrational desire of one's culture can one reevaluate it in order to discover one's own desire. Lacan suggests that individuals enact change when they become what I call "subjects of knowledge"; that is, they recognize that they are meaningless links in the signifying chain, blindly acting out a master signifier. Such recognition alters subjectivity by bringing into focus the cultural symptom of the master signifier (e.g., racism). When symptoms (attachment patterns related to the past) pass into speech, they can to some extent be reconfigured in the symbolic order. Reconfiguration occurs through acknowledgment or verbalization of how the gaze of the Other makes one an object and confines one to a prescribed role in society. Lacan states: "That the subject should come to recognize and to name his desire, that is the efficacious action of analysis. [. . .] In naming it, the subject creates, brings forth, a new presence in the world" (*Seminar* 228–29). Only by reconfiguring one's relationship to culture's desire and its implied lack can one let go of a dysfunctional system and create a new cultural or personal structure.

Both personal memory and cultural memory, lodged in the body, can activate trauma or Lacan's Real. However, nostalgic memory serves a protective function, providing a sense of imaginary fulfillment. Within Lacan's system, nostalgia (triggered by memory) represents a momentary fulfillment of an imaginary completeness. Memory, through the re-creation of imaginary wholeness, functions to fill a lack created in the symbolic order and social structure, and many of Morrison's characters revert to nostalgia for this psychic support. In this way, home functions as the positive gaze that the social structure does not provide. This positive gaze is a response to a lack in the symbolic structure and can support subjectivity, giving the black subject the agency to construct a self. Thus, the Real—equated with trauma—evokes a contrasting protective memory of a sufficient self that can give the subject agency. Home, then, connects to positive identity, a sense of self. It is fragile and shifting, yet it comes from a positive gaze that family and community can provide. It is constantly undercut not only by the symbolic structure, whose ideology erodes identity, but also by the bodily inherited trauma that bombards and overwhelms the subject. Subservient groups, and individuals in them, must process trauma to survive; reconstructed memory becomes a vehicle to protect the ego and support awareness of self. Cultural memory interacts with personal experience to shape subjectivity.

CULTURAL MEMORY: THE BODY FACTOR

Erik Erikson links the psychoanalytic with the cultural when he describes the mutual relationship between self and other, with subjectivity possessing both "a sustained feeling of inner sameness within oneself [. . . and at the same time] a persistent sharing of some kind of essential character with others" (qtd. in Volkan 32). Volkan elaborates that the "sense of identity that [. . .] individuals are terrified of losing and are driven to replace is [. . .] their 'core identity.' One's core identity provides one with an integrated self related to one's community. The loss of one's core identity is intolerable—it is psychological death" (32–33). According to Salman Akhtar, this core identity also represents "an inner solidarity with one's group and its ideals" (qtd. in Volkan 32). Thus, the identity of individuals takes shape in the context of their larger society. Volkan claims that core identity solidifies in adolescence, and because it is closely aligned with large-group identity or the individual's outer community, threats to the larger group "are perceived by members of that large group as *individually* wounding and *personally* endangering" (33). This fear on an individual level accounts for the vicious large-group responses to social unrest or deviation. Volkan concludes that "an individual's core identity and large-group identity develop alongside one another" (32). In sum, large-group identity molds and impacts an individual's identity.

As a result, the identity of a marginalized group shares characteristics of the larger, rejecting society, but personal subjectivity suffers when one's core identity incorporates negative images. As mentioned earlier, much has been written about how for blacks,

whiteness was desirable on one level and dreaded on another [. . . ;] by "wanting" to be like those who denigrated them, African Americans were both identifying with their oppressors and denying the pain of being reservoirs for the "bad" elements those oppressors had consigned to them, such as "sexual aggressiveness" and "intellectual inferiority." (Volkan 45)

The paradox of belonging to a marginalized culture within a larger culture creates conflicting cultural aspects of individual subjectivity. At the same time, members in the larger, dominant culture maintain *their* identity by rejecting a suppressed group and must accomplish this distance through an emphasis on difference. The dominant culture distances itself from marginalized groups largely through projection of its negative aspects outward onto others. Charles Brenner describes how projection works by saying that "people attribute to others wishes and impulses of their own which are unacceptable to them and which they unconsciously try to get rid of, as it were, by the mechanism of projection" (102). As a response to lack, projection represents a repetition of symbolic ritual that serves to protect against anxiety. Psychic enjoyment stems from the erasure of lack, propelling community members to project hatred onto blacks rather than question their culture. When people project unconscious and forbidden desires elsewhere, they protect themselves from lack and act to conserve constancy.

Projection helps members of the dominant society avoid lack, reinforcing the current symbolic structure and their place in it. Projection on a communal level results in targeting a group or in scapegoating, in which the "negative part of one's own psyche [. . .] is [. . .] transferred to the outside world and experienced as an outside object. It is combated, punished, and exterminated as 'the alien out there' instead of being dealt with as 'one's own inner problem'" (Neumann 50). Scapegoats come to represent projected "evil" and must be visible to the community to have a purging effect (51). In severe cases groups "tend to utilize blood as an equivalent to—rather than symbolic of—identity" (Volkan 84). The interconnection between individual and cultural identity explains much of violent social behavior and is an integral aspect of racial interactions on the larger American scene. Projection also functions within marginalized communities and families. For example, Macon scapegoats Pilate in *Song of Solomon*, Claudia's community scapegoats the Breedlove family in *The Bluest Eye*, men scapegoat women in *Paradise*, and the Bottom neighborhood scapegoats Shadrack and Sula in *Sula*.

Thus, individual and communal identities determine social interactions and personal self-concept. Memory, as we have discussed in terms of being stored in bodily and neuronal circuits, functions on individual, cultural, and generational levels to play a major role in the maintenance of subjectivity and as a mediator of trauma. According to Marianne Leuzinger-Bohleber and Rolf Pfeifer, memory is a combination of historical fact and the current emotional reworking of past events into present circumstances (3–4).[20] "Memory, then, is a theoretical construct that connects the state of the individual in the past and the influence the event had on the individual to the behaviour in the current situation" (11). Past experiences, triggered by sensory stimulation, are recategorized as related to current activity. It is important to consider memory "as a complex, dynamic, recategorising and interactive process, which is always 'embodied,' in other words based on actual sensory-motor experiences, and manifests itself in the behaviour of the organism" (27). That is, memory's bodily, sensory-motor component involves a recategorization or reactivation of past experiences. Prior sensory-motor experiences are reactivated and acted out in a response that constitutes memory. Memory reenacts a crucial bodily element.

This recategorization of past bodily experiences connects memory to the bodily repetition of trauma. That is, as memory reconstructs, and thereby repeats, traumatic events, the body reenacts the initial bodily stored trauma. Cooper claims that "[i]nitial events—basically *hypothesized* or reconstructed traumas—[work] as pathogenic memories" (43). Memory's reenactment of trauma preserves the initial impact. For example, Schoolteacher's presence or the image of his hat will trigger for Sethe the traumatic stealing of her milk, and she responds with the rawness of the initial bodily experience. Further, Caruth notes that "[t]he historical power of the trauma is not just that the experience is repeated after its forgetting, but that it is only in and through its inherent forgetting that it is first experienced at all" (*Unclaimed* 17). In other words, repressed trauma surfaces after the fact when it is acted out through action and memory. Therefore, the stored bodily aspect of memory accounts for the later materialization of trauma.[21]

Societies, like individuals, store memory in bodily rituals and shared experiences. Paul Connerton, in *How Societies Remember*, discusses the intricate web of past and present, with current experiences influencing or distorting the past even as past events and remembrances modify the present (2). While a society as a whole possesses certain rituals and shared memory, subgroups of a culture process and experience the past differently:

> The oral history of subordinate groups will produce another type of history: one in which not only will most of the details be different, but in which the

very construction of meaningful shapes will obey a different principle. Different details will emerge because they are inserted, as it were, into a different kind of narrative home. For it is essential in perceiving the existence of a culture of subordinate groups to see that this is a culture in which the life histories of its members have a different rhythm and that this rhythm is not patterned by the individual's intervention in the working of the dominant institutions. (19)

Despite a shared history, the different processing of that history results in a separate trauma. The larger group's narrative is distinct from that of subordinate groups. Notwithstanding a common history of racial divide, the white southern narrative differs from that of blacks who have processed slavery, segregation, discrimination, and poverty. Personal histories house identities. W. Fitzhugh Brundage describes the competing narratives of southern whites and blacks, with white subjectivity necessitating the silencing of black experiences. In this struggle for recognition, "black memory [. . . became] a form of cultural resistance [to southern heroic narrative]" (10). Brundage discusses how "[c]ollective remembering forges identity, justifies privilege, and sustains cultural norms. For individuals and groups alike, memory provides a genealogy of social identity" (4). In this way, "public space serves to reproduce social relations that define some members of a society as worthy of access to public life and others as unworthy" (6). Breaking the repetition of history requires new cultural performances, and one response included "black festivals [that] were virtual open-air classrooms in which blacks recalled their history" (88).

Consequently, the black community developed its own commemorative holidays, with "at least a half-dozen major holidays and countless smaller occasions during which southern African Americans celebrated their heroes and hallowed events" (61). Such sites of memory include anniversaries, celebrations, and other commemorative activities of past experiences, as well as a bodily performative re-enactment. Connerton refers to these performances as "employing at least three distinguishable modes of articulation: [. . .] calendrical, verbal and gestural re-enactment" (65).[22] Black cultural ritual and rites commemorate a traumatic past. However, blacks remain on the margins of national celebrations, and Connerton explains the difficult task of changing the master narrative, saying that "a community is reminded of its identity as represented by and told in a master narrative. [. . . which] is more than a story told and reflected on; it is a cult enacted" (70). In essence, changing the master narrative necessitates a change in bodily behavior and response, pointing to the libidinal aspect of a culture's ideology and ritual performance.[23]

If, as Connerton claims, "[h]abit is a knowledge and a remembering in the hands and in the body; and in the cultivation of habit it is our body which 'understands'" (95), cultural and personal memory are not intellectual or detached ideas, laws, and customs but rather physically encoded entities. Morrison has stated that writers capture how memory lodges in the emotions, "where we were, what valley we ran through, what the banks were like, the light that was there and the route back to our original place. It is emotional memory" ("Site of Memory" 119). In regards to the "hard wiring" effect of social interactions discussed earlier, Siegel's research shows that as "new synapses are formed in response to experience, we create the foundation for memory. In this way, experience, memory, and development are overlapping processes. Recent findings in neuroscience also suggest that new neurons growing in integrating regions of the brain may also continue to emerge across the lifespan" ("An Interpersonal" 2). Thus, alterations in environment and new experiences can reverse developmental deficits created by cultural habit.

Unfortunately, to protect a culture's habitual, bodily core identity, large groups will resort to violence in a reenacted version of their histories. Leaders who manipulate "large-group rituals in the service of maintaining, protecting, and repairing identity may create an atmosphere ripe for unspeakable, seemingly inhumane acts of violence" (Volkan 14). Such violence perpetuates the suffering of marginalized groups and reinforces ideology to protect the larger culture. Lynchings provide a good example of a large-group defensive mechanism after the defeat experienced by white southerners in the Civil War. After the Civil War, lynching became a means to preserve cultural separations and the "hierarchical power relationships based both on gender and on race" (J. Hall 156). To sustain their core identity, southern whites perpetuated color separation and inferior notions of blacks. Having lost their battle for the lifestyle of their ancestors, southerners fiercely reenacted codes of behavior.[24] Lynchings became a public reenactment, with all members of the community (white men, women, and children) endorsing these acts by group sanction: "Ordinarily, there were hundreds and sometimes thousands of spectators. It was not uncommon for railroads to run special 'excursion' trains to the site. The mass of whites not only signified their assent to the proceedings by their presence, but also exhibited an active sympathy with the execution. [. . .] Lynchers saw lynching as 'justice'" (Williamson 187). Cultural ritual and performance serve a protective function for the large group.

Post–Civil War fear of an altered social order coincided with concern about political change. It was during "Reconstruction, more than any other time, [that] whites lynched Afro-Americans because of their involvement in political affairs" (Wright 48). In addition to such mob rule, "[b]rutality from law enforcement officers was another form of intimidation blacks experienced in the 1870s and 1880s" (Lucas 294). Local ideology, played out in reenactment of the ideologies of prior generations, prevailed over national law. For example, in Kentucky, violence "in the years immediately following the Civil War stemmed from the prevalent belief of whites in the inferiority of blacks" (187). The enduring racism and bitterness on the part of the South over both its defeat in the Civil War and the national challenge to the southern way of life illustrates the complex and overwhelming "role of the chosen trauma—the collective mental representation of an event that has caused a large group to face drastic common losses, to feel helpless and victimized by another group, and to share a humiliating injury—in sustaining large-group identity and its cohesiveness" (Volkan 48). The scapegoating of blacks is one repercussion of the South's marginalization by the North.

While both the larger society and marginalized groups suffer from violent actions, those without power suffer the most. Home—a creation of an imaginary wholeness in response to the Real—appears in various manifestations as a protective mechanism. For African Americans, connections with Africa can provide such a home. Morrison states in "Rootedness" that ancestors in literature "are sort of timeless people whose relationships to the characters are benevolent, instructive, and protective, and they provide a certain kind of wisdom. [. . .] the presence or absence of that figure determined the success or the happiness of the character" (496). She adds, "When you kill the ancestor you kill yourself," and "if we don't keep in touch with the ancestor [. . .] we are, in fact, lost" (497). These African ancestors act as a mirror to reflect a positive and whole self and function as a home derived from place and custom. La Vinia Delois Jennings argues that such ancestral ties invade the self consciously or unconsciously and are inflected in body, speech, and action. "Morrison concerns herself with exigencies that the cultural contours of distinctly modern experiences place on her [. . .] to reunite significance and meaning with origins to (re)figure a modern, diasporic reality" (Jennings 184). Morrison's work strives to recover the ancestral core of black experience that slavery erased.[25]

Like ancestors, mothers in particular provide support for identity, but the separation of slave mothers and their children disrupts this connection. Thus, Peterson describes support for subjectivity as the communal act of mothering, from "female relatives, to friends close enough to be considered family, [...] and to women who look out for anyone in the community who needs looking after," claiming "the need for black women to support each other, to serve as surrogate mothers and othermothers, for only by extending mothering beyond kin and by practicing collective acts of mothering can the black community be sustained" (31–32, 44). Mothering and attachment, as outlined earlier, provide a supportive imaginary reflection of a self to combat the symbolic structure. The community offers similar support through cultural memory and rememory. Likewise, a mate or spouse, as well as children, can reflect a positive self, confirming one's existence. For example, in *Beloved* Sethe claims that Beloved, like the rest of her children, represents her "best thing," but Paul D, himself an imaginary mirror for Sethe, reminds her that she herself is her own "best thing" (272, 273). Sweet Home provides a nostalgic positive memory in *Beloved* because it represents a place where Sethe had some degree of agency and a sense of self. When Paul D tells Denver that "[i]t wasn't sweet and it sure wasn't home," Sethe adds, "But it's where we were [...]. All together. Comes back whether we want it to or not" (14). In Lacan's schema, the intrusion of negative experiences exposes the Real. This intrusion allows one to recognize the trauma created by cultural signification and in turn to develop one's own subjectivity. A concept of home as connected to memory and nostalgia functions to fulfill a lack and helps form a sense of self by providing a past and a positive self-concept. In this way, home provides safety and guards against trauma.

How Morrison's novels trace the success or failure to rebuild a self through home forms the basis of the following discussion. Exploring the experience of slavery and its aftermath, Morrison's work traces the lives of black Americans from childhood through old age, in a range of class and geographical situations, through the nineteenth and twentieth centuries.[26] She follows the struggle of blacks to create subjectivity without a positive gaze for them in the master narrative, and so my discussion begins with an investigation of how the abusive experience of slavery and its legacy of cultural rejection create trauma, low self-esteem, and anxiety for the black community on individual, familial, and group levels. *Beloved*'s depiction of slavery, from the Middle Passage to postslavery "freedom," captures the inherited and bodily aspects of communal trauma. Similarly, the discrimination against, and rejection of, freed blacks by white and black towns in *Paradise* produce trauma for the descendants of slaves. Both novels demonstrate how the generational transmission of slavery's trauma produces a cultural history that cannot be forgotten, despite repression or dissociation. *Beloved* and *Paradise* explore the problematic reconstruction of personal and communal identity and show the importance of remembering the past and the verbalization of trauma to establish a sense of self. Ruby's patriarchs in *Paradise* represent the problem of "freedom" in the aftermath of slavery. Morrison's text suggests the problematic task of re-creating a self that can function in the present while maintaining ties to original ancestors. Through rememory and the retelling of trauma stories, some characters confront Lacan's Real and thus name their own desire. In doing so, they reject the demand of white culture's master narrative. This new perspective provides the agency to act meaningfully in the world.

Personal memory and cultural rememory assist in the reenvisioning necessary for a positive self to counter and live with trauma, a burden that weighs on future generations. After considering the trauma of slavery and the initial postslavery generation, I explore the persistence of trauma for Morrison's twentieth-century blacks. In particular, Morrison's first three novels portray the effects of the greater white culture on children. I address how children contend with familial, community, and historical trauma in *The Bluest Eye, Sula,* and *Song of Solomon,* where young characters try to decode their culture in order to find self-satisfaction and love. Unfortunately, children in these novels act out in aggressive ways to protect themselves from cultural stereotypes and the social hierarchy of their culture; their aggression mirrors that of their parents and the greater white culture. Their core identities, defined by the deleterious larger white culture and shaped by their parents' trauma, exhibit low self-esteem and a sense of helplessness. These novels attest to children's psychic and bodily absorption of their parents' trauma, as well as the limited avenues to recovery and healing. The weakened family structure perpetuates separation, loss, abandonment, and faulty attachment. The aggression of children in these novels represents their need to gain control over the white gaze, which continues to dictate their lives. Jealousy, envy, projection, identification with whiteness, and racial self-hatred produce aggressive behavior in both children and adults.

The fabric of Morrison's communities consists of interwoven strands of private wounds, with each generation passing along familial as well as communal trauma to its youth. Trauma, attachment, and cultural theories explain the lingering effects of ancestral trauma. Siegel's research in particular suggests reconstructive paths to counter vulnerability and the need for protection, showing that

> [i]t is not just what happened to parents as children themselves that is the key, it is how parents have come to understand the impact of those events on their own lives that matters most. When parents have a compassionate understanding of themselves they are able to provide the emotionally sensitive, contingent communication that children need in order to thrive. ("Attachment" 35)

One response to firsthand and generationally transmitted trauma is to escape, either physically or mentally. In *Jazz* and *Tar Baby*, characters hope to escape trauma by relocating in order to reinvent themselves through new and different lives. My discussion of these novels illustrates the unsuccessful repression of memory by depicting the failure of individual attempts to escape trauma physically. *Jazz* and *Tar Baby* concern adult responses to the childhood trauma of being orphaned, ostracized, or discriminated against. Morrison's characters grapple with how to become adults who can protect themselves rather than remain dependent and in need of protection. However, moving to a different environment fails to separate them from either the source or reminders of traumatic experiences; thus, *Jazz* and *Tar Baby* illustrate that physical relocation does not erase trauma. Removal from the site of trauma does not remove "[t]he overflow from the abscess on American history [that] has not yet been absorbed, nor [. . .] the scar of slavery [that has not] healed" (Mayberry, *Can't I Love* 152). Characters store personal and familial traumas of loss and abuse, which they act out later in time.

Community and individual trauma of discrimination, poverty, abandonment, orphaning, and displacement continues in Morrison's novel *Love*. I investigate how home and memory connect to identity in this novel, where characters from different generations, including those of segregation, early integration, the civil rights movement, and the 1990s, experience displacement and search for subjectivity. *Love* chronicles how Cosey's Hotel and Resort, as a site of black personal and collective memory, serves as both a physical and a psychic space tied to self-concept and adequacy for the community and family members. In this novel, Morrison brings together the themes of abandonment, parenting, historical discrimination, poverty, and memory evident in her earlier novels to illustrate the reliance on the past and nostalgic memory for a sense of self. Although characters in *Love* are removed in time from slavery, the fragility of black subjectivity generated by fear and insecurity in white culture continues to play out. When parents cannot provide a safety zone, children inherit the fears of prior generations and bodily store parental trauma. Nostalgic memory helps to build positive self-images for individual characters as well as for the community.

Morrison's novels depict the hope for healing of the individual and the community, as well as the enormity of that process. She "addresses political issues in American society and [. . .] she takes a grand view of her role as a member of a community of writers, her belief in the power of language, and her vision of the future and literature's role in it" (Denard, *What Moves* xv). Taking her concerns to a global stage, Morrison continued to explore the concept of home in her curated exhibition "The Foreigner's Home," at the Louvre Museum, in Paris, in the fall of 2006. Accepting the invitation of the Louvre to renew its vision of collected art, Morrison created an exhibition encompassing ancient to contemporary art in multiple media. She posed the following question: how, throughout the ages, has the feeling of belonging and a sense of identity been put in jeopardy by the perils of history? Further, how do social, cultural, and political changes produce for individuals a sense of dispossession from their home? (Crombecque 39). Her exhibition examined how, throughout time, displaced and othered people create a home, paralleling my analysis of home as a healing response to trauma in her novels. The foreigner's home that is not a home represents Lacan's Real, which produces anxiety and trauma. Creating a home despite rejection mirrors Lacan's subject of knowledge who can move past culture's gaze to create a life based on personal, rather than cultural, desire.

In addition to Morrison's exhibition at the Louvre, her most recent novel, *A Mercy,* shows her continuing concern with home, subjectivity, and recovery from trauma. Setting her novel in an era before slavery was equated with race, Morrison examines the lasting individual psychic and communal social effects of ownership. Morrison's novel of dispossessed and transplanted people investigates each character's search for the safe haven of home. Creating a self and owning it, in spite of homelessness, constitutes the true mercy one can achieve. Nostalgic memories that constitute a positive sense of self provide the concept of home crucial to combating the trauma Morrison reveals in her novels.

In *Beloved,* perhaps Morrison's most viscerally disturbing work, Sethe verbalizes the function of nostalgia in her bittersweet memory of Sweet Home. Such "memory . . . [helps reclaim] a suppressed past and helps the process of re-visioning that is essential to gaining control over one's life and future" (Singh, Skerrett, and Hogan, *Memory, Narrative, and Identity* 19). Further, "personal memory shapes and is woven [into] group memory" (Singh, Skerrett, and Hogan, *Memory and Cultural Politics* 14). The reciprocal nature of personal and group memory lies in the fact that getting in touch with the "collective past means getting in touch with the individual experience of abandonment. [. . .] Remembering and mourning become signs of the subject's agency and recovery" (Grewal 142, 170). Intrusive nostalgic memory provides psychic relief because treatment for trauma involves helping the ego to feel safe and secure by building self-esteem and social connections. The memory of Sweet Home under the Garners' care serves this purpose, illustrating how nostalgic memory can furnish the distance from trauma necessary to rebuild subjectivity.

Morrison's characters portray the psychological and cultural obstacles to such reconstruction, as well as the hard-won personal victories available through verbalization of trauma and community sharing. Some characters are able to move beyond nostalgic memory and build lives in the present. To return to Morrison's essay "Home," she acknowledges that "matters of race and matters of home are priorities in my work" (4). Specifically, she states that the driving force of *Beloved* is "connection, acknowledgement, a paying-out of homage still due," the very elements necessary for recovery from trauma (7). Indeed, Morrison's imaginative search for "the concrete thrill of borderlessness—a kind of out of doors safety" has provided an ongoing hopeful thread interweaving her novels (9).

ONE

Shared Memory

Slavery and Large-Group Trauma in *Beloved* and *Paradise*

Characters in *Beloved* and *Paradise* discover that they must confront the trauma of slavery and discrimination in a personal and communal way, in each generation. Both novels demonstrate how generational transmission of trauma produces a cultural history that cannot be forgotten despite the will to repress it or dissociate from it. In *Beloved* communal memory of slave-ship horror and plantation life materializes in the shape of Beloved, whose return challenges the community to learn how to live with the trauma of slavery by processing the past in order to function in the present.[1] *Paradise* further explores whether one generation can preserve the memory of its forebears while accepting community change and contemporary behavior.[2] Morrison's communities illustrate that coping with trauma involves a reconstitution of the self, a process complicated by the institution of slavery, which systematically erased the personal identity of slaves. *Beloved* and *Paradise* explore this problematic reconstruction of personal and communal identity, which is crucial to healing and establishing subjectivity. While memory replays traumatic events, its reconstruction of those events can protect the ego; the recall of positive aspects of the past, tied to concepts of connections that mirror a positive self-image, helps to combat trauma and its lingering effects.

 Beloved is concerned with these issues of subjectivity in the characters of Sethe, Paul D, Baby Suggs, Denver, and Beloved. The novel narrates the story of their lives as slaves under the Garners at Sweet Home; their harsh treatment by Schoolteacher (Mr. Garner's replacement); their harrowing escapes; and their efforts to live in freedom with their traumatic memories of abuse. *Beloved* raises the question of how to recover from trauma and create an identity out of "nothing." For example, Baby Suggs, struggles to figure out how to locate her family when her son Halle buys her freedom. How can she locate her scattered children when she has not seen them since their infancy and does not know their names? The institution of slavery, because of its inhumane treatment of blacks, robs them of an identity separate from their white owners. According to Judith Herman, victims of "chronic trauma [. . .] may lose the sense that [they have] any self at all" (86). We see this phenomenon in Baby Suggs, who ponders having a

> sadness [. . .] at her center, the desolated center where the self that was no self made its home. [. . .] Could she sing? (Was it nice to hear when she did?) Was she pretty? Was she a good friend? Could she have been a loving mother? A faithful wife? Have I got a sister and does she favor me? If my mother knew me would she like me? (140)

She describes an erasure of self and a lack of connection with parents and siblings. Her core identity, shaped and defined by white slaveholders, lacks a sense of self outside of her inferior and subservient position.

Whites' projection of negative qualities onto black slaves reduces white anxiety at the expense of black self-esteem.[3] Jennifer Fleischner notes that "[g]rowing up a slave meant having to come to terms with the conflicting currents of identity and identification that arose out of the profoundly intimate relations that frequently bridged the worlds of slaveholder and slave, and the radical social, economic, and political gulfs segregating 'black' from 'white'" (4). Deprivation of personal identity was necessary to maintain the oppressive system.

Consequently, the protective function of the nuclear family is lost in the system of slavery. Families are separated, with members sold to different masters. Baby Suggs thinks that

> men and women were moved around like checkers. Anybody Baby Suggs knew, let alone loved, who hadn't run off or been hanged, got rented out, loaned out, bought up, brought back, stored up, mortgaged, won, stolen or seized. So Baby's eight children had six fathers. [. . .] nobody stopped playing checkers just because the pieces included her children. (23)

There is no possibility of an established nuclear family for Baby Suggs. Thus, she thinks that for seven of her eight children "it wasn't worth the trouble to try to learn features you would never see change into adulthood anyway" (139). Her last child, Halle, whom she is allowed to keep, works hard to buy his mother's freedom and thus provide a place, a home, an anchor, for his wife, Sethe, and their children when he can buy their freedom or they can escape.

Unlike Sethe, who knows how to reach Baby Suggs, most slaves lose their familial identity because they are given the names of their white masters and have no way to reconnect with their own families when freed.[4] In addition to losing their family name, slaves lack a connection with their mothers or fathers because parenting children in a nurturing family structure is in most cases impossible. A fellow slave at Sweet Home, Paul D, exemplifies how "the black male is left with nothing that's his own: not a self, a personal history, a real name. [. . .] Black females are in much the same position, as Sethe's memory of her own mother indicates. There is no personal address by which the child can call her" (Cummings 559). Essentially, the institution of slavery was built on the absence of a nuclear black home or family; confused parental identifications between slave and slave owner result, and "these cross-racial 'mother-like' bonds are torn between conflicting modes of attachment and rejection, hope and despair, trust and distrust" (Fleischner 178). In addition, black women often become the primary nurturers for white families, nursing and raising white babies. Displacement from a black nuclear family into a blurred role in the white owner's family derails a stable sense of selfhood.[5]

Taking the name of the white master further erases the black family name, and with it subjectivity. The newly freed Baby Suggs discusses her name with Mr. Garner:

> "Mr. Garner," she said, "why you all call me Jenny?"
>
> "'Cause that what's on your sales ticket, gal. Ain't that your name? What you call yourself?"
>
> "Nothing," she said. "I don't call myself nothing."
>
> Mr. Garner went red with laughter. "When I took you out of Carolina, Whitlow called you Jenny and Jenny Whitlow is what his bill said." (142)

She then tells him that she goes by her husband's name, Suggs, and that he called her "Baby." When Mr. Garner suggests that "Mrs. Baby Suggs ain't no name for a freed Negro," she thinks to herself that "Baby Suggs was all she had left of the 'husband' she claimed" (142). Going out in the world with his name is her only hope of ever finding him again: "how could he find or hear tell of her if she was calling herself some bill-of-sale name?" (142). However, Baby Suggs has no way to start looking for her children when she gains her freedom and so cannot create the home they never had. "Great God, she thought, where do I start?" (143). They have been sold or have perished, all without her family name. With Halle as her only familial link, she creates a home for him and his family, keeping her husband's name with the hope that Halle will be able to buy their freedom and join her in the future.

In contrast to Baby Suggs's situation, "Sethe had the amazing luck of six whole years of marriage to that 'somebody' son who had fathered every one of her children," which was a highly unusual circumstance (23). Even so, her early separation from her mother, coupled with the traumatic witnessing of her hanging, scar Sethe.[6] She suffers feelings of abandonment despite Nan's assurances that her mother's love protected her. Sethe wants her own body to have the mark her mother bears to preserve their connection. Her mother's physical pain and brutal death lodge in Sethe's psyche and will later produce a violent bodily response reminiscent of her mother. Nan's efforts to mother Sethe do not repair her traumatic separation from her mother.

When Mr. Garner dies, Sethe's intact family and subjectivity will collapse as a result of her assault by Schoolteacher's nephews and Halle's witnessing of this "stealing" of Sethe's milk. Although she will escape to the home Baby Suggs has made for Halle's family, white culture prohibits Sethe's family reunion when Schoolteacher arrives to reclaim his "property." In a repetition of her own mother's killing her children born to white fathers, Sethe would kill her children rather than see them returned to slavery.[7] With no other recourse for agency, Sethe's plan to "take us all to the other side where my own ma'am is" (203) not only asserts her subjectivity despite Schoolteacher's claim on them as property but also states her desire for the place of safety her mother and children will provide.

Just as Baby Suggs is separated from her children, Sethe is separated from her mother. She cannot remember sleeping in the same cabin and having her perform caretaking duties like fixing her hair. As she tells Beloved, "I didn't see her but a few times out in the fields and once when she was working indigo. By the time I woke up in the morning, she was in line. [. . .] She must of nursed me two or three weeks—that's the way the others did. Then she went back in rice and I sucked from another woman whose job it was" (60). Separating infants from their mothers prevents attachment, and the lack of parental attachment increases trauma and anxiety.[8] Sethe's early trauma, as well as her mother's, passes on to Denver.[9]

Slave parents learn not to get too emotionally attached so as to minimalize their feelings of loss. For this reason, the ex-slave Ella warns Sethe, "Don't love nothing" (92). One defense against family erasure is the passing on of oral narratives, such as the stories about Sethe's mother told to her by Nan in an African tongue, in the "same language her ma'am spoke, and which would never come back. [. . .] 'She threw them all away but you. [. . .] Without names, she threw them. You she gave the name of the black man. She put her arms around him. The others she did not put her arms around'" (62). In this way, Nan transmits Sethe's mother's love and sacrifice, preserving the ancestral, African home.[10] Without this nurturing, Sethe's mother would be merely a "woman in a felt hat" stretching "in the field" (98). With Nan's assistance, Sethe's memories will include her mother's language and physical markings.

Even so, the loss of family structure makes child rearing difficult for Sethe, because there is no community of women to consult. Sethe relies on her memory of "what I'd seen back where I was before Sweet Home. How the women did there" (160). These women relied on the shared knowledge of their community, but as the only woman at Sweet Home, Sethe had to depend on her own resources. When she is most bereft—of her murdered daughter, Baby Suggs, and her sons— Sethe will recall Nan's narrative of her mother to sustain her hold on her diminished self and to try to fabricate a sense of family and home. Nan reflects back a positive self for Sethe, who holds on to the threads of ancestral connection.

As a result of the destruction of the family unit, masters, overseers, sheriffs, and other white officials function as maltreating parents, creating physical and mental trauma for blacks in the slave system. Treated as children, called "boys" and infantilized, enslaved blacks take on the insecurities of children. Slave narratives often illustrate that "the African American slave narrator's first encounter with a white woman is actually represented as an engagement between a child and an adult" (Fleischner 175).[11] On a psychological level, the erasure of black identity by white culture overwhelms the black ego, creating anxiety and fear.

Later, freed slaves carry the generational memory of abuse, and their post-slavery reality reactivates the prior bodily experience and threat of real bodily harm. According to Marianne Leuzinger-Bohleber and Rolf Pfeifer, this memory "is not only a matter of internal processing of sensory signals, but of sensory and motor processes" (20). The reactivation of bodily stress accounts for self-protection through dissociation, the "voluntary thought suppression, minimization, and sometimes outright denial" that "alter[s] unbearable reality" (Herman

87). Memory is painful because it stimulates a "yearning for all that has been lost" in addition to bodily discomfort (89). For example, Sethe's memories of her mother are painful, and when she tells Beloved and Denver about her, she "had to do something with her hands because she was remembering something she had forgotten she knew" (*Beloved* 61). By repressing or dissociating herself from her trauma, Sethe combats the anxiety that results in her vulnerability, her lack of protection against a feeling of helplessness in the larger, white community.[12]

It is against this threat that Sethe acts to protect her children through a violent act. Kathleen Woodward explains that "[a]nger serves the function of appropriate self-defense and of retaliation" and that "unacknowledged shame leads to anger and often rage" (215, 217). Sethe's actions exemplify this anger and rage. Further, since "memories are reactivated when a person is exposed to a situation [. . .] reminiscent of the one when the original memory was stored," Schoolteacher's appearance triggers Sethe's violent response (Van der Kolk and Van der Hart 174). Her numbed back carries the scars of his whippings, and she can never forget the stealing of her milk. Both bodily assaults activate her response.

Trauma for the black community is not just the perception of bodily threat; it is the reality of bodily threat. Lynchings, whippings, rapes, and other forms of abuse were part of daily life for slaves. Stamp Paid, a freed slave who rescues others through the Underground Railroad, summarizes the legacy of slavery: "Whole towns wiped clean of Negroes; eighty-seven lynchings in one year alone in Kentucky; four colored schools burned to the ground; grown men whipped like children; children whipped like adults; black women raped by the crew; property taken, necks broken" (180).[13] *Beloved* chronicles such abuse with the hideous scars on Sethe's back; the physical and mental scars for Sethe's mother and Paul D from being forced to wear a horse's bit; Baby Suggs's broken hip, painful limp, and fear of being knocked down; and Sixo's lynching.[14] This physical abuse produces a psychological trauma that is absorbed by successive generations. Stamp Paid ponders all of the ills he has witnessed, capped by the brutality implied when he finds "a red ribbon knotted around a curl of wet woolly hair, clinging still to its bit of scalp. [. . .] 'What *are* these people?'" (180). His question about monstrous acts addresses the core of slave trauma and how to survive its impact.

Vamik Volkan's work suggests that the fixation on blood and the separation of black and white, along with other large-group rituals, including the violent acts of lynching, tarring and feathering, and castration, reinforce the ideology of a larger group that causes a subgroup to suffer. The southern white community has maintained its way of life through slavery and the treatment of black people as subhuman commodities.[15] Changing southern ideology would involve social displacement, with freedom for blacks threatening the economic as well as the psychological stability of the larger white culture. The mental and physical survival of the southern white population requires subservient blacks. Cultural memory of slavery reactivates on a bodily level a response to blacks in a particular way. The master narrative fosters a blind repetition of communal behavior that represents a ceding to the demand of the cultural symbolic order. Consequently, white actions represent an inherited response.[16]

Slavery and, later, racism result from the larger culture's projection of its own insecurities and weaknesses onto blacks, who become a scapegoated or targeted group. After the Civil War, without any precedents for living in a racially mixed society, it is difficult to know how to proceed. Paul D comments that "[t]he War had been over four or five years then, but nobody white or black seemed to know it" (52). Many men do not return from the war, and living conditions have deteriorated. Widows like Mrs. Garner cannot stay alone with blacks on their plantations if there are no white men to "protect" them. Schoolteacher's duty is not only to protect Mrs. Garner but also to maintain southern culture's separation from, and dehumanization of, slaves. His identity, like his community's, rests on reenacting his ancestral past of ownership and racism.

Thus, the larger culture maintains its identity at the expense of subgroups, compounding the latter's trauma. Memory, reenacted in community rituals, as Volkan and Paul Connerton claim, restores an ideal imaginary state for white culture as it represses the trauma of displacement and inadequacy. Memory, a sensory and motor reenactment of the past, supplies an ideal self and an escape from physical and mental trauma. Consequently, Sethe will think fondly of Sweet Home, where she shared a family life with Halle and warm interactions with the black and white community. Under the Garners' care, her core identity develops alongside the larger, white culture, and her desire for a wedding ceremony reflects her desire for the sanction of white culture and its standards for family. Feeling like a "daughter" to Mrs. Garner, Sethe remembers her disappointment when she "found out there wasn't going to be no ceremony, no preacher. Nothing. I thought there should be something—something to say it was right and true" (58). Sethe creates her own wedding equivalent—making a dress out of scraps, honeymooning with Halle in the corn—to claim her rights as a married woman. And Mrs. Garner acknowledges Sethe's identification as a daughter by giving her a pair of "diamond" earrings to commemorate the event.

Mrs. Garner's maternal relationship with Sethe illustrates that "the slave girl turns to her mistress in search of maternal care, self-esteem, and a sense of self" (Fleischner 8–9). Sethe's nostalgic memories of her "family" life at Sweet Home support her subjectivity. Her memory recategorizes past events to alleviate her current situation, allowing her to dissociate herself from her painful memories— the killing of her daughter, the stealing of her milk, Paul D in the spiked collar, and her own mother's abandonment of her.[17]

Paul D similarly buries his painful past, fearful that his nightmarish memories will overpower the present. His "past is hateful and humiliating, and has marked and damaged him. And yet it is the only past he has; it has also formed him and shaped his desires" (Berger 210). Memory, even painful memory, creates identity through reenactment. Trauma victims function through a process of splitting, in which the "memory of what has happened to them is pushed aside, externalized, repressed, placed in a box, given over to someone else. [. . .] each character splits into a 'core self' and 'alters,' none of whom possess the others' memories. Within each individual, there is no memory/knowledge that a split has taken place" (Koolish 173). But trauma resurfaces after the fact when acted out in memory or action. J. Brooks Bouson notes that "'rememories'—that is, spontaneous recurrences of the past," represent the resurfacing of trauma (3). Slavoj Žižek explains the process whereby

> the past (long-forgotten traumatic encounters) does determine the present, but the very mode of this determining is *overdetermined* by the present synchronous symbolic network. If the trace of an old encounter all of a sudden begins to exert impact, it is because the *present* symbolic universe of the subject is structured in a way that is susceptible to it. (*For They Know* 202)

Circumstances of the present moment trigger trauma and its sensory and motor memories.

In fact, "traumatic, memory [. . .] occurs automatically in situations which are reminiscent of the original traumatic situation. [. . .] When one element of a traumatic experience is evoked, all other elements follow automatically" (Van der Kolk and Van der Hart 163). It is the uncontrollable and repetitious nature of trauma that disrupts the daily lives of trauma survivors. What Morrison calls "rememory," the intrusive, uncontrollable repetition of cultural trauma, prevents the erasure of past trauma. Although Sethe would like to forget the painful past, she can only moderate her "rememories," not control them (95).

Morrison describes the bodily component of memory, and hence subjectivity, when she describes a memory of something as "what the nerves and the skin remember as well as how it appeared" ("Site" 119). Traumatic eruptions provide the opportunity to restructure the past so as to bodily relive a memory while subtly modifying it. That is, "remembering is a precondition for a process of recategorisation of unconscious traumatic experiences and therefore for a structural change of behaviour" (Leuzinger-Bohleber and Pfeifer 27). Attempts to completely escape from trauma physically and mentally must include a reliving of the traumatic experience. Healing comes from modifying this repetition, as "trauma is a repeated suffering of the event, but it is also a continual leaving of its site" (Caruth, *Trauma* 10). As memory alters, even incrementally, a sense of safety and well-being can surface.[18]

Morrison's text differentiates between personal memory and communal "rememory," the intrusion of a shared cultural past.[19] While memory pertains to the individual, rememory is shared with a community. Kate Cummings summarizes rememory as follows: "places are powerful histories" and that "history is what subjects bump into" (553). Caroline Rody aptly claims that "'Rememory' as trope postulates the interconnectedness of minds, past and present, and thus neatly conjoins the novel's supernatural vision with its aspiration to communal epic, realizing the 'collective memory' of which Morrison speaks" (101). The danger for Sethe is that "[r]e-memories often displace existing life, making the past more authentic than the present" (Furman 262). Thus, rememory represents the intrusive and repetitive aspects of the communal trauma of slavery. While rememory is disturbing, it ironically provides the source for the communal sharing of trauma necessary to survive it. The confrontation with traumatic memory can restore places of safety and comfort as well as horror. For example, Sethe and Paul D battle their final humiliations at Sweet Home with their nostalgic memory of their subjectivity under Garner's care.

When Sethe and Paul D leave Sweet Home, they reconstruct their identities through conflicting memories of this home, the place where they received a positive gaze from the Garners. In an interview with Morrison, Carolyn Denard refers to the evidence in Morrison's work of "both sides of memory"—"humiliation," or the negative, along with positive nostalgic fondness. Morrison agrees, describing her own parents' love-hate relationship with the South and their prior homes, referring to her mother's nostalgia mixed with fear and her father's recognition of violence and racism combined with the need to return South ("Interview").

Sethe considers how memories of Sweet Home intrude on everyday events, with the soothing memories blotting out the negative ones:

[A]nd suddenly there was Sweet Home rolling, rolling, rolling out before her eyes, and although there was not a leaf on that farm that did not make her want to scream, it rolled itself out before her in shameless beauty. It never looked as terrible as it was and it made her wonder if hell was a pretty place too. [. . .] Boys hanging from the most beautiful sycamores [. . .]. It shamed her—remembering the wonderful soughing trees rather than the boys. Try as she might to make it otherwise, the sycamores beat out the children every time and she could not forgive her memory for that. (6)

Sethe voices the paradox of having fond memories of Sweet Home despite the atrocities that decorate the landscape and that a place of such sorrow also contains beauty. For Sethe, the memory of Sweet Home creates nostalgia for a time and place that represent family because her courtship, marriage, and birth of her children take place there. The past can return either as rememory, that is, as uncontrolled communal trauma, or as nostalgic memory, which can protect and nourish the trauma victim. Sethe derives a positive sense of self from her life at Sweet Home, where she lived with her husband and children and received praise from Mrs. Garner. At Sweet Home, Sethe had her own space, a sense of being whole. She recalls a life in which "she picked some pretty growing thing" to have with her in the kitchen, picked to give her a sense of ownership, as if "some part of it [the kitchen] was hers" (22). This ownership, along with motherhood and family life, provides a sense of pride and adequacy. In hindsight, Sethe comments on the foolishness of believing that some part of Sweet Home belonged to her, but her positive memories of Sweet Home mirror a positive sense of self.

Since selective memory protects the ego against trauma by negating danger and life-threatening stimuli, the focus on family, shared experience, and home provides protection. Bitter but pleasing, Sweet Home figures as a past that defines, justifies, explains, and gives meaning to current experience. For Sethe, positive memories of Sweet Home provide momentary fulfillment of her lack. Unfortunately, Lacan's Real—in the form of Schoolteacher, who whips her, and his nephews, who steal her milk—manifests her sense of lack and undercuts her image of wholeness. Thus, Sethe will avoid memories that cause her to "break, fall or cry each time a hateful picture drifted in front of her face" (97). Following Sethe's traumatic departure from Sweet Home—the stealing of her milk, her subsequent whipping when she reports her abuse to Mrs. Garner, her near death giving birth to Denver en route—124 Bluestone Road provides a haven, an ideal place for Sethe's recovery as the soothing hands of Baby Suggs help her when "her spirits fell down under the weight of the things she remembered" (98). In addition, the community willingly assists her in the process of discovering a new self, teaching her how to face her days of freedom. When she reaches her new home at 124 Bluestone Road, Sethe marvels at how well she accomplished her task: "I did it. I got us all out. [...] Up till then it was the only thing I ever did on my own. Decided. And it came off right [...]. Me using my own head" (162). She wants to merge her newly freed and confident self with her family and new community, feeling that she has "milk enough for all" (198).

However, her safe and happy life will shatter after Beloved's murder, which follows the intrusion of the symbolic order in the form of Schoolteacher, who according to the Fugitive Slave Law can render Sethe and her children slaves. The larger white culture robs Sethe of her subjectivity. After this attack, 124 Bluestone Road transforms into a haunted house and a symbol of a negative self-concept as it becomes associated with Sethe's experiences as a slave, her time in jail after Beloved's murder, Baby Suggs's death, and the running away of Sethe's sons. Sethe's killing of her daughter ruptures her ties with her new community, which abandons her.[20] Severed from any ideal self, she experiences isolation and vulnerability.

Sethe's sense of worth can only be rebuilt with Paul D's love and the community's forgiveness and assistance. That is, through connection and communal "rememory" Sethe will be able to reconstitute a stable self.[21] Like the filter of memory, re-creation of the past through storytelling reinforces a sense of control by reproducing an imagined wholeness. For example, when Sethe tells Beloved about her earrings, Sethe "found herself wanting to, liking it" (58). Storytelling makes life bearable by producing an imaginary wholeness that counters Lacan's Real.[22] Reliving traumatic memories is a prerequisite for living in the present.[23] Sethe understands that the Real or trauma will always exist to threaten a secure self when she explains to Denver, that

Places [...] are still there. If a house burns down, it's gone, but the place—the picture of it—stays, and not just in my rememory, but out there, in the world. What I remember is a picture floating around out there outside my head. I mean, even if I don't think it, even if I die, the picture of what I did, or knew, or saw is still out there. Right in the place where it happened. (36)

Sethe's telling Denver about "the place" suggests not just the danger of cultural trauma but also the possibility of transgenerational healing. She recognizes the power of generational and community rememory and storytelling either to threaten or to overcome the erasure of self. Our stories—part fact, part fiction— shape our past and thus our memory. The fact that Paul D shares Sethe's story makes it bearable. That their collective past can be passed on to Denver brings the burden of healing into focus. Denver, plagued by the trauma she absorbs from Sethe and Baby Suggs as well as from her own fears about her mother's potential violence, will rely on her own early experiences in school to give her the agency she needs to leave 124 and get help.

Rememory reconstructs the large-group infliction of trauma on a subgroup. The verbalization and public recognition of this trauma makes the anxiety connected with it more manageable for the subgroup; community bonding provides recovery from trauma's assault. This community sharing—through rememory or through the confrontation of trauma through personal and communal memory —restores the shattered family network. For characters in *Beloved* to heal, each "must come to accept his or her memories. When each begins to remember and acknowledge their alter selves as part of their core self, they reintegrate" (Koolish 174). Thus, healing involves remembering: "The remedy is to remember, but to build strength and not weakness from these unsettling recollections" (Furman 270).[24] While Sethe seeks peace by avoiding the memory of how her violence put Baby Suggs in her deathbed and caused her boys to run away from home, she also envisions no longer having to justify killing her daughter.

Beloved's return restores Sethe's memory of the strong, capable person who escaped Sweet Home: "Now I can look at things again because she's here to see them too. [. . .] Funny how you lose sight of some things and memory others. I never will forget that whitegirl's hands. Amy" (201). Her memory favors the healing hands of Amy Denver over the trauma of her near death and birthing of Denver in a leaky boat. Remembering the positive revises Sethe's self-image and reactivates her capacity for love.[25] But to live in the present, symbolic world, Sethe must reshape memory and tell a new story. Paul D and the community will help Sethe to remember her traumatic past and to learn to live with it in the present. Communal rememory transforms traumatic personal memory. "The interlocking of integrity and trust in caretaking relationships completes the cycle of generations and regenerates the sense of human community which trauma destroys" (Herman 154). Since "[r]ecovery can take place only within the context of relationships," Sethe's reworking of her trauma assists Paul D and community members in their healing as well (133).[26]

Sethe's healing welcome by Baby Suggs—her bathing, feeding, and spiritual nurturing—represents the soothing aspect of home as a place of love and rejuvenation, and Sethe will rely on this memory when trauma overwhelms her. Sethe recalls how Baby Suggs's hands "bathed her in sections, wrapped her womb, combed her hair, oiled her nipples, stitched her clothes, cleaned her feet, greased her back and dropped just about anything they were doing to massage Sethe's nape when memories overwhelmed her; Baby Suggs soothed Sethe as a mother would care for a child (98). Under such care, Sethe returns from near death to the world of the living. Later, when Beloved has depleted her strength, Sethe thinks about Paul D's offer to bathe her. "There's nothing to rub now and no reason to. Nothing left to bathe, assuming he even knows how. Will he do it in sections? First her face, then her hands, her thighs, her feet, her back? [. . .] And if he bathes her in sections, will the parts hold?" (272). Reduced to a body in pieces, Sethe realizes that proper caretaking is her only hope of resuscitation. Cummings describes the importance of mothering to destroy colonization's effects, "for through it the subject is reconstituted" and it "is fundamental to the process" of healing (564, 568). The echo of her earlier return home to Baby Suggs suggests that together Sethe and Paul D can create a home—a sense of self despite the white gaze—with Denver.

Sethe's need to establish a home in Ohio, an identity apart from the slavery of Sweet Home, emboldens her to "protect" her young from Schoolteacher's scientific objectification: "No notebook for my babies" (198). However, once the outside white world invades her space and she reacts with violence, Sethe wonders whether she can ever be free of memories and breathe easy. Can she make her house into a home, a space where she can enjoy the moment? Dare she plan or *"count on something"* (38)? For Sethe, home is a psychic space that supports the ego. Paul D's arrival adds "new pictures and old rememories that broke her [Sethe's] heart" (95). A true home would be a space where she was free to have an inner life because Paul D would help rescue her from the dark side of memory. He tells Sethe, "I'll catch you 'fore you fall. Go as far inside as you need to, I'll hold your ankles. Make sure you get back out" (46). Paul D will provide the support and connectedness necessary to heal.[27]

Paul D's memory, like Sethe's, triggers trauma that he must repress in his search for a place to call home. He shares Sethe's positive memories of Sweet Home, stemming from his recognition there by Garner as a man and not an animal or a material object. Until the arrival of Schoolteacher, Sweet Home provides Paul D with an imaginary wholeness. But Schoolteacher strips Paul D of the dignity that Garner gave him, and his life on the road forces him to block all memory by storing all experience in a "tobacco tin lodged in his chest" (113). Paul D is sent to Alfred, Georgia, to join a chain gang for trying to kill the man to whom Schoolteacher sells him, and his memory represents both physical and psychic trauma. He fears remembering things that will reopen the tin and overwhelm him with memories of being put in the bit, of envying Rooster's freedom and sense of self, of witnessing Halle with the butter, and of his horrendous existence in Georgia. Unless he represses the voice of white culture and the demand of its master narrative, which defines blacks as subhuman, Paul D risks the reactivation of bodily and emotional pain.

Thus, Paul D attempts to bury each of these incidents to avert the weight of their trauma. Chained to forty-six other men, Paul D survives the mud slide that overtakes them by working with his fellow prisoners: "The chain that held them would save all or none" (110). As a community they escape, and their healing comes at the hands of some ostracized, sick Cherokee, for whom the "disease they suffered now was a mere inconvenience compared to the devastation they remembered. Still, they protected each other as best they could" (111). Their warmth and empathy provide a home and shelter for the escaped and hunted men. Paul D travels north until he gets to Delaware, where a woman "adopts" him, passing him off as her nephew. Thus, his next healing comes with the provision of a home: a woman, food, and a bed with "cotton sheets and two pillows" (131). Protection and security restore his humanity, and Paul D survives through his connectedness.

Yet he seeks a complete home with Sethe even though his confrontation with her makes him vulnerable, with "nothing else to hold on to. His tobacco tin, blown open, spilled contents that floated freely and made him their play and prey" (218). He can only truly recover from his trauma by building anew with Sethe, who shares his positive recollection of selfhood at Sweet Home. These memories will counter their post–Sweet Home lives, where they are "trespassers among the human race" in the view of white society (125). While at Garner's, he and the other slaves were "men," not "boys" (10). Garner defies the demand of his culture by treating his slaves as humans despite the ridicule he receives from his community. But their identity as men "rested on Garner being alive. Without his life each of theirs fell to pieces" (220). Garner's paternal nurturing of his men enveloped them with the protection children feel at home. Paul D can re-create this memory of security with the help of Sethe, who shared Garner's praise and mirrors a positive self in order to create a new life.

Paul D makes room for himself at 124 Bluestone Road by ridding it of its ghost as well as by standing up to Denver. By doing so, he makes 124 into a home rather than a house, restoring it to the possibility of family life. Sethe realizes that "[t]here was no room for any other thing or body until Paul D arrived and broke up the place, making room, shifting it, moving it over to someplace else, then standing in the place he had made" (39). Beloved will appear to jeopardize this home, but Paul D will ultimately claim his place beside Sethe, rescuing his own life along with those of Sethe and Denver. But the path to this place is filled with psychological obstacles that must be overcome. Both Paul D and Sethe must verbalize and come to terms with their trauma, learning how to live in the present despite their past. The image of Sethe, Paul D, and Denver holding hands on their outing to the carnival foreshadows their viability as a family, forecasting a future for them as a unit and as part of their community.

In addition to Beloved's hold on Sethe, Sethe's past killing of her daughter threatens a future life with Paul D. When he learns from Stamp Paid of her act, he leaves in horror, rejecting her for her animalistic behavior: "'You got two feet, Sethe, not four,' he said, and right then a forest sprang up between them; [...] Later he would wonder what made him say it. The calves of his youth? [...] How fast he had moved from his shame to hers" (165). Paul D must reject Sethe in order to reject reliving his own past sexual trauma. When he runs from Sethe, no one takes him in. He becomes, at this point, literally homeless, sleeping in the cellar of the church. Stamp Paid feels guilty about driving him off, Ella does not trust Sethe or her friends after her brutal murdering of her child, and the community distrusts people associated with a house filled with suffering spirits. Stamp Paid chides Ella, "You know all about it and don't give him a hand? That don't sound like you, Ella. Me and you been pulling coloredfolk out the water more'n twenty years. Now you tell me you can't offer a man a bed? A working man, too!" (186). The black community shuns Paul D in order to avoid reminders of slavery's painful treatment. As its members reject 124's ghost, Baby Suggs's good fortune, and Paul D's connection with Sethe, they unwittingly follow the demand of white culture, punishing themselves and other "trespassers." Only later, at the novel's close, will they break away from the voice of culture as they band together to assist Sethe. Their chant creates the voice of subjects who refuse their place as meaningless links in the master narrative.

Paul D is too proud to ask for help, and opening up to do so might unleash painful memories and break his spirit. Repressing need as well as his past holds him together: "It was some time before he could put Alfred, Georgia, Sixo, school-teacher, Halle, his brothers, Sethe, Mister, the taste of iron, the sight of butter, the smell of hickory, notebook paper, one by one, into the tobacco tin lodged in his chest. By the time he got to 124 nothing in this world could pry it open" (113). But when Stamp Paid finally finds him, Paul D is "holding his wrists between his knees and looking red-eyed," clearly at the end of his rope (188). With Stamp Paid's assistance, Paul D will begin to confront and rework his memories in order to rebuild his life, a life that includes someone that shares his past positive memories of a whole self at a place called Sweet Home. Susan Mayberry notes that "once he takes ownership of his head and his heart, he can slip back into Sethe's house" (*Can't I Love* 191). Talking with Stamp Paid, verbalizing events and the associated trauma, connects them and their shared suffering. Acknowledging the abusive white culture allows them to process their past and move on to live in the present as part of a postslavery community.

Just as the weight of the past threatens to break Paul D, life's afflictions have sent Baby Suggs to her bed, where she contemplates color to compensate for the bleakness that surrounds her. Throughout her life Baby Suggs has survived by blocking the memory of her eight children. For example, all she will let herself remember of her firstborn "is how she loved the burned bottom of bread" (5), and she refused to get attached to her others, except for Halle. Ultimately, Baby Suggs uses her painful past to create a present in which she learns to rebuild her life with self-love, and she inspires others in her community to "[l]ay all that mess down" and rebuild as well (86).[28] She uses her self-awareness to forge her life as a preacher and to assist others in loving themselves, creating an ideal imaginary image; she teaches others to see themselves differently from the way the larger, dominant culture views them.

At the end of her life, when she takes to contemplating color, Baby Suggs relinquishes her imaginary wholeness to her perceived lack in the symbolic structure and recognizes Lacan's ever-present Real, which reveals her fundamental nothingness. In her better days the celebration in the woods created a home for newly freed and displaced souls, where "Baby Suggs, holy, offered up to them her great big heart. [. . .] She told them that the only grace they could have was the grace they could imagine" (88). Like a parent, she mentors them to come into their own.[29] Yet, when she loses the support of the community after Sethe's daughter dies and her two sons run away, Baby Suggs "just up and quit" (177). The powerful trauma of black life in the white world returns with full force. "The heart that pumped out love, the mouth that spoke the Word, didn't count. [. . .] The whitefolks had tired her out at last" (180). Despite her earlier ability to embrace her postslavery life, Baby Suggs succumbs to her objectification by the larger culture. Volkan describes how white culture's "negative externalization and projection may evolve as a permanent part of the subjugated group's identity" (44). The depth of Baby Suggs's trauma illustrates the intensity of the struggle to protect the ego.

The trauma of the white world has molded Denver's young life in a different way. Even though she was born into freedom and a loving family, trauma pervades Denver's being: her traumatic birth during Sethe's escape; the traumatic return of Schoolteacher and her sister's murder; her time in jail with her mother; the abandonment by her brothers; and the death of Baby Suggs. She seeks a positive identity and utilizes the past to do so. Needing to escape the memory of Beloved's murder at Sethe's hands and her own imprisonment with her mother, Denver goes deaf when Nelson Lord confronts her with the horror of her mother's crime and their prison time.[30] Blotting out this negative image, Denver gains her positive sense of self from the stories her mother tells about her birth. She hates "the stories her mother told that did not concern herself, which is why Amy was all she ever asked about. The rest was a gleaming, powerful world made more so by Denver's absence from it. Not being in it, she hated it" (62). The story of her birth gives Denver a sense of belonging, safety, and home.

In contrast to the story of Amy, other stories reinforce Denver's sense of vulnerability. To avoid a feeling of being abandoned and defenseless, Denver will foreclose Sethe's and Paul D's talk of Sweet Home because it "belonged to them and not to her" (13). Their safe haven strips her of her safety net; if Paul D possesses Sethe and her memories, Denver fears that she herself will lack that protection. Joan Woodward describes how the bonds of maternal attachment are necessary for both physical survival and for psychological security. "If the loss of these bonds is threatened, both anxiety and anger are aroused. Their actual loss gives rise to sorrow, but their renewal is a source of joy" (8). Denver's survival depends on her attachment to Sethe.

Denver resents Paul D not only for taking her mother from her but also for running off her sister's ghost, "the only other company she had" (19). She creates her own safe space in the woods: "closed off from the hurt of the hurt world, Denver's imagination produced its own hunger and its own food, which she badly needed because loneliness wore her out. [. . .] Veiled and protected by the live green walls, she felt ripe and clear, and salvation was as easy as a wish" (28–29). Renewing her spirit with her own space, she will overcome her fears of abandonment and the outside world to go out the front door and seek financial income to protect Sethe and herself from Beloved's insatiable appetites. She realizes that they will die unless she acts. Sensing Baby Suggs's presence as she stands immobilized on her front porch, Denver overcomes her fear with the following exchange:

> But you said there was no defense.
> "There ain't."
> Then what do I do?
> "Know it, and go on out the yard. Go on." (244)

Memory of her grandmother's strength and encouragement provides Denver with the ego support she needs to act in the present.

Like Denver, who craves a home in order to feel protected and safe, Beloved seeks out 124 to make a home.[31] It is here that she comes to reclaim her identity—to have someone name her name. Coming from the nameless mass of the other side, Beloved seeks self-definition from Sethe and her memory. Sethe's stories can recapture the prior feeling of home through nostalgia or a masking of Lacan's Real. Consequently, Beloved searches for memories that will render her whole, relying on Sethe's storytelling about Sweet Home. These stories buffer the trauma of the fragmented self, unprotected and vulnerable. When her tooth comes out, "Beloved looked at the tooth and thought, This is it. Next would be her arm, her hand, a toe. Pieces of her would drop maybe one at a time, maybe all at once. [. . .] It is difficult keeping her head on her neck, her legs attached to her hips when she is by herself" (133). Beloved hangs on Sethe's stories to provide her with the missing memory that will prevent her from slipping into Lacan's Real as a body in pieces. In order to regain an imagined wholeness, Beloved needs Sethe's memory to reinstate her being; as Beloved says, "[T]he face I lost   she is my face smiling at me" (213). Her mother's love provides a safe haven. Beloved and Sethe reflect an imagined "ideal self" to each other, with Beloved feeling whole and Sethe feeling guilt-free and forgiven. Beloved returns seeking a home and a mother's love. By singing a song that Sethe made up and sang only to her children, Beloved establishes her place in Sethe's heart.

Beloved's returned presence also provides the space to examine traumatic acts in their social context. Verbalizing Sethe's extreme act as it relates to the larger cultural circumstances and the limited alternatives available enables Sethe to process her deed and work through her guilt. Others in her position also committed infanticide, and Sethe therefore repeats a generational acting out of violence as a means of protecting children. Sethe knows from Nan of her own mother's infanticide, remembering it as "[s]omething privately shameful that had seeped into a slit in her mind right behind the slap on her face and the circled cross" (61). To soothe the memory of her mother's death by hanging, Sethe also remembers that it was "Nan who took her hand and yanked her away from the pile before she could make out the mark. Nan was the one she knew best, who was around all day, who nursed babies, cooked, had one good arm and half of another" (62). The mothering Nan tendered will help Sethe to comprehend the chain of familial and cultural trauma that governs her own acts.

Nan represents how a nurturing community preserves and heals individuals so that they can function personally and as a group. Overcoming a negative self-concept through family or community support is paramount because a "child unconsciously takes into his or her own sense of self the images and functions of significant people in his or her environment" (Volkan 35–36). A protective family or home can assuage rejection by the larger community. Sweet Home and, ultimately, 124 Bluestone Road provide positive experiences of home because at both places the black community helps to create a positive identity. It is by reaching out to this community that Denver can save her mother and herself.

By leaving the house and entering the community, Denver finds a selfhood. She will realize later that "it was the word 'baby,' said softly [by Mrs. Jones] and with such kindness, that inaugurated her life in the world as a woman" (248). When Nelson Lord, who robbed her of her hearing earlier, says, "Take care of yourself, Denver" (252), Denver thinks, "It was a new thought, having a self to look out for and preserve" (252). These caring contacts have reconstituted her subjectivity. Thus, when her mother is immobilized by crisis, Denver receives her identity from those outside of her home, with her community providing her with the means to protect not only herself but her mother as well. Denver needs the help of her community to restore her home. In contrast, Paul D, having searched outside communities for a place in which to come into his own, will return to Sethe at 124 Bluestone Road to conquer the demons of the past. He needs a witness to his trauma in order to build a future, and with Sethe he can find a sense of self despite his traumatic memories, by "put[ting] his story next to hers" (273). Together, by verbalizing their trauma in white society, Sethe and Paul D can move forward in the symbolic order to have "some kind of tomorrow" with Denver (273).

As a family, Sethe, Paul D, and Denver can begin to heal from their past trauma and join with the community. At the novel's close, the neighbor women recognize their bond with Sethe and Denver, and they arrive in time to protect them as they did not when Schoolteacher came. Together they howl to verbalize their shared pain and trauma in order to keep the community safe.[32] The community struggles to redefine itself, to free itself of generational patterns and embodied trauma. As a community, the women rid themselves of the haunting Beloved, or past trauma; as a community, they will learn to live with her memory as well. Aoi Mori observes that "the community is presented as the source of racial empowerment" (103). By verbalizing the desire to be subjects rather than objects in white culture, community members voice a more rational desire. Healing comes from confronting the paradox that Deborah Guth describes as "the imperative to remember and the desperate need to forget" (585). While Paul D cannot replace Halle for Sethe and Denver, he can build a future with them that Halle would respect and admire.[33] "Trust and rememory, yes, the way she believed it could be [. . .]. Her story was bearable because it was his as well—to tell, to refine and tell again" (99). Shared remembrance is the route to a forgetting that allows one to live psychically intact in the present.[34]

"Disremembered and unaccounted for," Beloved fades from the community (274). But try as they might to erase her traumatic memory, the community cannot entirely do so.[35] In altered forms, the trauma she evoked remains and is a necessary component of the healing process. The statement that "[i]t was not a story to pass on" suggests that the community should not let it go (275). In her 1994 interview with Angels Carabi, Morrison claims that Beloved's representation of slavery is "a kind of healing experience. There are certain things that are repressed because they are unthinkable, and the only way to come free of that is to go back and deal with them. [. . .] And then that makes it possible to live completely. Part of you is dead if you don't remember. [. . .] So the pain is worth it because the healing is great" ("Interview" 38). Sam Durrant summarizes that "Beloved's presence as the materialization of racial memory ultimately allows Sethe and Paul D to dematerialize their own pasts" (101). Individuals as well as communities must heal in order to survive trauma. This process is especially challenging for those who have experienced the horrors of slavery firsthand. As we shall see in *Paradise,* future generations face similar challenges.

The community's ability to heal through narration and rememory at the end of *Beloved* sets the stage for a healing community in *Paradise,* where freed slaves and postslavery blacks escape from white oppression into an all-black world. However, the communities they create, first Haven and then Ruby, are fraught with unrest. *Paradise* presents two contrasting groups: the all-black town of Ruby and the community of women who live on its outskirts in a property formerly run by nuns and now called the Convent. Both groups suffer from trauma, one generationally transmitted and the other from firsthand experience. The men of Ruby carry their forefathers' trauma of the "Disallowing," their postslavery rejection by both white and black towns because they are considered too dark and too poor. The male descendants of these founding families cannot separate their own identities from this traumatic cut. They preserve the memory of both their ancestors' trauma and their monument, "the Oven," in the establishment of their own, all-black town.

But this "ideal," all-black community, forged to combat the trauma of discrimination, creates its own form of trauma. The men of Ruby destroy social harmony by discriminating against townsfolk with lighter skin tones, harnessing the actions of their women and children, worshipping the Oven and their ancestral past, and scapegoating the women at the Convent. They reinscribe the voice of white culture, reversing the hierarchy of color but preserving class status, failing to separate their own desire from that of their fathers, who themselves re-created an exclusionary world. By dedicating their town to the memory of their ancestors, the men of Ruby value the past and tradition over the current needs of community members, thus depriving their town of the safety and connectedness that it needs to thrive.[36]

In contrast to the men of Ruby, who want to live according to the ways of their forefathers, the women at the Convent seek to escape and forget the traumatic events of their past. Connie, who has been there since childhood and serves as a healer for those who find their way there, and the newcomers Mavis, Gigi, Seneca, and Pallas hope to reinvent themselves and to shed their traumatic pasts in order to create lives with a future. Michael K. Johnson comments that "the 'bodacious black Eves' speak a counternarrative to the American Adam's story of a patriarchal paradise established in the American West" (168). While both groups seek to escape the trauma of their communities and their private lives, only the women succeed. The distraught women who seek a haven at the Convent establish a sense of self and a strong community through empathy and recognition of one another's needs. They emerge as subjects of knowledge, able to move beyond their traumatic past lives. By refusing the demands of white culture, as well as that of Ruby's patriarchs, these victimized women receive positive imaginary selves from their communal space.[37] Both communities demonstrate the importance of establishing a home—a psychic space that provides safety, self-esteem, and connectedness—in order to move beyond trauma. Only supportive communities provide the healing necessary for future generations to grow and move beyond ancestral or firsthand trauma.

A seemingly honorable reverence for the founding fathers leads to the unraveling of the solidarity that Ruby needs for a hopeful future. In their efforts to avoid the trauma of rejection by both white and black communities that their forefathers experienced, the men of Ruby re-create the hierarchical, exclusive world that they seek to avoid. They act out their ancestors' trauma and inflict it on their women and children, as well as on the women at the Convent. Ironically, despite transporting home—the sacred Oven and ways of their fathers—any change or confrontation threatens the town's safety. The challenge for the community is to utilize collective memory to preserve the past yet live fully in the present. Without new rituals and traditions there can be no growth. For the townspeople of Ruby, home, figured as their ancestors' vision of Haven, reflects a positive imaginary self. Displaced by all-black towns that reject the "8-rock" men and women (194) as "too poor, too bedraggled-looking," the townspeople of Haven create their own home, and with it an imagined wholeness (14). Here, the Oven, passed down by their forefathers, becomes for them a symbol of home, self, and ancestry. Connerton describes "ritual *re-enactment*" as "a quality of cardinal importance in the shaping of communal memory" (61). But as the numbers of inhabitants dwindle, depleting Haven of its viability as a home, the townspeople must look elsewhere to establish their community. Despite its positive intentions, as a community Haven collapses. The population shrinks, and farming fails, offering an echo of black erasure in white culture.

The failure of this community to support its inhabitants financially as well as socially produces the trauma of unprotected helplessness. To avert this anxiety, the community moves en masse with the founding fathers' Oven to rebuild a supportive social structure by founding Ruby, a place where they can build new lives and establish a positive identity. Here there is no rejection; here they create an isolated but secure home. Built on the foundation of their fathers' Oven, the community provides safety from the memory of the Disallowing and protection in the wake of that rejection. Like the initial comfort of 124 Bluestone Road and the healing, newly freed community in *Beloved,* Haven and Ruby both eliminate a traumatic sense of victimhood and reinforce a feeling of control. In Lacanian terms, the all-black community evades encounters with the Real by establishing imaginary wholeness and minimizing the trauma of lack produced in the symbolic structure. The small, familylike community provides the nourishment and support needed for ego protection.[38] In addition, the all-black population enables the small group to supplant the larger culture.

The Oven "both nourished them and monumentalized what they had done" (7). Thus, it represents the triumph of community survival despite rejection by the outside world.[39] It voices their own desire for recognition as subjects. But as the community grows, its young people want to be counted, and they argue over the words inscribed on the Oven as well as over its purpose in the community. Their debate about whether the inscription should read "Beware the Furrow of His Brow" or "Be the Furrow of His Brow" or "We Are the Furrow of His Brow" indicates their need to inscribe themselves in the symbolic order of their ancestors (195, 298). They need such recognition by their elders to actively participate in community affairs. While elders like Steward Morgan "remembered every detail of the story his father and grandfather told, and had no trouble imagining the shame for himself" (95), the fourth-generation response is to combat discrimination by connecting with national movements, such as Black Power.

The original trauma of rejection produces vulnerability and helplessness. "It was the shame of seeing one's pregnant wife or sister or daughter refused shelter that had rocked them, and changed them for all time" (95). In addition to being refused aid, the Disallowing (the rejection by white society and other black societies) creates anxiety about surviving at all (194). In founding Ruby, Reverend Misner observes, "They think they have outfoxed the whiteman when in fact they imitate him. They think they are protecting their wives and children, when in fact they are maiming them" (306). By insisting on following the ways of their ancestors, the members of Ruby's patriarchy absorb and pass on their forefathers' trauma. Unwittingly, their new community repeats traumatic anxiety by discriminating against light-skinned blacks and by demanding allegiance to tradition; they unconsciously transmit trauma to their future generations, representing what Erik Hesse and Mary Main refer to as "a second-generation effect of their *parents'* own unresolved frightening experiences" (485). Pat Best thinks that "the Disallowing [. . .] was a burn whose scar tissue was numb by 1949, wasn't it? Oh, no" (194). Social forces in each generation will reactivate the original trauma.

Ruby also loses its protective sense of home when individuals value their own needs over those of the community. In times past, "Haven residents refused each other nothing, were vigilant to any need or shortage" (109). Safety and nurturing were the primary concerns, and the inhabitants of Ruby were "protective, God-loving, thrifty but not miserly. [. . .] They were pleased by the accomplishments of their neighbors" (160–61). Now, however, people take delight in the failure of others, gloating in complacency. The sense of a community in which people either succeed or fail together as a group has vanished. This lack of connectedness recreates both ancestral trauma and the projection mechanisms of the larger culture.

While the leaders of Ruby cannot see what is causing unrest, the newcomer, Reverend Misner, worries about how he can assist the town's leaders to be more flexible in order to nurture its women and young people. He ponders,

> Why such stubbornness, such venom against asserting rights, claiming a wider role in the affairs of black people? [. . .] Over and over and with the least provocation, they pulled from their stock of stories tales about the old folks, their grands and great-grands; their fathers and mothers. Dangerous confrontations, clever maneuvers. Testimonies to endurance, wit, skill and strength. Tales of luck and outrage. But why were there no stories to tell of themselves? About their own lives they shut up. Had nothing to say, pass on. As though past heroism was enough of a future to live by. As though, rather than children, they wanted duplicates. (161)

Yet their ancestors' triumphs and heroic deeds also contain their anxieties and the trauma of the Disallowing. By focusing on the need to live cut off from the world, the new generation harbors the inherent trauma of the past and becomes incapable of adapting and changing in the present. The women and children of Ruby realize the necessity of new memories to rejuvenate the community and make it *their* home, rather than just repeating or worshiping patterns from the past. By verbalizing their own desire to be subjects, they question the demand of Ruby's patriarchs.

Ruby's patriarchal hierarchy reserves power for the rich and the darkest-skinned members of the community. Thus, the identity of the women and children in this community rests on the men they marry, as Pat Best claims. Women suffer for their husbands' stubbornness, as when Pat Best's mother, Delia, dies because the 8-rock men refuse to seek help from the Convent. Their intractable thinking about Delia's light skin destroys the Best family.[40] Pat will later cause her daughter Billie Delia to run off by striking her with an iron, lashing out "to smash the young girl that lived in the minds of the 8-rocks, not the girl her daughter was" (204). Stereotypes about behavior and "place" in the community lore prevent people from living full lives, and Pat, her father, and her daughter all suffer from their assigned niche. The trauma of her mother's death and her daughter's presumed promiscuity render Pat defenseless despite her sheltered, all-black world. In its struggle to break free of national discrimination the town of Ruby "ends up as a conservative, patriarchal, thoroughly racialized, and violent community" (Dalsgard 233). Pat chronicles the genealogy of each family to map the community's pathology and traumatic history. This project allows her to verbalize her town's bad treatment of her family. Once she has completed it, she chooses to destroy it. However, she immediately realizes that she has deprived future generations of the knowledge she had reconstructed.

Like the Best family, others also suffer in this seemingly ideal community. Dovey and Steward Morgan have no children, and an unnamed friction haunts their home. Without his own progeny Steward cannot control the future. Yet, Dovey is Steward's home; he cannot sleep without her and agonizes over the fact that she prefers to sleep in town rather than at their ranch house. Their secure financial and leadership situations do not bring them happiness or peace, because they lack true connectedness with others. Likewise, Soane and Deacon "Deek" Morgan suffer despite their position of power because their sons have died in combat. Thinking that their boys were safer overseas than at home, they are devastated when their hopes for the future perish. The twin brothers Deek and Steward, each once a support for the other, have grown apart in their thinking, and Deek will eventually have to separate from his brother to form an independent and imaginary whole self and rebuild his home with Soane.

The lack of healthy progeny challenges the future of Ruby, which lies in the next generation. Sweetie Fleetwood's babies are sick, K.D.'s irresponsibility leads

Arnette to get an abortion, and Billie Delia refuses to choose a husband. Further, each character expresses insecurity and the need for a more stable home, indicating the failure of their parents to provide secure attachments.[41] The orphaned K.D., despite the support of his uncles and his place in the town's history, acts out for attention and love. Arnette clings to K.D. for security and a sense of self: "She believed she loved him absolutely because he was all she knew about her self— which was to say, everything she knew of her body was connected to him" (148). Billie Delia also is well aware that her community does not protect her. It has branded her unfairly as promiscuous and forced her to leave Ruby. These young people lack safety and protection; their rebellious behavior acts out their inherited trauma in an attempt to shake it. Their fourth-generation trauma illustrates Connerton's claim that the "narrative of one life is part of an interconnecting set of narratives; it is embedded in the story of those groups from which individuals derive their identity" (21).

This new generation falls victim to the inherited trauma of their parents, whose core identities contain two conflicting components: pride in ancestry and the reliving of ancestral trauma. By retelling tales of the Disallowing and their forebears' forging a new community in response to it, the men of Ruby verbalize their positive identification with the heroics and achievements of their ancestors. Like Denver in *Beloved,* who only wants to hear stories of her birth at the hands of Amy Denver, Ruby's patriarchy memorializes the tales of "their grands and great-grands" (161). However, the traumatic rejection by both black and white communities does not disappear with the founding of Haven. Despite the new symbolic structure, the trauma remains and is generationally passed on to their progeny. Thus, the founding fathers and their offspring, "haunted by the fear of abandonment or exploitation," harbor survivor trauma, a "hunger for protection and care" (Herman 111). The ancestral trauma underlying their secure environment can erupt at any time. Inherited trauma and a racist larger culture render Ruby's men vulnerable, and they respond with violence against the women at the Convent, whom they see as "sick" and a threat to their male-dominated bastion.

Thus, the women at the Convent become scapegoats, blamed for all of the ills that befall Ruby: "Before those heifers came to town this was a peaceable kingdom" (276). By projecting their own insecurities onto those at the Convent, the men store up their own positive image in order to protect their homes and families. They act out their ancestral trauma of degradation by lashing out. Yet this violence against others is not the answer to their problems. After the men attack the women at the Convent, the townspeople wonder, "How could so clean and blessed a mission devour itself and become the world they had escaped?" (292). By mirroring the large-group aggression that discriminated against their forefathers, the men of Ruby attempt to cope with and reverse their inherited trauma. But their efforts backfire, and just as "the nation's ideal desire to build a perfect community necessarily implies a violent repression of what it constitutes as its imperfect other," Ruby's isolationist standards for acceptance make victims of those who fail to measure up (Dalsgard 241). Although Ruby was founded to protect the egos of its inhabitants, it will do so at the expense of others, as projection theory explains. Rob Davidson describes Ruby's "rigidly controlled communal historiography predicated on the subordination of the individual to the group" (356). People work through transgenerational trauma most effectively by sharing narratives that can heal, rather than perpetuate, discrimination. Elizabeth Yukins discusses how Morrison "examines the inherent psychological discomfort that comes with having to reckon with historical trauma to which one was not an experiential witness" (238). Rather than rendering blind homage to the past, new generations must reenact their inherited past with a difference. Their customs, if they are truly to protect, require adaptation. Memory, rather than preserving a stagnant past, needs to incorporate the past in a way that benefits future generations. The community's narrative must acknowledge and reshape the past to serve current needs.[42]

In contrast to Ruby's community, the Convent physically and spiritually provides for the displaced women who seek a positive identity and new selves. Their family lives have created fragmented selves, bodies in pieces. This fragmentation represents the same psychic phenomenon Sethe and Beloved experience in *Beloved*; all of these women are victims of firsthand abuse. For the women who seek solace at the Convent, memories are painful, creating lack rather than providing fulfillment. Connie and the Convent space provide the healing necessary for these wounded women to reintegrate their selves. The women who settle at the Convent are escaping firsthand traumatic experiences that reduce them to victims: Mavis flees snickering children, an abusive husband, and guilt over smothering her babies; Gigi runs from a world of violent riots and a lost love; Seneca seeks healing from her early abandonment and sexual abuse in her foster home; Pallas escapes a restricting father, a rejecting mother, a deserting lover, and mocking schoolfriends; and Connie escapes her orphaned and abusive childhood to find stability and love with Mary Magna. The Convent serves as a vehicle for psychic healing by providing each woman with a positive imaginary self to counter Lacan's Real—their fundamental nothingness—and the trauma that characterizes their prior lives. To combat this trauma, the Convent protects them by providing a safe environment where they connect with others.

The novel closes with revised visions of these women, who have come into their own as subjects: Gigi and her father reunite; Mavis returns to guide her daughter Sally; Seneca is recognized by her sister Jean; Pallas, with her baby, returns to collect her shoes and leave her mother and Carlos behind; and Connie finds her ultimate peace with God. These images reinforce the need for an idealized self, often rendered through a nostalgic re-creation of the past. At the Convent, the women confront the painful reality of the past in order to move beyond it. Through the templates of their bodies, drawn according to Connie's instructions, the women graphically "verbalize" their unspeakable trauma. Their unseen bodily pain transfers to their body templates, freeing them from acting it out. By sharing their pain and empathizing with others, the women can heal and begin to function in the present as a community. Their success as a group contrasts with the failure of Ruby's mission. Repeated traumatic memory can limit day-to-day functioning, while rememory can lead to a shared release and renewal of possibilities. Therefore, each woman must form a new concept of home, one that replaces traumatic memory. Collectively the women experience rememory: each feels the other's pain, empathizing with past trauma.[43]

Thus the Convent women create a home that provides sustenance and comfort. As Hesse and Main suggest, trauma from both non-maltreating and abusive parents registers negatively in children, compromising their perceptions of safety and well-being. For example, Mavis's home life is plagued by poverty, fear, and inadequacy, and she operates in an unending cycle of poverty that the reporter who interviews her after her babies die sees but does not fathom. Mavis rejects Spam for "wieners" because "Spam ain't nothing for a working man to eat," missing the irony in the reporter's "And wieners are?" (24). She lies about Frank's coming home for supper every night and "wondered what that would be like: to have a husband who came home every day. For anything" (24). Despite her children and her married state, their home and nuclear family are inadequate.

Mavis feels unprotected, scared, and utterly incapable of coping. Her husband, Frank, views her as "the dumbest bitch on the planet," and when she runs away, she "felt her stupidity close in on her head like a dry sack" (37). Trying to escape her husband's wrath, her children's disrespect, and her guilt over suffocating her babies, Mavis seeks a new physical space in which to heal. When she ends up in Connie's kitchen, "she felt safe" (41). By praising her beautiful nails, Connie coaxes her into shelling pecans to give her confidence. This praise raises Mavis's self-esteem, as she watches "her suddenly beautiful hands" perform her task with skill (42). She chooses to stay at the Convent because of the comfort and support of home: "Connie had stuffed and roasted a chicken. But her decision to spend the night was mostly because of Mother" (46). From Connie's home-cooked food to the eerily soothing presence of the dying holy Mother Mary Magna, the Convent forms an instant home for Mavis. During the years she stays with Connie, Mavis will become a confident and capable woman. Her new, protective environment allows her to see herself as successful and competent.

Like Mavis, Grace ("Gigi") finds the Convent in the midst of an escape. She is running from the blood and violence in Oakland, California. While her first thought is to return to her grandfather in Alcorn, Mississippi, where she might find family love and solace, she gets sidetracked by a story told by a man on her train about the fabled "ecstasy" provided by two trees in Ruby, Oklahoma (66). She postpones her return home to investigate a possible source of pleasure to heal the pain of bloodshed and the loss of her love, Mickey. The Convent and Connie's kindness replace Gigi's family as a haven from the world's violence. Despite her constant tension and quarrels with Mavis (they fight like "siblings" for Connie's mothering love), Gigi stays at the Convent. While there, she regains her sense of control. Her constant battle with Mavis for Connie's attention and center stage, along with her unruly behavior, suggests a continuing struggle with her demons and perhaps a reenacting of physical trauma. Herman's comment that often "the story of the traumatic event surfaces not as a verbal narrative" but as an acting out (1) might explain much of Gigi's exhibitionist behavior. During her stay at the Convent, the love she might have found with K.D. vanishes when he is forced to marry Arnette. Her flaunting of her sexuality and her quarreling with the other women provide Gigi with the feedback she craves to make her feel wanted, needed, or worthy of attention. But she only finds inner peace when Connie forces her to confront the source of her trauma through her body template.

Seneca also ends up at the Convent accidentally, jumping off a truck to assist a clearly distraught and disoriented Sweetie. Reminded of her own childhood abandonment by her older sister, Seneca runs to aid Sweetie, whose despair is obvious. Seneca recalls her own trauma, when she was five, from having "spent four nights and five days knocking on every door in her building" looking for her sister (126). Blaming herself for being abandoned, Seneca hopes that "if she did everything right without being told, either Jean would walk in or when she knocked on one of the apartment doors, there'd she be! Smiling and holding out her arms" (127).[44] She craves physical love from her sole parental figure. She will have to settle for her sister's letter, with its comforting words, to let her know that she is loved. In her window perch, from which she scans the horizon for her sister, Seneca sees a crying woman, who mirrors her inner turmoil and becomes etched in her psyche. Sweetie's crying figure reactivates Seneca's previous trauma, and Seneca rushes to comfort and protect her, illustrating the sensory and motor aspects of memory. Her nurturing gestures, ones that she herself lacked in her own time of need, help Seneca to reenact and work through her own pain. She will spend her life placating others: "Always the peacemaker. The one who said yes or I don't mind or I'll go. Otherwise—what? They might not like her. Might cry. Might leave" (131). Her fear of abandonment, reactivated on a bodily level, controls her life.

In addition, her abuse in her foster home leads her to cut herself in order to achieve relief and garner sympathy. Internalizing blame for her abandonment and abuse, Seneca believes "that there was something inside her that made boys snatch her and men flash her" (261). She blames herself for failing her imprisoned boyfriend, Eddie Turtle, who she believes "knew how hopeless she was" (131). Only after his mother becomes a weeping woman and Seneca fights "the wails that continued to careen in her head" does she decide to flee that reenacted trauma (134). But at the bus station, before she can leave town, a man offers her a job, "complicated *and* easy" (136). She later thinks that her unworthiness led to her three weeks of play and abuse with Mrs. Fox. "The chauffeur had picked her up for Norma like a stray puppy. No, not even that. But like a pet you wanted to play with for a while—a little while—but not keep. Not love. Not name it. Just feed it, play with it, then return it to its own habitat" (138). Her low self-esteem and need to feel loved has kept Seneca a perpetual victim. When she lands at the Convent, she finally finds the home she has been lacking, people to call her by her name, feed her, and want her to stay: "Seneca? Come on, baby. We're waiting for you" (138). Morrison's echo here of Denver's encouragement from the word *baby* indicates the healing power of connection and mothering.

Pallas, the last and youngest to join the women at the Convent, lacks the parental love necessary to develop a healthy self-concept. She is abandoned by her mother, and her father's money is a poor substitute for love. Her lover, Carlos, compounds her trauma by having an affair with her mother. The adults in her life fail to protect her, leaving her vulnerable to further trauma when she runs away to escape. Pallas emerges from a lake barefoot, dazed, and covered with algae, unable to articulate her ordeal: "The nightmare event that forced her to hide in a lake had displaced for a while the betrayal, the hurt, that had driven her from her mother's house. She had not been able even to whisper it in the darkness of a candlelit room" (179). Brought to Demby by an Indian family, Pallas vomits behind the clinic where Billie Delia discovers her. Immediately Billie knows that the cure for what ails Pallas resides at the Convent. Sixteen-year-old Pallas will find the comfort there of "a grandmother rocking peacefully, of arms, a lap, a singing voice [soothing] her" (177). In this place that feels "like a protected domain," Pallas senses that "she might meet herself here—an unbridled, authentic self" (177). Connie's gentle rocking gives Pallas back her voice and the ability to verbalize her trauma. Although she returns home hoping to resume her life with her father, the rejection by her high-school peers leads her to return to the soothing comfort of the Convent. In that community of nurturing women, she can face her pregnancy and discover the inner strength to begin her own life, away from her parents and Carlos. The trauma that triggered her lingering nightmarish image of the prostitute with gold teeth on the mall escalator at Christmas will fade. Her erasure of herself in her mother's shadow will give way to a new sense of self.[45]

While Connie serves as the healing source for these women, she herself found solace at the Convent after being raped and kidnapped from her home in Portugal when she was nine. Sister Mary Magna protects and rears her at the Convent, becoming, both spiritually and figuratively, her mother. When Mary Magna dies,

> Consolata, fifty-four years old, was orphaned in a way she was not as a street baby and was never as a servant. [...] She had no identification, no insurance, no family, no work. [...] she felt like a curl of paper—nothing written on it— lying in the corner of an empty closet. They had promised to take care of her always but did not tell her that always was not all ways nor forever. (247–48)

Mother Mary Magna has provided Connie with her only positive identity. Connie's affair with Deek moves her to want to keep him with her, yet after she fixes up a place for them in the cellar, her need to consume him scares him away.[46]

Connie will return to her spiritual source of comfort, Mary Magna, who "rescue me from my body again. Twice she saves it" (263). Later, Connie in turn teaches the women to find their true selves, to heal the split between their broken bodies and their fractured spirits. The peace they find enables them to inhabit new selves and truer homes. Bessel Van der Kolk and Onno Van der Hart describe the importance of confronting traumatic memory in the healing process: "Traumatic memories are the unassimilated scraps of overwhelming experiences, which need to be integrated with existing mental schemes, and be transformed into narrative language. It appears that, in order for this to occur successfully, the traumatized person has to return to the memory often in order to complete it" (176). As a welcome rain washes them clean of their trauma-filled pasts, they become "holy women dancing in hot sweet rain" (283). With a mercy similar to the one Baby Suggs preached in *Beloved,* the women learn to love themselves. By articulating their pain and nurturing their souls, they release themselves from the bonds of their trauma. Their liberation enables them to work together in harmony as a community, each performing a necessary role; "the Convent women were no longer haunted" (266).[47]

In the protected environment of the Convent, the women heal themselves by confronting individual trauma and forming a supportive community. The novel closes with images of the women finding peace by reuniting with family members on their own terms. These healing reunions transform traumatic memory. In contrast, Deek and his brother in Ruby must separate at the end in order to forge their own paths and rebuild their lives with the lessons of trauma. Consciously or unconsciously, individual, family, and community trauma shape lives and the choices people make. Trauma leaves the ego unprotected, and without a source of nurture people cannot recover from trauma. Inherited or otherwise, trauma— from the threats of the white world to the personal trauma of rape, abuse, dislocation, and loss of family members—never disappears. The men of Ruby rigidly cling to the ways of their ancestors out of a positive identification with their strength and heroic acts. Consequently, their unacknowledged inherited trauma cannot be resolved. The shared rememory of their ancestors' firsthand trauma supports their actions but not those of their children, who need to redefine their community. In contrast, the women at the Convent create a space of their own in which to rebuild their lives, recover from firsthand trauma, and live in the present. Memory and rememory assist in the reenvisioning necessary to re-create a positive self to counter and live with trauma.

In both *Beloved* and *Paradise* the psychic entity of home serves to moderate trauma. The pervasive scapegoating of marginalized subgroups by the larger culture and conflicting components of core identity perpetuate generational trauma. As Morrison stated in a 1978 interview, "We have a tendency to carry those things from the past around with us. Sometimes we look them in the face and sometimes we do not, but [. . .] moral resurrection [. . .] is possible only by confrontation with the dead past" (Shange 48). This confrontation of the past provides the healing that Herman describes: "Remembering and telling the truth about terrible events are prerequisites both for the restoration of the social order and for the healing of individual victims" (1). Ultimately, the imaginary ideal self that furnishes the foundation of a positive self-image emerges after recognition of the Real of one's existence, a process aided by memory—and rememory. According to Herman, "Sharing the traumatic experience with others is a precondition for the restitution of a sense of a meaningful world," making communal sharing of trauma a necessary component of healing (70). Unfortunately, inherited trauma, even from non-maltreating parents, as Hesse and Main contend, perpetuates its generational transmission. In several novels, Morrison investigates the ramifications of the personal and societal trauma that plays out in children. As we will see in the next chapter, *The Bluest Eye, Sula,* and *Song of Solomon* evidence how, generations after slavery, children struggle with the familial, community, and national trauma of its legacy.

TWO

Inherited and Generational Trauma

Coming of Age in *The Bluest Eye, Sula,* and *Song of Solomon*

The cultural and individual traumas experienced during slavery and in postslavery discrimination depicted in *Beloved* and *Paradise* also appear in *The Bluest Eye, Sula,* and *Song of Solomon.* As Dennis Foster suggests in his work on trauma and memory, "[T]he traumas of slavery persist as mute presences for African Americans, [and] the racism that produced those traumas persists as well" (746). In Morrison's novels children learn about American culture, their black communities, and their own self-worth through the legacy of racial discrimination.[1] They must come to terms with economic and social stereotyping while trying to develop their own values and beliefs. Historical and familial inherited trauma complicates their personal lives, as they struggle to discover a unique self. In their search for knowledge of who they are as individuals, they long for the protection, safety, and love that will preserve a singular "self."[2]

Unfortunately, in *The Bluest Eye, Sula,* and *Song of Solomon* children act out in aggressive ways to protect themselves, and their aggression mirrors that of their parents and the greater white culture.[3] Their core identities, defined by the damaging larger white culture and shaped by their parents' trauma, exhibit low self-esteem and a sense of helplessness. Aggression functions as a bodily acting out of trauma and provides a temporary positive imaginary self. Aggressive acts project pain and self-hatred onto others, and this release of bodily cultural and personal trauma provides the home necessary for finding a temporary self. However, Morrison's texts indicate that aggressive responses do not lead to healing.

Another means of coping is to seek a friend to provide feedback and support for an intact identity. In *The Bluest Eye,* for example, Pecola asks Claudia and Frieda McTear how to be worthy of love, and not finding a friend who can serve as a soulmate, she creates an imaginary one. In *Sula,* Sula and Nel instinctively function as the two halves that make a whole. In *Song of Solomon,* Guitar serves as a confidant to Milkman and one vehicle for his journey to self-exploration. Children absorb and inherit the trauma that white culture produces for the black community. The aggressive behavior that trauma begets does not lead to recovery or healing.

In *The Bluest Eye,* the schoolmates Pecola Breedlove and Claudia and Frieda McTear process the ways in which their black population and the larger white one judge people by shades of skin color and economic status. Through their daily interactions the girls perceive that they are somehow "lesser" than others.[4] The novel begins with the simplistic premise of the Dick-and-Jane elementary-school primer that families are made up of a father, a mother, and children living together happily in a well-kept home: "Here is the house. It is green and white. It has a red door. It is very pretty. Here is the family. Mother, Father, Dick, and Jane live in the green-and-white house. They are very happy" (3). The subsequent linguistic disintegration of the passage suggests that this reality does not exist for everyone in American culture: "Hereisthehouseitisgreenandwhiteithasareddoor itisveryprettyhereisthefamilymotherfatherdickandjaneliveinthegreenandwhite housetheyareveryhappy" (4). Morrison's text speaks to the disconnect between middle-class mainstream society and those from disadvantaged sectors, for whom learning about their place in the social hierarchy, as well as about predominant cultural stereotypes, becomes an integral part of growing up. Understanding the greater culture's disdain is easier than comprehending the black community's replication of rejection and contempt.

The Bluest Eye chronicles the sad story of the Breedlove family and their neighbors in Lorain, Ohio. As the darkest-skinned and most economically impoverished family in this black community, the Breedloves serve as a scapegoat for the frustrations and pain that the greater white culture generates. Deemed ugly by her family and community, eleven-year-old Pecola searches for love and acceptance but finds only scorn for her poverty and physical appearance. Rejected by parents, teachers, shopkeepers, and schoolmates, Pecola prays for the blue eyes that society sanctions. Ignored by her mother, Pauline, deserted by her brother, Sammy, raped and impregnated by her father, Cholly, and abandoned by her friends Claudia and Frieda, Pecola finally undergoes a psychotic break that allows her to attain her imagined beauty. Unlike Pecola, who is at last protected in her isolated world, Claudia and Frieda try to process the community's guilt in the demise of the Breedlove family. They attempt to come to terms with the fact that "*since* why *is difficult to handle, one must take refuge in* how" (6).

Claudia's community monitors the Breedloves through gossip, and the confidential phrase *"Quiet as it's kept"* suggests the community's culpability in the family's demise (5). Claudia comes to understand the mechanism of projection: "All of our waste which we dumped on her and which she absorbed. And all of our beauty, which was hers first and which she gave to us. All of us—all who knew her—felt so wholesome after we cleaned ourselves on her. We were so beautiful when we stood astride her ugliness. [. . .] We honed our egos on her" (205). In a manner parallel to the white culture's treatment of blacks, Pecola's community members usurp her ego in the service of their own. Isolated at school, Pecola is "the only member of her class who sat alone at a double desk" (45). This isolation by her teachers leads her classmates to avoid her. Both groups favor the company of Maureen Peal, a "high-yellow dream child" (62). Although she was born with six fingers on each hand and has a "dog tooth," Maureen's deformities are fixable; she can excel in white culture because she is light-skinned and wealthy (63).

The black community's admiration for Maureen's light color creates lack in Claudia, Frieda, and Pecola. This fixation with shades of color replicates the hierarchy of white culture, a structure that the children perceive as strange. They "could not comprehend this unworthiness. Jealousy we understood and thought natural—a desire to have what somebody else had; but envy was a strange, new feeling for us" (74). Envy, the mechanism of wanting to destroy what someone else has, reflects the aggression that distinguishes it from jealousy. Simon Clarke elaborates on envy in race relations:

We perceive others as possessing something good that has been stolen from us; ways of life, jobs, even culture; we try to take it back, but we cannot have it all so we destroy it in envy. The racist in envy seeks to destroy the good that he cannot have. The racist, unable to enjoy cultural difference[,] is an embodiment of envy; making bad what is good and destroying what he cannot have because he is unable to accept and share. (166–67)

Claudia pinpoints the larger cultural mechanism of envy and its embodiment in the social construction of beauty when she reflects that "[t]he *Thing* to fear was the *Thing* that made *her* beautiful, and not us" (74). This thing, "the ideology of racial devaluation," leads Claudia to "misdirected anger and violence" (Baille 26–27). Her aggressive attacks on her neighbor and her own doll serve to protect Claudia's sense of an intact, worthy self.

Claudia, Pecola, and their classmates come to understand "whiteness" as the thing to fear. Kalpana Seshadri-Crooks explains the psychic structure of race in terms of whiteness as a master signifier:

> [T]he structure of racial difference is founded on a master signifier—White-ness—that produces a logic of differential relations. [. . .] the unconscious sig-nifier Whiteness, which founds the logic of racial difference, promises whole-ness. [. . .] what guarantees Whiteness its place as a master signifier is visual difference. The phenotype secures our belief in racial difference, thereby per-petuating our desire for Whiteness. (20–21)

Cultures define people against the standard of whiteness, and to "be a raced sub-ject is to be subjected to the signifier Whiteness" (25). Subjects internalize this master signifier, and "we can assume the prevalence of a master signifier that is 'introjected,' that we identify with in our unconscious, and which gives us our sense of having a racial identity" (27). All members of a society operate in relation to this master signifier. According to Leester Thomas, Morrison's text reveals the "contagious effects of self-hatred and loathing within the nuclear family itself," as well as the "annihilating effects of self-inflicted hatred" (52). Rejection from the white gaze "destroys Pecola's entry into her external world and in turn cripples an interior self-relation" (Doyle 201). Similarly, Cat Moses claims that the "novel's central paucity is the community's lack of self-love, a lack precipitated by the im-position of a master aesthetic that privileges the light skin and blue eyes inherent in the community's internalization of this master aesthetic" (634).

Pecola internalizes her culture's standard of whiteness, believing that if she had the blue eyes of the beloved Shirley Temple and the Mary Jane candies, people's behavior might change. In her rejected state, Pecola identifies with the weeds: "Nobody loves the head of a dandelion" (47). Unloved and outcast, Pe-cola processes the trauma of discrimination and contempt. She senses distaste "lurking in the eyes of all white people. So. The distaste must be for her, her blackness" (49). Even the dandelions "do not look at her and do not send love back" (50). Her only protection is to consume white culture: "To eat the candy is somehow to eat the eyes, eat Mary Jane. Love Mary Jane. Be Mary Jane" (50). Pecola perceives the rejecting larger culture to be her only resource for love, be-cause her own family's structure fails to give her ego support. In their research on attachment theory, Mauricio Cortina and Giovanni Liotti describe the effect of parenting on children's self-esteem:

To the extent that attachment figures are trusting and emotionally attentive to the needs and communications of their children, positive images of the self are formed. On the other hand, if children feel abandoned or attachment figures are not able to attend to infant needs, an image of self as unworthy of love and others as unreliable will be gradually constructed. (5)

Pecola is therefore caught in a double bind: neither her greater culture nor her family can provide her with the resources necessary to develop a lovable self. She intuits that her only avenue for love or acceptance is somehow to achieve white-ness, and she focuses on receiving blue eyes as her means to do so. Farhad Dalal's research on race affirms that "[t]he fact that everything of consequence is white, means that the colonized has to do everything in his power to make himself white, inside and out" (96). Consequently, Pecola consumes inordinate amounts of milk and Mary Jane candies in order to access whiteness.[5]

Pecola's racial self-hatred illustrates the extent of white intrusion on her ego. David Marriott writes that "the pain and anger that intrusion provokes derives not from something missing, but from the addition of something undesirable and dirty that fragments the body by destroying all positive semblances of self. The aggressivity this intrusion unleashes introduces a new dynamic into the structure of the personality" (419). He gives an example of a young girl who physically attempts to remove blackness from her skin by rubbing it raw; in doing so she

is punishing and denying her black body precisely because she unconsciously believes herself to be white. The girl's fantasy is not simply an imaginary or delusionary identification with whiteness: It represents the intrusion, into her unconscious, of phobias that racist cultures project onto the bodies of black people. The clash between seeing oneself—and being seen—as black manifests itself in the form of an "aggravated identity-confusion," whose symptom is a disabling hypochondria that the girl's attempt to scrub herself white fully illustrates. (421–22)

Thus, the psychic intrusion of whiteness results in a twofold negative consequence: self-loathing and aggressivity. The self-loathing threatens to damage the ego beyond repair, while the aggressivity produces an often punishable acting out. Unlike white aggressive behavior, which may sometimes be culturally sanctioned, black aggression reinforces the threatening stereotype of black violence and the danger to whites that the greater culture maintains exists. According to

Ruth Rosenberg, this novel presents "a world that permits the foreclosure of childhood, that imposes a premature adulthood," where a young girl like Pecola who has "been either a victim or a witness of aggression [. . .] learns strategies of defending herself more vigorously than someone who has never been so vulnerable" (442).

For Pecola, the blue eyes that she covets represent acceptance by, and success in, white culture through the lighter skin tones that often lead to greater economic stability. The ability of some blacks to achieve social success weakens the black community through the creation of "a black underclass mired in poverty and possibly at risk of permanent exclusion from full participation in the wider society" (Allen 49). In his study on racial inequality, Walter Allen finds that the legacy of slavery and discrimination "is apparent in the persistent deprivation of blacks, relative to whites, in educational attainment, occupational distribution, patterns of employment, income levels and geographic location. Continuing patterns of discrimination merge with accumulated disadvantages to sustain black deprivation" (57). Economics becomes a vehicle for black exclusion, and those blacks who achieve financial success often identify with white culture while abandoning the black community.[6]

Morrison's text picks up on this phenomenon in its presentation of a stereotype of the upwardly mobile black woman:

They come from Mobile. Aiken. From Newport News. From Marietta. From Meridian. And the sound of these places in their mouths make you think of love. When you ask them where they are from, they tilt their heads and say "Mobile" and you think you've been kissed. [. . .] They are thin brown girls who have looked long at hollyhocks in the backyards of Meridian, Mobile, Aiken, and Baton Rouge. [. . .] They go to land-grant colleges, normal schools, and learn how to do the white man's work with refinement: home economics to prepare his food; teacher education to instruct black children in obedience; music to soothe the weary master and entertain his blunted soul. Here they learn [. . .] how to behave. (81–83)

To fit into white society, these middle- and upper-class blacks will perform as whites, fulfilling their role as objects in the signifying chain. Accepting the demand of the master narrative, they internalize the ideology of white culture and modify their actions. These women are socially constructed to learn "[t]he careful development of thrift, patience, high morals, and good manners. In short, how to get rid of the funkiness. The dreadful funkiness of passion, the funkiness of nature, the funkiness of the wide range of human emotions" (83). The desire to get rid of the "funkiness" represents "the self's desire to hurt the imago of the body in a passionate bid to escape it" (Marriott 419). Christopher Douglas explains that "Geraldine can't change her race, but she can try to change her culture, and this process is described as loss rather than a gain or transformation" (144).[7] In *The Bluest Eye* Geraldine escapes by avoiding human contact or emotions. She will make love with her husband so as not "to touch or feel too much of him" (84) and "did not allow her baby, Junior, to cry. [. . .] Geraldine did not talk to him, coo to him, or indulge him in kissing bouts, but she saw that every other desire was fulfilled" (86). As she blindly acts out white cultural demand, her lack of emotional attachment and motherly love produces aggression in her child.

For example, Junior realizes that his mother loves the cat more than she loves him and "learned how to direct his hatred of his mother to the cat" (86). His torturing of his cat, and later Pecola, attests to his aggressive response to his isolation and loneliness. He "threw a big black cat right in her face. She sucked in her breath in fear and surprise and felt fur in her mouth. The cat clawed her face and chest" (89–90). When he finds Pecola soothing the cat, Junior "snatched the cat by one of its hind legs and began to swing it around his head in a circle," later throwing it "full force against the window" (90–91). His actions reflect his lack of a loving interaction with his mother. While "children with a secure history tend to gravitate toward peer relationships that are based on equality and cooperation[, . . .] children with avoidant or resistant attachment histories gravitate toward dominance and control, in which the dominant peers are bullies and tend to have histories of an avoidant attachment (that minimizes attachment needs)" (Cortina and Liotti 10). Junior's minimization of his attachment needs plays out in his victimization of others. By refusing to let Junior play with lower-class children, Geraldine further weakens his ability to connect with his peers. Barred from playing with other black children, Junior gets pleasure from being mean and "enjoyed bullying girls" (87).

His aggression mirrors that of white culture, and he perpetuates the cycle of racial separation and abuse that he absorbs from his mother. When she finds Pecola in her home, Geraldine focuses on "the dirty torn dress, the plaits sticking out on her head, hair matted where the plaits had come undone, the muddy shoes with the wad of gum peeping out from between the cheap soles, the soiled socks, one of which had been walked down into the heel of the shoe" (91). Pecola represents Lacan's Real, the ultimate objectification of blacks by white culture, and Geraldine defends herself by punishing Pecola: "'Get out,' she said, her voice quiet. 'You nasty little black bitch. Get out of my house'" (92). Her verbal abuse of Pecola bespeaks the trauma white culture heaps on blacks, and Pecola reacts with fear and horror.

Unlike the "elite" blacks, those of lesser means in the community concern themselves not with getting rid of the "funkiness" but with paying bills and meeting basic needs. Claudia's father works hard to keep his family safe in winter: "Wolf killer turned hawk fighter, he worked night and day to keep one from the door and the other from under the windowsills" (61). Her mother, charitably taking in Pecola when she is temporarily homeless, rants about the expense when Pecola drinks three quarts of milk. Claudia can understand the concern with money better than she can comprehend her mother's desire to embrace white culture, as represented in the Shirley Temple doll that her mother prizes but Claudia despises. Claudia dissects the doll "to see what it was that all the world said was lovable. Break off the tiny fingers, bend the flat feet, loosen the hair, twist the head around" (21). When adults scold her for being unappreciative and destructive, she wonders at the adults' attachment to the doll: "How strong was their outrage. Tears threatened to erase the aloofness of their authority. The emotion of years of unfulfilled longing preened in their voices" (21).[8] For her elders, possession of the Shirley Temple doll represents their desire to be part of white culture; Claudia rejects their desire for her own. She envies the doll's lovability and wants to destroy the doll if she cannot have the same love and admiration. Just as Junior treats the cat and Pecola sadistically, Claudia attacks the doll. Later in life Claudia will succumb to the norm, realizing that in her "conversion from pristine sadism to fabricated hatred, to fraudulent love. [...] the change was adjustment without improvement" (23). Her understanding of white "repressive strategies calculated to restore and protect white dominance" (Allen 65) makes her a subject of knowledge capable of becoming a subject with agency at some future time; in contrast, Pecola cannot separate her own desire from that of white culture.

Claudia's observation that because they were children "[n]obody paid us any attention" summarizes the black community's treatment by white culture (191). Despite their attempts to assimilate, the reality is that in the face of the greater culture, "we were not strong, only aggressive; we were not free, merely licensed;

we were not compassionate, we were polite; not good, but well behaved" (205). Her description of her community echoes the white slave owners' views of their slaves, suggesting an inherited status held over from the institution of slavery. The legacy of slavery and the master signifier of whiteness is "for the black child, disavowal—the inability to accept its own blackness, and for the white child, phobia—the inability to introject the other's image" (Seshadri-Crooks 31). Racial difference embeds a separation and hierarchy affecting blacks and whites on the psychic level.

The black trauma of culturally not existing as people for whites creates a psychic struggle to overcome invisibility and powerlessness and to achieve a self worthy of recognition. Research on children suggests that "the need to be recognized and valued by others becomes both a *biological necessity* and a *psychological imperative:* the need to be valued as persons" (Cortina and Liotti 26, emphasis mine). The social pattern of rejection encompasses each generation of blacks, including the defenseless children. Marriott explains the black psychic phenomenon as follows: "[T]hey cannot love themselves as black but are made to hate themselves as white. The dangerous split in black identity between black abjection and white superegoic ideal thus registers as a failure of the black ego to accept the reality of its abjection" (423). Robbed of value and love themselves, parents cannot instill lovability and worthiness in their children. Like the bodily transmission of trauma, psychic inheritance creates an ongoing cycle of deprivation and need.

As the epitome of what white culture rejects—the darkest skin and the direst economic situation—the Breedloves embody trauma. Living in an abandoned store, the family represents Lacan's Real, the body in pieces: "Each member of the family in his own cell of consciousness, each making his own patchwork quilt of reality—collecting fragments of experience here, pieces of information there. From the tiny impressions gleaned from one another, they created a sense of belonging and tried to make do with the way they found each other" (34). In stark contrast to the happy family of the Dick-and-Jane primer, the Breedloves do not gel as a family. "There were no memories among those pieces. Certainly no memories to be cherished. Occasionally an item provoked a physical reaction" (36). Rather than storing soothing, healing memories of love and support, the Breedlove house fosters aggression and hatred. Their torn couch, delivered in its damaged condition and representative of their social standing, functions like a sore tooth, diffusing "its own pain to other parts of the body" (36). Memories in this house are violently physical, not emotionally loving. While the ideal house of Dick and Jane represents a comforting home, the Breedlove house—abandoned and devoid of memories—does not.

Cholly and Pauline Breedlove work out their aggression through their physical violence and constant fighting with each other. Bereft of other alternatives, Pauline is Cholly's scapegoat, and he is hers:

> She needed Cholly's sins desperately. The lower he sank, the wilder and more irresponsible he became, the more splendid she and her task became. [. . .] No less did Cholly need her. She was one of the few things abhorrent to him that he could touch and therefore hurt. He poured out on her the sum of all his inarticulate fury and aborted desires. Hating her, he could leave himself intact. (42)

Their encounters mirror the larger culture's need for someone to project weaknesses onto and the symbiotic relationship of usurping another's subjectivity in the service of one's own.[9]

When Cholly burns down their house, the Breedloves hit rock bottom, for "[i]f you are put out, you go somewhere else; if you are outdoors, there is no place to go" (17). Cholly, "having put his family outdoors, had catapulted himself beyond the reaches of human consideration" (18), ensuring their place as community pariahs. Their homeless state reflects the plight of black Americans: "without cultural/racial identity; without family bonding; and finally, without self-esteem and, consequently, self-realization" (Thomas 53). Being homeless reenacts prior insecurities for both Cholly and Pauline. Pecola inherits their personal trauma, and her own social interactions magnify and perpetuate the cycle of helplessness and loss that they bequeath her. Her parents' constant fighting makes "Pecola tighten her stomach muscles and ration her breath" (40). She bodily stores the trauma that they act out. When her schoolmates taunt her, Pecola bodily reacts to their insults: "She seemed to fold into herself, like a pleated wing" (73).[10]

Sammy's response to the fighting is to continually run away, while Pecola experiments "with methods of endurance. Though the methods varied, the pain was as consistent as it was deep. She struggled between an overwhelming desire that one would kill the other, and a profound wish that she herself could die" (43). Both of these responses involve physical harm. Finally, she wishes to disappear, to fade bodily, one piece at a time: "Her fingers went, one by one; then her arms disappeared all the way to the elbow. Her feet now. [. . .] Only her tight, tight eyes were left. They were always left" (45). Her fantasy reflects the body in pieces and her lack of an integrated self. She resigns herself to the fact that she will never escape, for "as long as she was ugly, she would have to stay with these people" (45). Her entire family internalizes the negativity the community heaps on them, and their belief that they are ugly "came from conviction" (39). Katherine McKittrick writes that "[b]odies and homes [. . .] carry within them, and throughout them, racialised hierarchies, thus producing gendered and racialised behaviour and expectations that may or may not defy oppressive ideals" (127). The Breedloves act out in their bodies and their home life the dominant culture's social order of difference.

Cholly's trauma begins with his mother's abandonment: "When Cholly was four days old, his mother wrapped him in two blankets and one newspaper and placed him on a junk heap by the railroad" (132). Rescued by his Aunt Jimmy, Cholly grows up with her positive influence and that of the drayman, Blue Jack. "Cholly loved Blue. Long after he was a man, he remembered the good times they had had" (134). But despite early positive experiences, the greater culture will traumatize Cholly during his first sexual encounter. What should have been a cherished memory becomes a moment of humiliation, when two white men shine flashlights on him with Darlene and say, "[G]et on wid it. An' make it good, nigger, make it good" (148). Confirming his place in the social structure, the "flashlight wormed its way into his guts and turned the sweet taste of muscadine into rotten fetid bile" (148). The intrusion of the gaze of the Other "violently evacuates the subject [. . .], leaving an empty space where before there was arguably a self, or at least a proper name" (Marriott 426).

During this encounter Cholly directs his hatred toward Darlene. "Never did he once consider directing his hatred toward the hunters. Such an emotion would have destroyed him. They were big, white, armed men. He was small, black, helpless. His subconscious knew what his conscious mind did not guess—that hating them would have consumed him, burned him up like a piece of soft coal" (150–51). Farhad Dalal discusses this phenomenon of directing hatred and aggression either inward or away from the object of pain: "[N]ot only is the colonizer venerated, he is also *feared* because of his power. Thus the aggression, which cannot be expressed 'upwards' because the consequences are too threatening, gets turned either inwards or outwards in a horizontal direction" (99). Laura Doyle elaborates, saying that Cholly becomes "undone by a racialized gaze, precisely in his moment of entry into the world of embraces, of sexuality" (202), resulting in the "racialized seizure of the intimate encounter" (203).[11] Hatred and aggression lead to self-hatred or mistreatment of loved ones. In white culture, Cholly cannot avoid functioning as a small, helpless child in need of protection.[12] Later in life, any "half-remembrance of this episode, along with myriad other humiliations, defeats, and emasculations, could stir him into flights of depravity" (42–43). His rape of Pecola reenacts his own "rape" in his first sexual experience. Pecola literally absorbs his sexual trauma.

Humiliated, orphaned, and fearing that he may have impregnated Darlene, Cholly flees to find his father. Hoping for a healing reunion, Cholly tries to imagine the exchange: "How would he know him? Would he look like a larger version of himself? At that moment Cholly could not remember what his own self looked like" (154). The erasure of self by his recent trauma, compounded with Aunt Jimmy's death, has left Cholly in his original orphaned state: "He could not remember his mother's name. Had he ever known it? What could he say? Whose boy was he?" (155–56). When his father rejects him, he experiences a traumatic bodily response, crying and losing control of his bowels. In this infantile state he is soothed by thoughts of Aunt Jimmy's nurturing love: "With a longing that almost split him open, he thought of her handing him a bit of smoked hock out of her dish. He remembered just how she held it—clumsy-like, in three fingers, but with so much affection. [...] And then the tears rushed down his cheeks, to make a bouquet under his chin" (158). Aunt Jimmy's loving care and psychic support, the only home he has ever known, register as a bodily attachment.

Yet his connections to Aunt Jimmy and Blue do not suffice. Cholly lacks a consistent parenting model and so fails as a parent himself: "having never watched any parent raise himself, he could not even comprehend what such a relationship should be" (160). In their research on children Andrew Eisen and Charles Schaefer have found that "[s]ecure relationships have protective value and may help to immunize youngsters from developing later separation anxiety and related problems" (17). Unable to grow into a parent himself, Cholly remains unconnected to his children. "Had he not been alone in the world since he was thirteen [...] he might have felt a stable connection between himself and the children" (160–61). His own self-hatred leads to his aggressive assault on his daughter, as he confuses her with Pauline. When Pecola repeats her mother's gesture of rubbing her foot on her leg, Cholly feels the same "tenderness, a protectiveness" that he had felt when he first met Pauline (162). But this feeling quickly dissolves into a "hatred mixed with tenderness" (163), the merging of love and aggression that he felt toward Darlene and that he and Pauline have acted out in their constant fighting, which results in the rape of his daughter.[13]

Pauline's aggressive behavior also stems from childhood trauma. The ninth of eleven children born in Alabama, she experiences physical trauma when, at two years old, a nail punctures her foot. This injury renders her different, making her an outsider to her own family, and explains "why she alone of all the children had no nickname; why there were no funny jokes and anecdotes about funny things she had done; why no one ever remarked on her food preferences [. . .]. Her general feeling of separateness and unworthiness she blamed on her foot" (110–11). While Pauline's trauma begins as a bodily injury, it translates into emotional abandonment, and "she never felt at home anywhere, or that she belonged anyplace" (111). When her family moves to Kentucky, Pauline most misses the sensory reminders of home, and she dreams of a rescuing "Presence, an all-embracing tenderness with strength and a promise of rest" (113). Cholly's arrival signals this protective renewal of home because *"when Cholly come up and tickled my foot, it was like them berries, that lemonade, them streaks of green the june bugs made, all come together"* (115). In their early days, "Pauline and Cholly loved each other. He seemed to relish her company" (115). Each provides a positive imaginary self for the other, mirroring self-worth.

But when they move north in search of work, loneliness sets in. Pauline cannot adjust to the fact that the whites up North are *"everywhere—next door, downstairs, all over the streets—and colored folks few and far between. Northern colored folk was different too. Dicty-like. No better than whites for meanness. They could make you feel just as no-count, 'cept I didn't expect it from them"* (117). Pauline might expect rejection from white culture, but not from her black community. Her loneliness in the North reenacts her isolated youth. "In her loneliness, she turned to her husband for reassurance, entertainment, for things to fill the vacant places" (117). But Cholly, having his own friends and work to occupy him, rejects Pauline's dependence on him. She finds herself lacking any mirror for self-esteem.

To stave her sense of isolation and nonexistence when she is pregnant, Pauline speaks to her babies in utero, *"just friendly talk"* (124). But when she loses her tooth while eating candy at the movies, she loses hope of ever meeting the expectations of the larger culture. *"I don't believe I ever did get over that. There I was, five months pregnant, trying to look like Jean Harlow, and a front tooth gone. Everything went then. Look like I just didn't care no more after that. I let my hair go back, plaited it up, and settled down to just being ugly"* (123). Although she loves her children, Pauline admits, *"Sometimes I'd catch myself hollering at them and beating them, and I'd feel sorry for them, but I couldn't seem to stop"* (124). Aggressive behavior takes over in physical expression of her trauma and frustration. With her lost tooth, Pauline resigns herself to being ugly, and she passes this legacy on to Sammy and Pecola. They inherit the bodily trauma of Pauline's early lack of familial attachment, her disconnection to northern culture, and her conviction of "ugliness."

Pauline compensates for these losses as her children cannot, through her position in the Fisher home at Lake Shore Park. "It was her good fortune to find a permanent job in the home of a well-to-do family whose members were affectionate, appreciative, and generous" (127). In her role as the "ideal servant," she reactivates her childhood coping mechanism of arranging things: "Here she could arrange things, clean things, line things up in neat rows. [. . .] Here she found beauty, order, cleanliness, and praise" (127). Her work with the Fishers represents a bodily repetition of her childhood competence. In addition, they "even gave her what she had never had—a nickname—Polly," filling her childhood lack of one (128). As Jennifer Gillan observes, "The role of Polly becomes a substitute for what Pauline wants: a satisfying and substantial self" (291). Thus, Pauline finds a home of imaginary support at her workplace at the expense and exclusion of her own family. "More and more she neglected her house, her children, her man—they were like the afterthoughts one has just before sleep, [. . .] the dark edges that made the daily life with the Fishers lighter, more delicate, more lovely" (127). Her imaginary self cannot exist in her own home.

Rather than bestowing her joy on her children, she endows them with fear: "Pauline kept this order, this beauty, for herself, a private world, and never introduced it into her storefront, or to her children. [. . .] Into her son she beat a loud desire to run away, and into her daughter she beat a fear of growing up, fear of other people, fear of life" (128). Sadly, she cannot love or comfort her own children as she can soothe the Fisher's young daughter with "honey in her words" (109). Her own environment, where her family fulfills the scapegoat role for the black community, lacks the positive mirror of the Fisher home. As it was for the slaves that preceded her, white culture is available only through service. While Pauline occasionally has nostalgic pangs for her early life with Cholly, the memory has faded: *"Only thing I miss sometimes is that rainbow. But like I say, I don't recollect it much anymore"* (131). Aggression and self-hatred have replaced their former intimacy. The research of Eisen and Schaefer suggests that Pauline lacks the "sensitivity, positive attitude, synchrony, mutuality, support, and stimulation" needed "to promote secure mother-infant relationships," and such a family environment "may result in a diminished sense of personal control in the youngster" (17).[14] Pecola and Sammy try to gain control in self-destructive ways.

With her mother unavailable to her for assistance, Pecola seeks help from Soaphead Church, whose ancestors were bent on purifying the race by marrying partners with lighter skin tones. A hapless misanthrope, he has settled into a life of assisting others in an imperfect world: "His business was dread. [. . .] Singly they found their way to his door, wrapped each in a shroud stitched with anger, yearning, pride, vengeance, loneliness, misery, defeat, and hunger" (172). His own trauma is the result of two abandonments: his mother's early death and his wife's desertion. Soaphead never knew his mother, and all that he has from her is a pendant. The keepsakes from all of the important people in his life provide his only human contact besides the contact he has with his clients. These things, rather than memories, provide comfort and confirm his existence. His misanthropy mirrors the meanness of white culture, and he settles on loving things, not people: "his disdain of human contact had converted itself into a craving for things humans had touched" (165). Pecola's request, however, creates a "surge of love and understanding [. . .] quickly replaced by anger. Anger that he was powerless to help her" (174). He articulates the helplessness of blacks in white culture and attempts to achieve what God has not: "I did what You did not, could not, would not do: I looked at that ugly little black girl, and I loved her" (182).

But his generous gift of blue eyes to Pecola cannot combat her internalized ugliness or her lack of family support. From the moment of Pecola's birth, despite her being a *"right smart baby,"* Pauline rejects her because *"Lord she was ugly"* (126). Pecola's negative self-concept is reinforced in school when her classmates taunt her. "It was their contempt for their own blackness that gave the first insult its teeth. They seemed to have taken all of their smoothly cultivated ignorance, their exquisitely learned self-hatred, their elaborately designed hopelessness and sucked it all up into a fiery cone of scorn" (65). Their projection compounds Pecola's core identity, which will not allow her to be worthy of social acceptance. After her father rapes her, Pecola endures the traumatic physical and emotional rejection by her mother, as Pauline refuses to look at Pecola and does not believe her story. The community also puts some of the blame on Pecola and hopes that the baby will die, because it is "[b]ound to be the ugliest thing walking" (189). Only her friends Claudia and Frieda "felt a need for someone to want the black baby to live—just to counteract the universal love of white baby dolls, Shirley Temples, and Maureen Peals" (190). Yet even they fail her and thus "tried to see her without looking at her, and never, never went near" (204). Even though "his touch was fatal," Cholly "was the one who loved her enough to touch her, envelop her, give something of himself to her" (206). While her father's rape is shocking and traumatic, her mother's rejection and the community's blame and desertion leave Pecola totally defenseless.

When Pecola finally finds sanctuary in her psychotic state, she asks her other half, "suppose my eyes aren't blue enough?" (203).[15] We see that even in the safety of her psychic split Pecola fears rejection despite her belief that she has blue eyes. Pecola's dismissal by all segments of her black community denotes its pervasive sense of inadequacy in the larger culture. Claudia describes the plight of the black community when she observes that the "soil is bad for certain kinds of flowers. Certain seeds it will not nurture, certain fruit it will not bear, and when the land kills of its own volition, we acquiesce and say the victim had no right to live" (206). Aggression in the white culture breeds aggression in the black one, an acting out of trauma not fully verbalized. Claudia instinctively harbors aggression toward the hierarchical social structure. Just as she dislikes the Shirley Temple doll, Claudia resents the unfair privilege of the light-skinned Maureen Peal: "when I thought of the unearned haughtiness in her eyes, I plotted accidental slammings of locker doors on her hand" (63).[16] She and her sister, Frieda, also compete with their white neighbor Rosemary for the upper hand. When they get candy, they will not share with her, flaunting their good fortune by showing off where Rosemary can see them: "We always did our Candy Dance there so Rosemary could see us and get jealous" (76). These responses indicate the need for acceptance in the community and the greater culture.

Claudia and Frieda learn about their stratified culture when Pecola temporarily stays with them after Cholly burns down the Breedlove house. When Pecola raises the issue of love, Claudia realizes that there are concepts she has yet to grasp. "Pecola asked a question that had never entered my mind. 'How do you do that? I mean, how do you get somebody to love you?' But Frieda was asleep. And I didn't know" (32). This theme of defining love—familial, community, and societal—surfaces throughout the story. As the palliative for trauma, love and connectedness become crucial elements in the girls' development. In her search for love Pecola befriends the three whores, who are kind to her because she "loved them, visited them, and ran their errands. They, in turn, did not despise her" (50–51). Their acceptance of her provides a positive, if limited, mirror for Pecola, who enjoys being with them because they talk openly with her and laugh deeply. Their banter about men causes Pecola to wonder, "What did love feel like? [. . .] How do grown-ups act when they love each other?" (57). Her parents are a poor model, since they show little love to each other or to her. Thinking about her parents in bed, she ponders the fact that Cholly's painful noises "were not nearly as bad as the no noise at all from her mother. It was as though she was not even there. Maybe that was love. Choking sounds and silence" (57). Despite the brutality of their relationship, Pauline stays with Cholly for intimacy and his touch. Their lovemaking gives her a self: *"I feel him loving me. Just me. [. . .] he has let go of all he has, and give it to me. To me. To me. When he does, I feel a power. I be strong, I be pretty"* (130). Although the tenderness is gone by the time Cholly runs off at the story's end, Pauline misses him. In a tragic repetition of the forced separation of families during slavery, the Breedlove unit comes undone. The precedent of separation resurfaces to impede family coherence.[17]

While her parents have a more stable relationship than the Breedloves', Claudia also has difficulty defining love. She knows that when she is sick, her mother tends to her but does so with anger. "I do not know that she is not angry at me, but at my sickness" (11). Claudia's sickness represents her mother's own vulnerability: the challenge of medical costs and lost work time, as well as caring for Claudia properly. Preoccupied with financial obligations and keeping their children safe, the McTears have little time for frivolous warmth or playfulness. Unselfconscious ease does not exist for blacks in this society. Her mother expresses generations of pain when she sings the blues, and her soulful singing comforts Claudia. Claudia's mother provides a consistent and ready response to her needs. In addition, their intact family unit provides both Claudia and her mother with her father's support.[18]

But all of the segments of Claudia's black community sorely need the soft touch of others, rather than the harsh contacts that surround them, in order to build the protective self-esteem and memories that can alleviate trauma. In addition to the psychic trauma of living in a white culture, Claudia's community absorbs the trauma the Breedloves suffer, for "the symptoms of trauma may influence and/or disturb those who bear witness to them" (Ball 19).[19] Pecola's trauma touches Claudia and her sister, despite their attempts to look the other way. Cortina and Liotti explain that witnessing trauma creates a neurological reaction: "the same mirror neurons are activated when we prick a finger with a needle, or when we see someone pricked with a needle or simply when someone tells us that the finger of a person was pricked with a needle" (22). The cultural legacy of trauma produces a community incapable of nurturing its members.

With the loss of their friend and their innocence, Claudia and Frieda recognize the community's lack of love and the negative seeds it sows. As we saw in *Beloved* and *Paradise,* only when community members overcome the need for scapegoats can they work together to create a protective environment. The devastating outcome of *The Bluest Eye,* in which Pecola's psychic split from reality thwarts any self-love, provides little hope for Claudia that her community can nurture those in need. With her destruction of the Shirley Temple doll, we see hope for Claudia in her recognition of her arbitrary signification and the demand of her culture. Despite her resignation to the master narrative, Claudia's self-reflection shows that she has the strength to pursue her own desire. Kathleen Woodward summarizes the bleakness of this environment, observing that in *The Bluest Eye* "shame leads either to lacerating violence or to debilitating depression. [. . .] shame takes on the intense form of racial humiliation or the numbing form of pervasive daily racism, resulting either in trauma or chronic discrimination, neither of which can be overcome" (217). The girls never adequately verbalize their grief or mourn Pecola. Morrison's work progresses from the debilitating cycle of trauma in *The Bluest Eye* to the tentative self-love in *Sula* and its possibility in *Song of Solomon.*

Sula narrates the struggles of a black community in Ohio between 1919 and 1965. Primarily, it tells the story of two childhood friends, Nel Wright and Sula Peace, spiritual soulmates who go their separate ways when Nel marries but reunite ten years later. In addition, it exposes the small-mindedness of the black community toward Shadrack, a veteran suffering from post-traumatic stress disorder; Nel's mother, Helene, the financially comfortable newcomer from New Orleans; and Sula and her grandmother Eva. The novel depicts the cultural trauma of being black in a post–World War I white society, as well as the physical and emotional personal trauma of loss, abandonment, and family dysfunction. While the community in some ways resembles the one in *The Bluest Eye,* in *Sula* the possibility for personal agency emerges to provide a glimmer of hope for individual development.

The novel opens with the destruction of "the Bottom," the black community's land, to make way for suburban development. A tone of loss and reminiscence, through community tales about the pool hall and Reba's Grill, frames the story.

While this black community literally becomes homeless, it masks the pain of dislocation with humor in its perpetuation of the white man's "joke" that set up the community in the first place. According to community lore, a "white farmer promised freedom and a piece of bottom land to his slave if he would perform some very difficult chores" (5). When it came time to honor this agreement, the farmer, not wanting to relinquish the rich bottom land, cheated the slave by telling him that the high, rocky, windy land was "the bottom of heaven—best land there is" (5). Thus the joke that begot the town forms the self-deprecating humor that "folks tell on themselves when the rain doesn't come, or comes for weeks, and they're looking for a little comfort somehow" (5). The ability to recognize one's plight with humor helps to ease the pain.[20] Once settled in their space, the black community members go about the chore of living their daily lives, much as Claudia's parents and community members do in *The Bluest Eye.*

This framing of the novel encompasses the trauma of black life in white culture: scapegoat, butt of jokes, a lesser other. The story of the traumatized black veteran, Shadrack, reinforces the lack of self that constitutes the core of black identity.[21] Shadrack's trauma results from seeing, in World War I France, a fellow soldier get his head blown off and the subsequent headless body, running "on, with energy and grace, ignoring altogether the drip and slide of brain tissue down its back" (8). As Shadrack recovers in the hospital, he becomes Lacan's body in pieces when he senses that he has no control over his hands or other body parts: "anything could be anywhere" (8). He breaks down and cries when he emerges from the hospital and realizes that "he didn't even know who or what he was . . . with no past, no language, no tribe, no source, no address book, no comb, no pencil, no clock, [. . .] and nothing nothing nothing to do" (12). Like the freed slaves in *Beloved* and the orphaned Cholly in *The Bluest Eye,* Shadrack lacks a sense of self and has no clear idea of how to live in the world.

In order to reenter life after the war, Shadrack needs to see a reflected self to know that he exists. Looking into the toilet, Shadrack sees his "grave black face. A black so definite, so unequivocal, it astonished him. He had been harboring a skittish apprehension that he was not real—that he didn't exist at all. But when the blackness greeted him with its indisputable presence, he wanted nothing more" (13). Through the mirrored reflection of the water, Shadrack forms an intact self that the larger culture denies him. Having survived Lacan's Real of nothingness, he can begin anew by "making a place for fear as a way of controlling it. [. . .] It was not death or dying that frightened him, but the unexpectedness of both"

(14). To commemorate his triumph, and as a yearly reminder of the precarious-ness of life and his own identity, he establishes National Suicide Day, a day when "everybody could get it out of the way and the rest of the year would be safe and free" (14). In doing so he verbalizes his own past trauma, as well as his black com-munity's perilous status in the greater culture.[22]

Recovered enough to function in daily life, Shadrack isolates himself from society, living on its fringes in an eccentric and independent way. While the black community initially shuns him, they eventually learn how to live with him: "Once the people understood the boundaries and nature of his madness, they could fit him, so to speak, into the scheme of things" (15). Just as the greater white culture calculates its relationship with blacks in terms of boundaries, so Shadrack's com-munity negotiates an alliance with him, absorbing his idiosyncrasies into their routines. "Suicide Day became a part of the fabric of life up in the Bottom of Medallion, Ohio" (16). Shadrack creates a new home for himself. The commu-nity members separate themselves from Shadrack just as those in *The Bluest Eye* kept a distance from the Breedloves and Pecola, but without the vicious aggres-sive projection.

Individual lives in the Bottom harbor unique personal traumas, which are passed down with communal trauma. For example, Nel's mother, Helene Sabat Wright, constricts Nel's experiences based on her own fearful past. The daughter of a "Creole whore" (17), Helene is taken from her mother's brothel and raised by her Christian grandmother. When Wiley Wright, a ship's cook on the Great Lakes line, falls in love with and marries Helene, both she and her grandmother are pleased about her move to Medallion, to "a lovely house with a brick porch and real lace curtains at the window" (17). Helene Wright makes a proper home (much like the Dick-and-Jane house in *The Bluest Eye*) for her husband, even though he is home "only three days out of every sixteen" (17). Her new home alleviates the trauma of her rejecting mother, a "painted canary who never said a word of greeting or affection" (26), but it does not erase her earlier trauma.[23] To compensate for her early lack of motherly love, Helene overprotects her own daughter, Nel, by raising her strictly: "Any enthusiasms that little Nel showed were calmed by the mother until she drove her daughter's imagination under-ground" (18). In order to avoid her own mother's weaknesses and her own early trauma, Helene bars any "funkiness" in Nel to ensure that Nel "had no aggres-sion. Her parents had succeeded in rubbing down to a dull glow any sparkle or splutter she had" (83).[24]

Like Geraldine and the other middle-class women in *The Bluest Eye,* Helene represses her earlier trauma by blending with the greater culture. She tries to mold Nel physically as well as socially when she makes Nel "pull her nose" and put a clothespin on it at night so she can have "a nice nose" later in life, and every Saturday Nel endures "the hateful hot comb" (55).[25] Helene aims for a "[w]hiteness [that] offers a totality, a fullness that masquerades as being," so as to reduce her cultural and personal anxiety (Seshadri-Crooks 45). Yet despite Helene's good works in the community, her effort to perform adequately in the white world draws contempt from the "people in the Bottom[, who] refused to say Helene. They called her Helen Wright and left it at that" (18). In her attempt to compensate for her early deficits in life and to find acceptance in the greater culture, Helene reaps the disdain of her own community. She remains an outsider, a scapegoated other whom the community can single out in order to ease its own pain. This aggressive response, while milder than the one toward the Breedloves in *The Bluest Eye,* nonetheless serves the function of projection.

Helene's trauma is twofold. White culture's restrictions compound her mother's rejection. When Helene must leave her complacent life in Medallion to return to New Orleans because her beloved grandmother is dying, her earlier memories of white cruelty to blacks in the South are triggered. Needing protection as she ventures into the harsh white world of her youth, Helene makes a dress to protect herself on the trip south in the hope that her demeanor will ward off evil. She tries to fabricate a culturally acceptable [white] body image.[26] But her train ride south reactivates her childhood trauma and unfortunately creates a similar trauma for Nel. Helene and Nel mistakenly enter the train through the "whites only" car, and the conductor's treatment of them rekindles Helene's memory of discrimination. When the conductor calls her "gal," "[a]ll the old vulnerabilities, all the old fears of being somehow flawed gathered in her stomach and made her hands tremble" (20). His words provoke a bodily reenactment of her painful experiences, and her automatic response is to placate the conductor through apologies and smiles, "[l]ike a street pup that wags its tail at the very doorjamb of the butcher shop he has been kicked away from" (21). Her response shows how "in dangerous situations a behavioral reaction is activated before the danger is registered as a feeling (anxiety or fear)" (Cortina and Liotti 4).

When Nel perceives the disdain of the black soldiers on the train toward her mother for her submissive response, she experiences the trauma of rejection that her mother tries to evade. Nel fears that "if *she* [her mother] were really custard, then there was a chance that Nel was too" (22). Faced with Lacan's Real by witnessing her mother melt into a body in pieces, Nel "resolved to be on guard—always. She wanted to make certain that no man ever looked at her that way. That no midnight eyes or marbled flesh would ever accost her and turn her into jelly" (22). Nel's trauma comes from watching her mother's trauma in the greater community, where "culture determines and maintains the imago associated with blackness" (Marriott 420).[27] When they discover that there are no toilets for the "colored" and that they must go in the grass with the other blacks, Nel further experiences the degradation of the greater culture that Helene has avoided by living in Ohio.

Nel's best friend, Sula, lives in a less regimented home but nonetheless absorbs the traumas of both her mother, Hannah, and her grandmother, Eva. As the matriarch of that family, Eva is led by her trauma—her husband BoyBoy's abandonment and dire poverty—to the desperate acts of leaving her three children under the age of five for eighteen months and sacrificing her leg for the lifetime insurance she collects to support her family.[28] Her options in white culture leave her few avenues for financial security, and she responds to her trauma with an aggressive attack on herself. But Eva later works through her abandonment trauma when BoyBoy returns three years after his desertion. She realizes when she sees a flashy, big-city, insensitive womanizer that she hates him. Her hatred of BoyBoy brings her relief: "Hating BoyBoy, she could get on with it, and have the safety, the thrill, the consistency of that hatred as long as she wanted or needed it to define and strengthen her" (36). By projecting her hatred and anger onto BoyBoy, Eva experiences imaginary fulfillment. Like Shadrack, who is able to recognize and then move beyond his trauma, Eva comes to terms with her place in the master narrative, settling down to the task of raising her children and establishing her place in the community.

Unfortunately, Eva's abandonment of her three young children—Pearl, Plum, and Hannah—for eighteen months creates attachment trauma for them, in addition to their absorption of Eva's own trauma.[29] In her absence, Eva fails to provide her children with the "*proximity,* [. . .] *safe haven* [. . .] and *secure base* that they need" (Siegel, "An Interpersonal" 37). Pearl leaves for Flint, Michigan, and never returns. Plum perhaps suffers the most, because he will have the additional burden of postwar trauma. He returns from war traumatized and addicted to drugs. Although he served his country during wartime, he cannot find a place to live meaningfully when he returns home. His need for his mother to heal him over-

powers Eva and leads her to set Plum on fire. Claiming that she killed Plum because "[t]here wasn't space for him in my womb. And he was crawlin' back," Eva
voices Plum's failure to mature into an independent man (71).[30] Unlike Shadrack,
who heals himself of postwar trauma through recognition of personal and community trauma, Plum cannot stand on his own. Eva protects Plum from death by
overdose or a perhaps worse fate by administering her own mercy killing. However, she takes no joy from the act: "But I held him close first. Real close. Sweet
Plum. My baby boy" (72). Eva's killing of Plum is reminiscent of slave infanticide:
she kills him out of mother love, claiming him on her own terms and not those of
the larger society.[31]

Knowing that Eva has killed Plum, Hannah asks Eva if she ever loved them.
"I know you fed us and all. I was talkin' 'bout something else. Like. Like. Playin'
with us. Did you ever, you know, play with us?" (68). Eva's heated response defends her actions. By focusing on feeding them and taking care of their physical
needs, Eva parented as best she could. Eva explains that there was no time for
play, because surviving was a serious business. "You want me to tinkle you under
the jaw and forget 'bout them sores in your mouth? Pearl was shittin' worms and
I was supposed to play rang-around-the-rosie?" (69).[32] While Hannah knows that
Eva has been a steady presence for her, she senses some deficit of playful bonding
with her mother.[33] Hannah's mothering of Sula will take a backseat to the fulfillment of her own need for playful touching.

When Hannah's husband dies, Sula is three. Hannah fills her loneliness and
meets her attachment needs by having sex with men on a regular basis. Like the
whores in *The Bluest Eye*, Hannah needs "some touching every day" (44). The
"Peace women loved all men. It was manlove that Eva bequeathed to her daughters" (41). Hannah takes daylight lovers and teaches Sula "that sex was pleasant
and frequent, but otherwise unremarkable" (44). The community views Hannah as generous in her affairs, as she does not steal husbands but just borrows
them. Perhaps Hannah's weak emotional bond to Eva accounts for her comment
about her own daughter: "I love Sula. I just don't like her" (57).[34] In a repetition
of Hannah's questioning of Eva's love, Sula now doubts Hannah. Sula learns from
her mother's rejecting comment that "there was no other that you could count
on" (118–19). Since a "sense of self emerges directly from self-other interactions,"
with "communication within attachment relationships [being] the primary experience" (Siegel, "An Interpersonal" 31), Sula, like Hannah, lacks the safe haven or
secure space that parental attachment provides.

The cycle of abandonment trauma that Eva endures thus continues two generations later with three events in Sula's life: Hannah's biting statement of dislike;
Shadrack's possible witnessing of Sula's part in Chicken Little's accidental death;
and Ajax's forsaking of their relationship. Sula's actions attempt to compensate
for her vulnerability. Without her mother's support, Sula turns to Nel to create
a sense of self. Each girl mirrors a firm identity for the other, and they "had difficulty distinguishing one's thoughts from the other's" (83). Morrison has com-
mented that "there was a little bit of both in each of those two women [...]. But
each one lacked something the other one had" (Stepto 13). Unlike most friends,
the girls do not quarrel over boys or express jealousy. Emotionally, they bond to
form a supportive relationship.[35]

Sula and Nel will share a life trauma of guilt when Chicken Little joins their
play by the river. Sula befriends him, first climbing a tree with him and then
swinging him. When her grip fails, he flies into the water and drowns as both
Nel and Sula stand by and watch. The death of Chicken Little teaches Sula that
"there was no self to count on either. She had no center, no speck around which
to grow" (119).[36] Like Sethe and other freed slaves in *Beloved* and Shadrack when
he returns from war, in her core identity Sula lacks an integrated self. Sula perceives her vulnerability on two levels. First, Chicken Little's quick disappearance
suggests her own physical vulnerability. Second, the possibility that Shadrack has
witnessed her failure to save Chicken Little creates a psychological vulnerability regarding the safety of her secret. Although Shadrack says "always" to assure
Sula of permanency so that she will not fear death, Sula and Nel will harbor the
traumatic memory of Chicken Little's sudden death and their part in it forever:
"the bubbly laughter and the press of fingers in the palm would stay aboveground
forever" (66). The brevity of life and the finality of death mark the girls.

Sula also realizes the tenuousness of her friendship with Nel. "She had clung
to Nel as the closest thing to both an other and a self, only to discover that she
and Nel were not one and the same thing" (119). Sula's response to lack and vulnerability has been to create attachment bonds through Nel, relying on her as a
caretaker. "Whenever I was scared before, you knew just what to do" (101). In a
reciprocal way, Nel perks up when Sula returns, sensing the return of her other
half: "Talking to Sula had always been a conversation with herself. [...] Sula never
competed; she simply helped others define themselves. [...] humor returned"
(95). The recovery of her former self includes her ability to laugh, an outlet for
life's trials that dissolves daily setbacks. "It had been the longest time since she

had had a rib-scraping laugh. She had forgotten how deep and down it could be" (98). Their childhood bond has weathered time and separation, restoring perhaps through nostalgic memory a carefree aspect of youth and a positive mirror.

But Sula's physical attachment needs go beyond Nel. Having absorbed from her mother that sex is an uneventful, routine act, Sula sleeps indiscriminately with whomever she chooses. She insults the women by sleeping with their husbands once and discarding them, and her lack of empathy makes her wonder what all the fuss is about when she sleeps with Jude.[37] While Hannah uses sex to connect through touching, Sula uses sex to escape her numbness by creating sadness in order to feel alive. Only later will Sula realize that it is through sex that she finds "misery and the ability to feel deep sorrow. She had not always been aware that it was sadness that she yearned for" (122). Thus, for Sula sex becomes an expression of grief, a "verbalization" of the trauma of her mother's abandonment. After her sexual encounters, Sula withdraws into a "privateness in which she met herself, welcomed herself, and joined herself in matchless harmony" (123). Carolyn Jones describes Sula's sexuality as "a place where she recovers the self that her mother took away, the self on which she can depend. It is the way to experience and to mourn the death of her dislocated self that Shadrack promised she would never experience" (622).

Through her sexual liaisons, Sula bodily creates a sense of being that did not exist before and temporarily fills her emptiness. Unfortunately for her friendship with Nel, Sula counts Nel's husband, Jude, among her conquests. Nel takes this act as a personal betrayal: "And you didn't love me enough to leave him alone. To let him love me" (145). Sula, on the other hand, merely seeks to penetrate her numbness. Joan Woodward's research finds that weak maternal attachments leave some children "unable to fully comprehend how others feel" (18). In addition, reactions to the loss of primary attachment figures include numbness, yearning, searching, anger, disorganization, despair, and detachment (19). The last straw for the community comes when Sula sleeps with white men, for there "was nothing lower she could do, nothing filthier" (113). This final act of rebellion, in a repetition of slaveholders' defilement of black women, secures Sula's position as community pariah. Her search for bodily pleasure that mirrors a positive imaginary self unleashes the pent-up aggression in her community as Sula becomes its scapegoat.

Circumscribed from childhood by both black and white communities, Sula learns to protect herself by acting in aggressive ways. For example, to protect Nel and herself from the boys who taunt them, she cuts off the tip of her finger. She later thinks, "The one time she tried to protect Nel, she had cut off her own finger tip and earned not Nel's gratitude but her disgust" (141). This misunderstanding by Nel of Sula's intent resembles Eva's sacrificing her leg to protect her family, an act that garners disgust in return. Sula repeats her grandmother's self-mutilation as a means of protection.[38] At other times, Sula responds with a numbness that immobilizes her. Just as she and Nel stand by and watch Chicken Little drown, Sula later watches her mother burn. "I stood there watching her burn and was thrilled. I wanted her to keep on jerking like that, to keep on dancing" (147). Numbed by her abandonment trauma, Sula finds emotional release as she watches transfixed. "Sula had watched Hannah burn not because she was paralyzed, but because she was interested" (78). Her fascination with her mother's pain helps to overcome her numbness by making Sula feel more alive, just as the greater culture inflicts pain on the black community as a mode of projection. Nel later ponders this protective mechanism when she thinks about Chicken Little's death: "Why didn't I feel bad when it happened? How come it felt so good to see him fall?" (170). Scapegoating performs the function of saving oneself at the expense of the other. "Just as the water closed peacefully over the turbulence of Chicken Little's body, so had contentment washed over her enjoyment" (170). Nel voices how her community uses Sula as a scapegoat and the violence that accompanies the process. Patricia McKee summarizes this phenomenon when she writes that

> people in the Bottom distribute their moral variations among themselves in order to contain what they could project into the white population only at the risk of their own lives. What they contain is not only the evil that would more accurately be located outside their community but their own rage, which, because limitless, cannot be stopped once let loose. (13)

Thus, Sula actually performs a valuable service for her community.

Sula's vulnerability surfaces when she falls in love with Ajax. He finds her interesting and aloof, like his mother. Sula likes the fact that he talks to her and sees her as a whole person. Absorbing a sense of self from his attention, Sula cultivates their relationship, feeling a connection that has been lacking in her other sexual dalliances. When Sula makes love to Ajax, she thinks: *"I will water your soil, keep it rich and moist. But how much? How much water to keep the loam moist? And how much loam will I need to keep my water still? And when do the two make mud?"* (131).

She imagines rubbing his black body to uncover a layer of gold, then alabaster, finally reaching the layer of loam that forms his core. Ajax's gaze may make Sula whole, but she usurps his identity in the service of her own. As in white abuse of blacks, Sula wants to carve Ajax to fulfill her own needs. He responds to her actions by leaving her.

With Ajax's abandonment, "he had left nothing but his stunning absence. An absence so decorative, so ornate, it was difficult for her to understand how she had ever endured, without falling dead or being consumed, his magnificent presence" (134). Ajax's desertion of Sula is like BoyBoy's desertion of Eva: both men dodge responsibility in favor of life in the big city and reject domestication. Sula's final blow comes when she discovers that she had not even known his name. Having called him Ajax all her life, she learns that his name was Albert Jacks. "A. Jacks" (135). Sula feels empty of all significance: "there is nothing I did know and I have known nothing ever at all since the one thing I wanted was to know his name so how could he help but leave me since he was making love to a woman who didn't even know his name" (136). His desertion leaves her like the paper dolls of her childhood, whose heads came off: "I lost it just like the dolls" (136). Reduced to a body in pieces, Sula cannot recover despite her attempt to mother herself by singing until, "touched by her own lullaby, she grew drowsy" (137). She will never leave her bed again. Sula's only comfort comes from looking at Eva's boarded window, an ironic connection to the grandmother she feared so much that she committed her to an institution.[39] Despite her prior fears, this familial connection soothes Sula, coming full circle to Sula's generational absorption of Eva's trauma. Sula's weakness with Ajax parallels Nel's vulnerability when she loses Jude.

Jude's abandonment reactivates the trauma Nel felt as a child on the train with her mother.[40] His parting look of disdain and hatred sears Nel: "if only you had not looked at me the way the soldiers did on the train" (105). Reliving her mother's meltdown, Nel imagines that she herself must be custard if she provokes that hateful look from Jude. Initially, after that trip, Nel had discovered a sense of self: "I'm me. I'm not their daughter. I'm not Nel. I'm me. Me" (28). Just as Shadrack's toilet-bowl mirror produces a cohesive self in the midst of trauma, Nel becomes a separate entity. Realizing that she is lonely and vulnerable, she will find a friendship to meet her needs. "The trip, perhaps, or her new found me-ness, gave her the strength to cultivate a friend in spite of her mother" (29). Unfortunately, when Jude leaves her, Nel's loss of Sula doubles her pain: "To lose

Jude and not have Sula to talk to about it because it was Sula that he had left her for" (110). She loses both of her positive mirrors.

In her grief, Nel thinks about the function of mourning: "The body must move and throw itself about, the eyes must roll, the hands should have no peace, and the throat should release all the yearning, despair and outrage that accompany the stupidity of loss" (107). She describes the bodily response that trauma triggers, as well as the need to verbalize trauma in order to move through it. She needs to mourn for the loss of Jude, to express her grief. Nel waits for "a deeply personal cry for one's own pain. A loud, strident: 'Why me?'" (108) and speaks of "the flake in her throat" (109). Nel sleeps with her children for their comfort and for hers, to keep away the "gray ball hovering just there. [...] Quiet, gray, dirty. A ball of muddy strings, but without weight, fluffy but terrible in its malevolence" (109). Like Sula, Nel becomes a body in pieces, a shell of her former self, "with no thighs and no heart just her brain raveling away" (111). Years later, visiting Sula in the cemetery, Nel realizes her misplaced loss, and her earlier trauma erupts:

> A soft ball of fur broke and scattered like dandelion spores in the breeze. "All that time, all that time, I thought I was missing Jude." And the loss pressed down on her chest and came up into her throat. "We was girls together," she said as though explaining something. "O Lord, Sula," she cried, "girl, girl, girl-girlgirl." It was a fine cry—loud and long—but it had no bottom and it had no top, just circles and circles of sorrow. (174)

Her verbalization allows Nel to grieve at last for her multiple losses.[41]

Both Nel and Sula need an inner core to rely on, but the outer culture's discrimination deprives them of one. Further, a weakened family structure, modeled on separation, loss, abandonment, and faulty attachment, leaves the girls unable to protect themselves.[42] They have been left to mother and heal themselves. Cut off from their families and the community, they have no other recourse but to lean on each other. "Because each had discovered years before that they were neither white nor male, and that all freedom and triumph was forbidden to them, they had set about creating something else to be" (52). Sula and Nel, both lonely only children, dream of having a friend and find "each other to grow on" (52). Such a friend combats loneliness as well as rejection.[43] Like Claudia and Frieda in *The Bluest Eye*, the girls must unravel culture's knot on their own. Unlike Denver in *Beloved*, who recruits community members to save her mother and herself, Nel and Sula work out their healing, less successfully, on their own, in different ways.

Sula's self-sufficient loneliness contrasts with Nel's devastating one. Describing the difference between them, Sula tells Nel that "my lonely is *mine*. Now your lonely is somebody else's. Made by somebody else and handed to you. Ain't that something? A secondhand lonely" (143). Sula's loneliness is of her own making, and while she identifies the loneliness at the core of everyone's being, she explains that it is the agency of that loneliness that matters. Cut off from her community because of her controversial behavior, Sula gains the distance to judge her community. She challenges Nel's community-sanctioned notions of right and wrong: "About who was good. How you know it was you? [...] I mean maybe it wasn't you. Maybe it was me" (146). Judged by community—and thus white—standards, Sula rebels in order to build a separate self. When Nel asks about Sula's defiance, "What have you got to show for it?" Sula reaffirms that her independence was worth the price: "Show? To who? Girl, I got my mind. And what goes on in it. Which is to say, I got me" (143). Sula believes that whether one is good or mean is inconsequential: "Being good to somebody is just like being mean to somebody. Risky. You don't get nothing for it" (144–45). She feels she has gained nothing from her kindness to Chicken Little, her love for Ajax, or her protective friendship with Nel. While Sula approaches knowledge of her position in the symbolic structure, her vulnerability after Ajax leaves deprives her of agency.

"Being good" should make a difference, especially for a community to thrive. If people in the Bottom had been nicer to Sula, perhaps they would not have suffered after her death. Initially, their use of Sula as a scapegoat strengthens their cohesiveness: "Once the source of their personal misfortune was identified, they had leave to protect and love one another. They began to cherish their husbands and wives, protect their children, repair their homes and in general band together against the devil in their midst" (117–18). Sula serves as the other that they must combat.[44] She bears the sins of her forebears, with the community describing her as having "Eva's arrogance and Hannah's self-indulgence" (118). But Sula tells Nel that the community will miss her when she is gone, when they will need another scapegoat to project their weaknesses onto and save them from themselves. "Oh, they'll love me all right. It will take time, but they'll love me" (145). Projection perpetuates a cycle of rejection and weakens the community. The townspeople will love her when they have admitted their own evil thoughts and deeds, "after all the black men fuck all the white ones; when all the white women kiss all the black ones; when the guards have raped all the jail-birds and after all the whores make love to their grannies; after all the faggots get their mothers' trim [. . .] then there'll be a little love left over for me" (145–46). Having deserted her at her death, they will later appreciate her function in their lives.

In fact, after Sula dies the community suffers: "Without her mockery, affection for others sank into flaccid disrepair" (153). They revert to their old ways and bad habits. Eventually, the Bottom as a community falls apart when young people go off and the white developers move in. People need to love and help each other, but they do not know how. They will have to work through trauma "by telling stories, narratives that inevitably appropriate the past and help the community learn to live into their future" (Foster 746). As in Claudia's community in *The Bluest Eye*, seeds will not grow in this soil; the river has killed the fish, and the environment does not nourish.

This lack of nurture prevents healing, and without access to financial stability the cycle of poverty, discrimination, and abuse perpetuates itself. But strong family ties and community sharing can combat such trauma. *Song of Solomon* depicts the need for a shared history on which to build a future.[45] This novel follows the coming of age of Macon "Milkman" Dead III as he discovers his family history. Having grown up affluent and educated, Milkman knows nothing of his grandfather's life as a slave and the trauma his father, Macon Dead Jr., and his aunt, Pilate, endured. Similarly, he begins to learn about the ordeals his mother, Ruth, has withstood despite her privileged position in society. As he unearths his ancestors' trauma of slavery, Milkman also discovers a cultural legacy of discrimination that he cannot escape. His interactions with his best friend, Guitar, his cousin, Hagar, and his sisters, Magdalena and Corinthians, provide the insight he needs in order to mature. Hope for a vital future lies in contributing to the community, learning how to protect oneself without harming others. Milkman learns this lesson primarily from the balanced perspective of his father's sister, Pilate.

The novel opens with the erasure of black culture in white society, depicting discrimination as well as separation. When Ruth Dead goes into labor in front of the whites-only Mercy Hospital, on Mains Avenue, Milkman becomes the first black to be born there. Community lore calls this street Not Doctor Street because when Ruth's father, Dr. Foster, had practiced there, his patients had referred to it as Doctor Street. But the greater culture, in its concern for separation and propriety, decree that "'Doctor Street' was never used in any official capacity," and the edict that the street "would always be known as Mains Avenue and not

Doctor Street" creates a lasting nickname (4). By referring to it thereafter as Not Doctor Street, the black community establishes "a way to keep their memories alive and please the city legislators as well" (4). This opening vignette establishes the conflict between the greater culture and the black community. The unfolding story indicates that the roots of this conflict derive from previous generations and layers of discrimination, familial dysfunction, and abuse. Karyn Ball writes that "both individuals and groups retain partial memories from personal and collective experiences, and [. . .] memory-images and narratives provide both the content and impetus of political and moral claims about historical oppression in the past and present" (8). Each generation inherits a renewed version of the personal and cultural trauma dating from slavery.

Postslavery times were understandably disruptive for both the black and white populations, with disruptions occurring on economic and psychological levels. In a shattered postwar economy blacks posed a threat to the white labor force; the destruction of an agrarian society produced a struggle to find suitable work. Psychologically, whites also feared an upheaval. Marriott describes the black other as "an instinctual component of the white psyche, linked inextricably to the psychic processes in which aggressive drives associated with phobic anxiety and fear become psychically effective through a racial object or delegate" (427). Projection onto the black other perpetuates the post-Reconstruction discrimination that continues to plague society. For example, Macon's assistant, Freddie, explains why he was raised in jail: "You know they ain't even got an orphanage in Jacksonville where colored babies can go? They have to put 'em in jail" (109). Adequate facilities for blacks are not available. A member of the Seven Days enumerates the material items and the luxury lifestyle that are inaccessible to blacks: "no private coach [. . . no] special toilet and your own special-made eight-foot bed either. And [. . . no] valet and a cook and a secretary to travel with you and do everything you say" (60). Society maintains the cultural practice of separation.

Despite his father's money and position in society, Milkman is stopped by the police when he is out driving simply because he is black. To get him out of jail, Pilate plays a subservient black, fabricating a story about how she retrieved her husband's bones after his lynching. Milkman marvels at her "Aunt Jemima act" and "the fact that she was both adept at it and willing to do it—for him" (209).[46] Her performance brings home two important lessons for Milkman. First, Pilate willingly humiliates herself for him because he is family. Second, his own interactions with the malevolent larger culture have been limited. Guitar sums up their situation as follows: "The cards are stacked against us and just trying to stay in the game, stay alive and in the game, makes us do funny things" (87). Milkman becomes aware of the vulnerability of black men, realizing that "[e]ach man in that room knew he was subject to being picked up as he walked the street" (101). Following Emmit Till's brutal killing, a group of blacks calling themselves the Seven Days vows to balance the violence by killing a white for each subsequent black death. The mission of the Seven Days is "about trying to make a world where one day white people will think before they lynch" (160). Milkman's friend Guitar explains the ongoing sociopolitical problems to Milkman when he points out the labor abuse that produces the tea that Milkman takes for granted: "Like Louisiana cotton. Except the black men picking it wear diapers and turbans. All over India that's all you see. Bushes with little bitsy white tea bags blossoming" (114). Marriott explains the problem in psychological terms: "[B]lack men must die so that the aggressive structure of white repression and sublimation of libidinal drives can remain in place" (428).[47]

Guitar joins the Seven Days in his attempt to challenge white culture's easy dismissal of blacks. When his father is cut in two in a sawmill accident, Guitar is only four years old, but the trauma registers on a bodily level. He recalls how

> his mother had smiled and shown that willingness to love the man who was responsible for dividing his father up throughout eternity. [...] It was the fact that instead of life insurance, the sawmill owner gave his mother forty dollars "to tide you and them kids over," and she took it happily and bought each of them a big peppermint stick on the very day of the funeral. (224–25)

Just as Nel realizes in *Sula* that her mother can turn to custard when she must placate the train conductor, Guitar cannot forgive his mother's gratitude for her handout from white authority. He associates candy with this subservience, and it makes him sick forever after. Thinking about the candy, he "felt the nausea all over again" (225). The bodily memory of the candy produces "beads of sweat" and "dry heaving" (61–62). Shortly after his father's death, Guitar's mother leaves the family. "She ran away. Just ran away. My aunt took care of us until my grandmother could get there. Then my grandmother took care of us. Then Uncle Billy came. [...] So it was hard for me to latch on to a woman. Because I thought if I loved anything it would die" (307). Deserting the family in a time of grief, Guitar's mother increases the family's stress by disrupting a secure attachment for her children, and the movement from caretaker to caretaker compounds Guitar's trauma of loss. Years later, Guitar connects his personal and cultural trauma with the violent activities of the Seven Days.[48]

As we saw in *Paradise* and *The Bluest Eye,* the black community creates its own hierarchy, which mimics white culture. Ruth's father, a successful doctor, "didn't give a damn" about the blacks in his town (71). His main concern when his grandchildren are born is that they be light-skinned. Identifying with the white aggressor rather than with his own community, Dr. Foster forms no personal ties. When his daughter marries Macon, Dr. Foster's interest lies in Macon's financial success. An elitist like Dr. Foster, Macon thinks like a white man and lacks empathy with his black community members. Guitar describes Macon's separation to Milkman: "I don't have to tell you that your father is a very strange Negro. He'll reap the benefits of what we sow, and there's nothing we can do about that. He behaves like a white man, thinks like a white man" (223). What troubles Guitar is why Macon emulates those responsible for his father's death.[49] In defense of his father, Milkman says that his father "doesn't care whether a white man lives or swallows lye. He just wants what they have" (224). He fixates on material goods and takes pleasure in ownership, not the objects themselves. For example, rides in the car every Sunday are a duty and "had become rituals and much too important for Macon to enjoy" (31). In his emulation of whites, Macon buys vacation property, cementing the gap between the haves and the have-nots. Taking his financial security for granted, Milkman only realizes the impact of black-on-black discrimination when Guitar challenges him on this point; Guitar's roots in Alabama are a long way from Milkman's party set in Honore. Cars, education, home ownership, and leisure time are not the norm for Milkman's community.

When Milkman leaves his place of privilege to uncover his past, he discovers the layers of trauma embedded in the black community.[50] Slavery, Reconstruction, discrimination, and poverty compound personal family dysfunction. Milkman's journey traces his own family's traumatic past back to his original ancestor, his great-grandfather Solomon, who flew out of slavery to return to Africa, leaving his wife, Ryna, and twenty-one children behind. He "stood up in the fields one day, ran up some hill, spun around a couple of times, and was lifted up in the air" (323). Solomon's attempt to take the youngest child, Jake, with him fails, but Jake drops to safety on the porch of a neighbor, Heddy. Heddy raises Jake along with her daughter Sing. Like many blacks separated from their family during slavery, "neither one of them knew their own father, Jake nor Sing" (322). They head north together and marry, renamed by a drunken guard's error en route. Similar to the accidental naming of Baby Suggs as "Jenny" in *Beloved,* Jake's papers stamp him as Macon Dead.

In these postslavery times, with people dispersed and arbitrarily named, finding someone proves a formidable task. Milkman learns that one aftermath of slavery is the inability to trace one's roots: "It's a wonder anybody knows who anybody is" (324). But Sing decides that they should keep the new name, hoping that it "would wipe out the past" (54). Thus, Macon Dead names his son Macon Dead Jr. When Sing dies in childbirth, Macon Dead names their daughter according to ancestral tradition, taking the first name that he points to in the Bible: Pilate. Although Jake's new name bears the stain of slavery, his daughter receives a name according to black cultural custom. Milkman later learns the importance of Pilate's earring, which bears her written name: it represents her ability to claim her own identity.

Despite his freedom, hard work, physical stamina, and profitable farm, Macon Dead Sr. fails to escape the cycle of racial abuse founded in slavery. Because of his inability to read, Macon unknowingly signs his land over to a devious white family. Refusing to leave his land, Macon dies when he is shot while sitting on his fence. As witnesses to this traumatic event, Macon Dead Jr. and Pilate will harbor this burden forever. Their father's death leaves Macon and Pilate "homeless. Bewildered and grieving, they went to the house of the closest colored person they knew: Circe, the midwife who had delivered them both and who was there when their mother died and when Pilate was named" (166). Circe, who represents the only family tie they have, provides the comfort they need to recover and survive. Although they go their separate ways, Macon and Pilate will pass on the firsthand and inherited trauma that they carry with them. Their father's vulnerability, as well as their own, shapes the way they approach life.

Macon's actions toward others derive from his early trauma. He recalls the "numbness that had settled on him when he saw the man he loved and admired fall off the fence; something wild ran through him when he watched the body twitching in the dirt" (50–51).[51] Having never shared this story with his son, Macon now understands that it is time to verbalize not only the memory of his struggle to develop the land and raise Pilate but also the memory of his father's violent death. As his memory floods back, Macon realizes that "[f]or years you can't remember nothing. Then just like that, it all comes back to you" (52).[52] Milkman notices that his father's voice softens as he tells of his early home life in a rural and more community-oriented culture. In the sharing, Milkman feels close to his father: "Milkman felt close and confidential now that his father had talked to him in a relaxed and intimate way" (54). This sharing helps ease Milkman's own sense of abandonment by his father, as he begins to see the seeds of Macon's distress. Macon's business dealings have been influenced by the knowledge that his father worked for sixteen years only to be tricked out of the fruits of his labor.[53]

Thus, Macon Dead Jr. inherits his father's traumatic history in white culture, which produces a legacy of ownership. He tells Milkman, "Own things. And let the things you own own other things. Then you'll own yourself and other people too" (55). Macon's response to the greater culture is to emulate it, cutting himself off from others in his obsession with accumulating wealth to protect himself. Joseph Brown comments that Macon's father's experience makes him want "to own things and people. To accomplish this he must reject his family, his past (the knowledge of his origins), and the support of his community" (718).[54] He acts out his trauma with hatred and aggression in his interactions with his family and community. Just as Cholly hates Darlene rather than the white aggressor in *The Bluest Eye,* "Macon kept each member of his family awkward with fear. His hatred of his wife glittered and sparked in every word he spoke to her. The disappointment he felt in his daughters sifted down on them like ash, dulling their buttery complexions and choking the lilt out of what should have been girlish voices" (10). His home becomes a place of trauma and confinement rather than one of nurturing and love. Macon also turns on his sister, Pilate, once a source of love and support. Believing that she has betrayed him by stealing some gold they found in a cave shortly after their father's death, Macon disowns her. "At one time she had been the dearest thing in the world to him. Now she was odd, murky, and worst of all, unkempt. A regular source of embarrassment" (20). Blinded by the larger culture's values, Macon cannot recapture his familial love. In brief moments of nostalgia, listening to Pilate sing, "Macon felt himself softening under the weight of memory and music" (30). But although memory moves and rivets him, it does not alter his hardened core. His possessions mirror back a positive imaginary fulfillment, making him merciless in his determination to "own things" and collect his rents. Guitar's grandmother sums up his estrangement from the black community when she says, "A nigger in business is a terrible thing to see" (22).

Unlike her brother, Pilate responds to their father's death by reaching out to others. Initially, Pilate misses the bodily comfort of home and food when they are in hiding with Circe. "Craving certain specific foods had almost devastated her" (167). As a twelve-year-old child, she verbalizes this loss by crying, mourning for what no longer exists. When her brother rejects her, Pilate resigns herself to a life of wandering. Born without a navel, Pilate is rejected as some type of evil. Her lack of a navel "isolated her. Already without family, she was further isolated from her people, for, except for the relative bliss on the island, every other resource was denied her: partnership in marriage, confessional friendship, and communal religion" (148). Marked as other, Pilate confronts Lacan's Real, her insignificance and utter isolation. Bereft of parents and her brother, rejected by each community she settles into, Pilate can rely on no one but herself. As a subject of this knowledge, she gains agency as she builds her own identity with the help of her father's ghost, who comes to her in times of need.[55] For example, when she is in the cave with Macon, her father warns her that stealing the gold would be wrong. When her daughter Reba is born, he comes to comfort her by saying, "Sing. Sing" and "You just can't fly on off and leave a body" (147).

Singing to herself for company and comfort, Pilate takes her father's moral lesson to heart. Only later does she realize that his words reflect two sources of her trauma: her dead mother, Sing (whose name she does not know), and her dead father. She is unaware that the bones she goes to collect are her father's, not those of the stranger she and Macon accidentally kill.[56] Through her singing and caretaking of her father's remains, Pilate supports her being with her parents' love. Rather than hating others as her brother does, Pilate has responded to trauma— her mother's death at her birth, her father's brutal slaying, her brother's rejecting hatred, her isolation because of her marked body—with love for all. Her missing navel articulates her trauma, as does her singing, and perhaps it is this articulation that enables her to find inner peace. In contrast to Macon's prison of a house, Pilate creates a true home, "the only one he [Milkman] knew that achieved comfort without one article of comfort in it. [. . .] peace was there, energy, singing, and now his own remembrances" (301). Pilate moves to be near Macon when her granddaughter Hagar is born, staying on after he rejects her because she senses that Ruth "was dying of lovelessness" (151).[57] With or without Macon's sanction, Pilate will provide the anchor of home for her daughter and granddaughter as well as for Ruth.[58]

From these opposing models—his father's ruthless materialism and his aunt's bounteous love—Milkman will assess his own behavior and place in the world. His mother, Ruth, provides him with additional insight. When she loses her mother, Ruth looks to her father for love and attention. He becomes her life-line for self-esteem. But Ruth feels vulnerable and anxious when her father and Macon become uncomfortable with her inappropriate attention. To better understand his mother's unhappiness, Milkman follows her at night to her father's grave. These visits briefly restore her sense that she is worthy of love; reconnecting with her father's memory renews her. With Macon, she lives cut off from human touch or warm connection. Blaming Macon for her father's death—she claims Macon threw away his medicine—Ruth fears the brutal side of him that tried to abort Milkman. She finds sanctuary with Pilate, whose "house had been a haven [. . .] a safe harbor" (135). Bereft and vulnerable, Ruth nurses Milkman until he is five because it gives her "the distinct impression that his lips were pulling from her a thread of light. It was as though she were a cauldron issuing spinning gold" (13). Like the jarring watermark on the table that reminds her of her vulnerability but also gives her a sense of being alive, nursing Milkman counters the numbing response to trauma.[59] Her prolonged nursing of Milkman places her need to connect before Milkman's own needs.

Protected by her father and restricted by her husband, Ruth remains dependent and childlike. Her daughters, Lena and Corinthians, imprisoned by Macon's position and wealth, also lack independent maturity. The girls make velvet roses, which they sell to local stores, an activity that they will grow to loathe for the isolation and elitism the roses represent. Lena resents Milkman's freedom to interact with the world, vocalizing her pent-up frustration years later when she finally chastises him. Recalling how he peed on her during one of the family outings, she tells Milkman, "I wanted to kill you. I even tried to once or twice" (213). Milkman represents the man's world she can never possess, because her place as black and female binds her.[60] She recalls how Macon "would parade us like virgins through Babylon, then humiliate us like whores in Babylon" (216). Viewing them as objects of his success in the greater culture, Macon fails to establish an emotional connection with his children. In return, they lack the positive mirror they need to exist as subjects.

Corinthians suffers because her parents see her as "a prize for a professional man of color" (188). In her community, men find her "a little too elegant. Bryn Mawr in 1940. France in 1939. That was a bit much" (188). Money and class separate the girls from other blacks. "Magdalene called Lena seemed resigned to her life, but when Corinthians woke up one day to find herself a forty-two-year-old maker of rose petals, she suffered a severe depression which lasted until she made up her mind to get out of the house" (189). When she takes a job as a maid out in the world, Corinthians must choose between a flesh-and-blood poor man and her former pedestal life. Life with Porter wins out: "She banged her knuckles until they ached to get the attention of the living flesh behind the glass, and would have smashed her fist through the window just to touch him, feel his heat, the only thing that could protect her from a smothering death of dry roses" (198–99). Like the whores in *The Bluest Eye* and Sula's mother, Corinthians recognizes the overwhelming need for a human touch. Porter makes Corinthians feel "bathed, scoured, vacuumed, and for the first time simple" (199). He returns a loving gaze that has been lacking, and "[i]n place of vanity she now felt a self-esteem that was quite new" (201). In choosing Porter, Corinthians chooses to grow up, something her mother and sister have not done. In fact, in her circle of isolated women "[s]he didn't know any grown-up women. Every woman she knew was a doll baby" (196). In contrast, she gains agency as a subject of knowledge, processing her position as a woman in her black community, as well as her place as object in the master narrative of white culture.

While Macon's women become isolated through wealth and position, his niece Hagar's isolation comes from her status as social outsider, in part connected to Pilate's bootlegging business. Although Pilate and Reba deny her nothing, Hagar claims that some of her "days were hungry ones" (48). Lack of a best friend or social circle leaves a loneliness that Milkman eventually soothes. Unfortunately, when he discards her for the light-skinned, copper-haired rich women at Honore, Hagar lacks the inner core identity to survive. Seshadri-Crooks describes the development of this lack of self-esteem: "[T]o be subjected to Whiteness means that race impacts on the bodily ego as a regime of visibility. Certain marks of the body then become privileged and anxious sites of meaning" (36). Pilate tells Hagar that Milkman "can't value you more than you value yourself" (306). But Hagar views Milkman as her "home in this world" and cannot survive without his protective gaze (137). Just as Sula does when Ajax leaves her, Hagar takes to her bed. Although Pilate and Reba "offered her all they had: love murmurs and a protective shade," Hagar will not recover (315).[61] Pilate mourns Hagar by publicly announcing her grief: "Pilate trumpeted for the sky itself to hear, 'And she was *loved!*'" (319). But mother love was not enough to combat the deficient self-concept created by the greater culture. "Neither Pilate nor Reba knew that Hagar was not like them. Not strong enough, like Pilate, nor simple enough, like Reba, to make up her life as they had" (307). In addition to her loving mother and grandmother, Hagar needs community to survive, "a chorus of mamas, grandma-mas, aunts, cousins, sisters, neighbors, Sunday school teachers, best girl friends, and what all to give her the strength life demanded of her—and the humor with which to live it" (307). The love and support of the community enable children to grow and thrive.[62]

Manipulative family dynamics force Milkman to research his roots; he real-izes that "all he knew in the world about the world was what other people had told him" (120). Thinking about his strange family interactions, Milkman suddenly has a bodily memory of his late nursing: "Cold sweat broke out on his neck. [...] He had remembered something. Or believed he remembered something" (77). This somatic response recalls the earlier event responsible for his nickname. He also begins to understand his mother's vulnerability and her need to connect through human touch. "He had never loved his mother, but had always known that she had loved him. [...] He wondered if there was anyone in the world who liked him. Liked him for himself alone" (78–79). Milkman's mother conceives him to hold on to his father; her nursing, which fulfills her needs, produces a weak at-tachment to Milkman. Ruth admits to herself that "[h]er son had never been a person to her, a separate real person. He had always been a passion. Because she had been so desperate to lie with her husband and have another baby by him, the son she bore was first off a wished-for bond between herself and Macon, some-thing to hold them together and reinstate their sex lives" (131). As a result, other than the prolonged nursing, she has not had real communication with Milk-man. Milkman feels this lack, looking in the mirror at his face, thinking, "Taken apart, it looked all right. [...] But it lacked coherence, a coming together of the features into a total self" (69). Thus, his journey includes a search for a likable, integrated self.[63]

As a child, isolated like his sisters, Milkman never played with his contempo-raries: "his velvet suit separated him from the other children" (264). This isola-tion from other blacks by class recurs in Shalimar, where his car, whiskey, and clothes separate him: "They looked at his skin and saw it was as black as theirs, but they knew he had the heart of the white men who came to pick them up in the trucks when they needed anonymous, faceless laborers" (266). He looks longingly at the children playing in Shalimar and regrets the childhood he never had. When Milkman realizes his personal connection to the children's song, he gets "as excited as a child confronted with boxes and boxes of presents under the skirt of a Christmas tree. [...] He was grinning. His eyes were shining. He was as eager and happy as he had ever been in his life" (304). Through the innocent play of the children, Milkman recaptures the experiences of a childhood that escaped him. The singing children "reminded him of the gap in his own childhood" (299). Reliving these experiences helps him to grow up, as he begins to understand not only himself but also his parents' trauma. As an adult he now understands that his father's wealth has kept him from developing into an independent and socially responsible individual.

In Shalimar, Milkman partakes in a communal memory he did not experience at home. When his friends had discussed Emmit Till's murder, he was not able to relate to their shared trauma: "The men began to trade tales of atrocities, first stories they had heard, then those they'd witnessed, and finally the things that had happened to themselves. A litany of personal humiliation, outrage, and anger turned sicklelike back to themselves as humor" (82). Their narration tempers their pain through verbalization of trauma and through humor. When he experiences genuine hospitality in the South, Milkman wonders why blacks ever left. He senses that people there are valued for themselves rather than for their material goods. But he fails to see that like Sweet Home in *Beloved,* the South contains painful memories that wound even as they connect. A pillar of this tight-knit southern community, Reverend Cooper greets Milkman as one of their own: "I know your people!" (229). Reverend Cooper's stories of Pilate, her earring, and his father change how Milkman perceives history: "Milkman felt a glow listening to a story come from this man that he'd heard many times before but only half listened to" (231). Milkman experiences a connection, a home, and a positive sense of identity.

But when he gets to Shalimar, his ancestors' "original home," he is vulnerable, not protected as he was in Danville: "here, in his 'home,' he was unknown, unloved, and damn near killed" (270). Vulnerable for the first time in his life, Milkman will begin to take risks. For example, he goes hunting with the men who mock him, letting them completely re-dress him in their clothes. By relinquishing his past Milkman can relive the stages of maturity: vulnerability, testing, self-worth, and empathy for others. In the woods, "[t]here was nothing [. . .] to help him—not his money, his car, his father's reputation, his suit, or his shoes. In fact they hampered him" (277). He develops the "ability to separate out, of all the things there were to sense, the one that life itself might depend on" (277). In doing so he connects with nature and others. His ability to laugh with the hunters enables him to walk without his limp. He matures, so that his response will be not numbness but the ability to relate to and love others: "he did feel connected, as though there was some cord or pulse or information they shared. Back home he had never felt that way, as though he belonged to anyplace or anybody. He'd always considered himself the outsider in his family" (293). The community of his ancestors allows him to connect to his own. Pilate's ability to make sense of her life passes on to Milkman.

With his new self-insight, Milkman realizes that he usurped Hagar's ego in the service of his own. He begins to think nostalgically about how the traumas of his mother and father have shaped his life. For example, his mother's deficiency in attachment and mothering stemmed from her own deprivation, and Milkman now can imagine how she might have felt and acted: "And suppose he were married and his wife refused him for fifteen years. His mother had been able to live through that by a long nursing of her son, some occasional visits to a graveyard. What might she have been like had her husband loved her?" (300). Milkman's understanding of his mother will help him move forward, as will his new understanding of the close attachment that Macon had with his father and that Macon's zeal for ownership was an expression of that extreme love. His father loved property "to excess because he loved his father to excess. Owning, building, acquiring—that was his life, his future, his present, and all the history he knew. That he distorted life, bent it, for the sake of gain, was a measure of his loss at his father's death" (300). Macon's stories take on a new meaning. Rather than being mere boasting about his former hard work, they represent an expression of love: "That he loved his father; had an intimate relationship with him; that his father loved him, trusted him, and found him worthy of working 'right alongside' him" (234). His father's bragging represents a verbalization of his loss, and he softens in the telling because it rehumanizes him, allowing him to connect with his past. Mirroring white aggression, Macon's acting out has been his only outlet for his grief and loss.

Milkman's initiation into his shared history joins him to his culture. The children's song and game become his too: "But I can play it now. It's my game now" (327). And he will play responsibly. While identifying with his flying ancestor, Milkman knows that desertion hurts those left behind.[64] He comprehends that Pilate's earlier lesson on how to cook the perfect egg involves finding a fitting balance. Members of a community have to come together in their own right, accommodating one another's needs and traumatic history. In this way people can heal with "supportive, empathic, emotionally meaningful, relationships that encour-

age authenticity and the nurturing of direct forms of compassionate communication" (Siegel, "Attachment" 31). Family and connection are keys to success. The
safety of community support, which provides the sense of a true home, allows for
a verbalization and coming to terms with trauma. Unlike Macon, who shuts down
emotionally when his father dies, Pilate develops empathy and love. Milkman rejects his father's harmful response for the nurturing response of Pilate.[65] Cheryl
Wall writes about the buried history present in black songs and the mining of
family history that Morrison's novel reflects. Milkman's growth stems from how
well he "has learned [. . .] the 'other ways of knowing' that Pilate has taught [. . .
and] how to 'be' in the world" (Wall 231–32). Milkman's "body, reborn, begins to
act as a register and collector of ephemeral bits of knowledge," and "these bits of
knowledge combine in unexpected ways, producing a visceral sense of history as
present and living, an understanding not available through official or structured
channels of knowing" (Hogue 125). Pilate's guidance and cultural knowledge of
his ancestral past enable Milkman to become a responsible adult. The next chapter traces how the journeys of characters in *Jazz* and *Tar Baby* reflect a similar
search for a grown-up, self-sufficient identity and how community connections
and finding a home contribute to this process.

THREE

Searching for Safety

The Persistence of Slave Trauma in *Jazz* and *Tar Baby*

While aggressive responses constitute an attempt to gain control over damaging social forces, they do not provide a productive solution to white culture's othering. Another kind of response to firsthand and generationally transmitted trauma is to physically escape with the hope that moving to another environment will eliminate either sources or reminders of traumatic experiences. However, both *Jazz* and *Tar Baby* illustrate that physical relocation does not erase trauma; people must verbalize and acknowledge personal and cultural trauma in order to mature and function in daily life. The lack of positive mirroring in the symbolic order continues to plague the black population, as characters in these novels suffer from the childhood trauma of being orphaned, ostracized, or discriminated against. Characters grapple with how to grow up to become adults who can protect themselves rather than remain dependent and in need of protection. Nostalgic as well as painful memories, along with the formation of new family units, provide characters the space to verbalize how the core trauma of slavery plays out in their daily lives. Thus, community connections enable characters to begin the healing process and to develop a sense of self. While people can never totally eliminate the bodily response to the cultural trauma of slavery's residue, recognizing the gap between their own desire and the master narrative allows them to create new homes in which to mature and find some type of peace.[1]

Morrison explores the motif of maturation and self-love in *Jazz*, where the slave legacy of abandonment and being orphaned abounds. Characters seek new homes, connections, and love in order to counter their sense of lack and loss. *Jazz* chronicles the hope of black migration north and the escape from southern life to a more promising life in "the City" (a tacit reference to New York's Harlem).[2] In this vibrant place, where a supportive black community gives back love, a positive self, and comfort, the abandoned and the orphaned find new families, subjectivity, and, consequently, homes. Exiting the South unites blacks as a group, but although the City provides work, new connections, and new possible family units, this escape does not erase personal and cultural trauma.[3] Orphans still need to heal by gaining self-esteem, and it is only when individuals heal that the community can heal as well.[4] The City, as surrogate parent, provides the nurturing space to combat trauma. Jazz music, the voice of the City, operates as the vehicle for verbalization of personal and cultural trauma. Jazz functions as rememory, with its riff and refrain representing the reenactment of prior traumas and the forging of a community bond through the vocalization of individual trauma.[5] Jazz music articulates the desire of black culture in response to the white master narrative. When one relives trauma in personal memory and community rememory, the healing power of connectedness furnishes the foundation for personal growth and self-love.[6]

The novel opens with the conversational narrator confiding the secrets of the neighborhood and introducing the major players in the story to come.[7] Much in the style of *The Bluest Eye*'s "Quiet as it's kept," we learn that Joe Trace killed his young girlfriend Dorcas; that his wife, Violet, attacked her in her coffin; that Dorcas's aunt, Alice Manfred, has forgiven them both; and that a new young girl, Dorcas's friend Felice, has taken to visiting the Trace apartment. It will take the full telling of their story to move beyond gossip to an understanding of need and motivation.[8] In addition, the narrator describes the parenting function of the City, which is "there to back and frame you no matter what you do. [. . .] All you have to do is heed the design—the way it's laid out for you, considerate, mindful of where you want to go and what you might need tomorrow" (8–9). In this close-knit community "people knock on each other's doors to see if anything is needed or can be had," and "everything you want is right where you are: the church, the store, the party, the women, the men, the postbox (but no high schools), the furniture store, street newspaper vendors, the bootleg houses (but no banks), the beauty parlors, the barbershops, the juke joints, the ice wagons, the rag collectors" (10). The black community here takes care of its own, despite the neglect of the larger culture, which deprives it of education and economic security. Working together, community members combat the master narrative.[9]

Like an encouraging parent, "the City [. . .] danced with them, proving already how much it loved them. Like a million more they could hardly wait to get there and love it back" (32). In the City's positive gaze self-esteem develops, and people "feel more like themselves, more like the people they always believed they were" (35). Faith in future possibilities heals old wounds, and "[p]art of why they loved it was the specter they left behind" (33). The City provides the "wave of black people running from want and violence" the space in which to reinvent themselves, paralleling the inventiveness of jazz music (33). For those finding sanctuary in the City, "perfect was not the word. It was better than that" (107). However, the promise of escape that the City affords disintegrates on an individual level when past trauma erupts. Relocation does not cure an injured core identity. The generationally inherited trauma of slavery and the abandonment it produced resurfaces again and again. *Jazz* repeatedly relates this abandonment narrative, interweaving stories of pain and loss. A refrain emerges: we are all orphans. Each character's personal story provides the solo improvisation of the riff.

The displacement of slavery and the uprootedness of postslavery life portrayed in *Beloved* and *Paradise* appear in *Jazz,* where four generations struggle to recover. The personal stories that intersect and leave unresolved questions of parentage attest to the disruptions of family life associated with slavery. The slave practice of separating children from their mothers at birth forms the kernel of abandonment trauma. For those not separated at birth, mothers were often sold or forced to accompany their masters for various reasons. For example, True Belle, Violet's grandmother, must abandon her daughters and her husband to follow her master's daughter, Vera Gray, to Baltimore; she does not return for eighteen years. In these cases parents do not willingly desert their children; nonetheless, the children feel abandoned, and trauma results. Such trauma leaves people feeling "that they have lost an important measure of control over the circumstances of their own lives and are thus very vulnerable" (K. Erikson 194). This loss of control and the resulting vulnerability surface as a bodily and emotional reenactment of personal and cultural trauma. The search for a positive parental gaze takes over as a lifelong mission, complicated by the larger culture's rejection of blackness.

When Vera Gray forces True Belle to follow her to Baltimore, she instigates a cycle of abandonment and loss for three generations of True Belle's family, ultimately terminating future progeny. As Vera Gray's property, True Belle has no choice but to accompany her to Baltimore and care for Vera's son, fathered by one of her father's slaves. Vera's father must send her away when she becomes pregnant, because "there were seven mulatto children on his land" (141). Fearing that she has conceived this child with her half-brother, he quickly rids his home of possible scandal. One of the consequences of this banishment is that True Belle must leave her husband and two daughters. While absent from her own family,

True Belle serves as the spiritual mother for Vera's child, Golden Gray. Claiming that Golden is an orphan that they have taken in, both women dote on him, carefully observing him for racial markers that might curtail his ability to "pass." But while they lavish Golden with attention and love, two young children, left with their aunt, will struggle to recover from their loss. Rose Dear and May, aged eight and ten when their mother leaves, do not see her again for eighteen years, when Golden Gray is old enough to set out to find his father. Golden Gray's own story of loss intersects with that of True Belle's children.

Raised as a white man, Golden Gray searches for his black father with mixed emotions, instinctively separating himself from blackness on various occasions. Yet he does not desert Wild, the pregnant black woman he encounters, despite "holding his breath against infection or odor or something. Something that might touch or penetrate him" (144). Perhaps he rescues the woman because "True Belle had been his first and major love, which may be why two gallops beyond that hair, that skin, their absence was unthinkable" (150). He protects Wild out of nostalgia for True Belle and his attachment to her. His bodily stored memory reactivates and propels him to assist Wild. When he meets his father, Henry Les-Troy, a tracker, a "hunter's hunter," he recognizes his mixed blood and realizes that there is more than one kind of black person "like himself" (168, 149). While Golden has been able to choose to live as a white man, his father cannot pass and warns his son that he has to make a choice. When Golden says, "I don't want to be a free nigger; I want to be a free man," his father replies, "Don't we all. Look. Be what you want—white or black. Choose. But if you choose black, you got to act black" (173). Acting black presents a challenge for Golden, who has been raised with the cultural notion that blacks are inferior and that material goods are more important than lesser humans. Thus, "he thinks first of his clothes, and not the woman, [. . .] worrying about his coat and not tending to the girl" (151–55). Honor, the young black boy who does occasional work for Henry, assumes that Golden is white because of Golden's "smileless smile," which he associates with white dismissal (156). Brought up in the larger white culture, Golden has learned to separate himself from blacks through body language.

Yet the pain of parental loss overpowers him, and he succumbs in a bodily way to an emotional life hidden from him until this moment: "Only now, he thought, now that I know I have a father, do I feel his absence: the place where he should have been and was not. Before, I thought everybody was one-armed, like me. [. . .] I don't need the arm. But I do need to know what it could have been like to have had it" (158). An orphan's need for parental love will trump racial hatred, and Golden thinks, "What do I care what the color of his skin is, or his contact with my mother? When I see him, or what is left of him, I will tell him all about the missing part of me and listen for his crying shame. I will exchange then; let him have mine and take his as my own and we will both be free, arm-tangled and whole" (159). He envisions a reunion that will heal both parties.[10] When Golden confronts his father for abandoning him and his mother, Henry explains, "I never knew you were in the world" (170). Cultural racial taboos prevented Henry from looking for Vera or from even declaring his love for her. Although Golden is free to leave and live with prestige and power in the larger culture, he stays with his father and the abandoned woman Wild, "[f]or the safety at first, then for the company. Then for himself—with a kind of confident, enabling, serene power that flicks like a razor and then hides" (161). With his father and Wild, Golden becomes a subject of knowledge, recognizing his black roots and articulating the desire to embrace them. He bonds with them and finds peace; perhaps his original bonding with True Belle prepares him for this new subjectivity.

At first glance, this story of Golden Gray disrupts the story of Joe and Violet, already in progress. But as close as they are and as much as they have been through together, Joe and Violet have never shared crucial stories with each other: he has never shared the story of his mother's abandonment, and she has never revealed the story of her mother's suicide or information about True Belle and Golden Gray. These gaps in personal history suggest the difficulty of articulating one's core trauma. The digression here provides the information not only about Violet's ancestry and extended family but also about the interconnectedness of her past with Joe's, given that Wild may be Joe's mother. When Wild gives birth, she rejects the baby; "the woman would not hold the baby or look at it" (170).[11] Wild's abandoning of the baby resonates with Joe's abandonment by his mother. The narrator tells us that Joe had

made three solitary journeys to find her. In Vienna he had lived first with the fear of her, then the joke of her, finally the obsession, followed by rejection of her. Nobody told Joe she was his mother. Not outright; but Hunters Hunter looked right in his eyes one evening and said, "She got reasons. Even if she crazy. Crazy people got reasons." (175)

Whether Henry LesTroy—Hunters Hunter—is Joe's father or just his mentor remains unclear, but the connection to Golden Gray compounds Joe's link to Violet.

The generational legacy of trauma that Joe and Violet experience starts with True Belle's slave status and plays out in her granddaughter. True Belle's forced desertion of her daughters, Rose Dear and May, results in Rose Dear's suicide and her granddaughter Violet's decision to remain childless.[12] Without a husband at home or her mother to guide her, Rose Dear succumbs to desperate finances. When the bill collectors arrive, "they just tipped her out of it like the way you get the cat off the seat if you don't want to touch it or pick it up in your arms" (98). The bill collectors' fear of contagion resembles what Golden Gray feels when he finds Wild. Helpless and hopeless, Rose Dear denies the reality around her through dissociation. Her five children are "huddled in an abandoned shack, [...] thoroughly dependent upon the few neighbors left in 1888" (98). Even though True Belle arrives home just in time to rescue the family, she cannot save Rose Dear, who four years later "jumped in the well and missed all the fun" (99). She commits suicide just two weeks before her husband returns with the fortune he set out to find, acting out the bodily impact of her mother's abandonment in this violence to herself.[13] Violet thinks about what would drive her mother to such a violent act, one that leaves her children so completely on their own, and asks, could her mother have gotten stuck in a place "where you know you are not and never again will be loved by anybody who can choose to do it? Where everything is over but the talking?" (110). Violet identifies with her mother's sense of unworthiness and her refusal to live a life without love.[14]

Rose Dear internalizes the idea that she is unlovable, having been deserted by both her mother and her husband, a desertion that Violet feels as well. Violet thinks about her absent father, "He'd be in his seventies now. [...] this phantom father" (100). Violet's initial response to her mother's death is to take charge of her life. "She had been a snappy, determined girl and a hardworking young woman" (23). To be near Joe, she works in Tyrell. "It was there she became the powerfully strong young woman who could handle mules, bale hay and chop wood as good as any man" (105). Although Violet rejects her mother's weakness, the scars of her mother's desertion remain. As the narrator muses, "[T]he children of suicides are hard to please and quick to believe no one loves them because they are not really here" (4). Without the positive gaze of the Other to mirror their subjectivity, these children feel that they do not exist at all, but are merely shells of substantive people.

Violet bodily stores her mother's trauma. Doubting that she is lovable, Violet wants "to be the woman my mother didn't stay around long enough to see. That one. The one she would have liked and the one I used to like before" (208). She seeks an ideal self, the one before the body in pieces. Fearing her own inability to love, Violet decides against having children so that she cannot abandon them, thereby protecting her unborn children from possible trauma and abuse. Her self-worth suffers with the added rejection by her grandmother True Belle, who chooses to love Golden Gray over Violet. Violet claims, "My grandmother fed me stories about a little blond child. He was a boy, but I thought of him as a girl sometimes, as a brother, sometimes as a boyfriend. He lived inside my mind" (208). He was "my own golden boy, who I never ever saw but who tore up my girlhood as surely as if we'd been the best of lovers" (97). Like her phantom father, Golden Gray's powerful specter augments her trauma.

Joe's trauma, like Violet's, stems from maternal abandonment. Whether the parental abandonment results from suicide, natural death, murder, forced separation, or desertion, abandoned children experience a similar trauma.[15] Despite the kindness of his adoptive parents, Rhoda and Frank Williams, who have raised him along with their other six children, Joe's sense of lack from his mother's rejection propels him on an unending search for her acknowledgment:

> Just a sign, he said, just show me your hand. [. . .] She wouldn't even have to say the word "mother." Nothing like that. All she had to do was give him a sign, her hand thrust through the leaves, the white flowers, would be enough to say that she knew him to be the one, the son she had fourteen years ago, and ran away from, but not too far. (37)

His need to be named becomes his unfulfilled desire: "'Give me a sign, then. You don't have to say nothing. Let me see your hand. Just stick it out someplace and I'll go; I promise. A sign. [. . .] You my mother?' Yes. No. Both. Either. But not this nothing" (178). Joe echoes Lacan's notion that subjectivity comes from the Other. Like Beloved, who asks Paul D to "call me my name" (116), Joe voices his need to be signified, as this recognition will validate his worthiness.

Joe changes his name—his signification—from the adoptive Williams to Trace, because his parents had "disappeared without a trace. The way I heard it I understood her to mean the 'trace' they disappeared without was me" (124). Yet despite his act of agency in naming himself, Joe needs parental love. He tells his surrogate brother Victory, "They got to pick me out. From all of you all, they got to pick me. I'm Trace, what they went off without" (124). Joe needs to come to terms with the fact that "nobody came looking for me either. I never knew my own daddy" (125). He faults his mother for being "[t]oo brain-blasted to do what the meanest sow managed: nurse what she birthed" (179). In the end, it is not his mother who will pick him out but Violet, and Joe concedes that he marries her as a mother substitute, "me saying, 'All right, Violet, I'll marry you,' just because I couldn't see whether a wildwoman put out her hand or not" (181). Throughout his life, women sense that Joe needs mothering, and the day he meets Dorcas, the women in the apartment "flicked lint off my jacket, pressed me on the shoulder to make me sit down. It's a way they have of mending you, fixing what they think needs repair" (122). But his ease with women has yet to fix Joe. His inability to fill his lack, despite his unending search, illustrates the power of the positive gaze of Lacan's Other, which gives love and enables one to love oneself. The protective power of early attachment supports this self-love.[16]

Joe's quest is not only for his mother but also for the ability to verbalize his trauma in order to name his own desire. "It's not a thing you tell except maybe to a tight friend, somebody you knew from before, long time ago" (121). Joe may feel safe with someone he has known throughout his life, yet he cannot reveal all of his pain to Violet. Thus, Dorcas offers an avenue for vocalization, as he can tell her things he has not been able to share with Violet. "I couldn't talk to anybody but Dorcas and I told her things I hadn't told myself" (123). He wonders whether things would have gone differently had he been able to talk to his boyhood friend Victory and not kept his feelings shut up inside. Joe and Violet share the same abandonment trauma—Wild's rejection and Rose Dear's suicide—but their inability to talk about these traumatic, connected strands of their lives eventually leads Joe to Dorcas as an outlet. When Joe kills Dorcas, he bodily acts out his trauma, generating a release, a physical verbalization of his mourning for and anger toward his mother.[17] His trauma leads to a violent acting out as his means of verbalization. Joe's constant crying after Dorcas's death further reenacts tears of loss for his mother. When Felice asks Joe, "Why'd you shoot at her if you loved her?" Joe replies, "Scared. Didn't know how to love anybody" (213).[18] The cycle of abandonment continues; lack of attachment leads to a failure to adequately provide love or feel secure.

Even though the social ties of the City promise an imaginary wholeness, the personal family unit is necessary to provide subjectivity. The larger culture's rejection of black life compounds the black struggle for recognition. For example, Dorcas bleeds to death because the ambulance that Felice calls for does not come until the next morning.[19] Felice's father tells her that there are two kinds of white people: "The ones that feel sorry for you and the ones that don't. And both amount to the same thing. Nowhere in between is respect" (204). For the larger culture to endorse black subjectivity, it must return a positive, reinforcing gaze that will activate psychic healing and growth on both the cultural and the personal level. While personal nostalgic memories can create imagined wholeness, characters in *Jazz* recall only painful ones, illustrating how memory constitutes bodily enactment of stored sensory-motor impulses. Violet and Joe's early courtship and marriage constitute a rare happy memory, but when Joe tries to remember when he and Violet were young, "he has a tough time trying to catch what it felt like" (29). A sense of loss replaces nostalgic memory. Joe's adopted family does not fill the gap left by the parents who abandoned him, just as Violet's grandmother and Dorcas's aunt and Felice's grandparents fail to suffice.

After Dorcas dies, Violet lets all of her birds go, even the parrot who only said "I love you" (92). Ignoring its wretched and loving cry as it freezes to death outside, Violet abandons the parrot and her other charges in her desperation, repeating her mother's abandonment of her own children in her despair. In addition, Violet's stabbing of Dorcas parallels Joe's bodily reenactment of trauma. Violet says she stabs Dorcas because she "[l]ost the lady [. . .]. Put her down someplace and forgot where" (211). Having lost her own subjectivity, Violet wants to discover what Joe found in Dorcas that she herself lacked. She confronts Lacan's Real of her trauma to discover what is still unlovable about her.[20] In her search, Violet will reunite with Joe with the help of Alice Manfred and Felice. Violet says of her arrival at Alice's apartment, an unlikely place for her to show up, "I had to sit down somewhere. I thought I could do it here. That you would let me and you did" (82). Her need to connect matches Alice's. "When Violet came to visit (and Alice never knew when that might be) something opened up. [. . . Violet was] the only visitor she looked forward to" (83). Alice, abandoned by her husband, confides in Violet, telling her that she "had never picked up a knife," yet "every day and every night for seven months she, Alice Manfred, was starving for blood" (86). Empathizing with Violet's need to hurt the other woman rather than her husband, Alice takes Violet under her wing.[21] She advises Violet to stay with Joe: "You got anything left to you to love, anything at all, do it" (112). Alice shares her insight that love and self-love are the restorative agents that come with maturity. Lucille P. Fultz says that this mother-daughter type of relationship provides mutual healing for Alice and Violet. "If Violet is to regain a semblance of a coherent self, she must find it in human companionship and conversation—talking is a necessary part of the cure" (75). The need to connect with others resounds in a community of deserted souls; Alice and Felice mutually need Violet and Joe.

Representing a fourth generation of this story, Dorcas and Felice harbor a similar trauma of abandonment, betrayal, and loss rooted in slavery's racial separation. Dorcas's parents die during the riots in East St. Louis in 1917, and her aunt, Alice Manfred, raises her.[22] As she watches from her best friend's window, the fire consumes her house and her mother, and Dorcas "yelled to her mother that the box of dolls, the box of dolls was up there on the dresser can we get them? Mama?" (38). Losing her parents as well as her symbolic babies, she never verbalizes the trauma: "She never said. Never said anything about it. She went to two funerals in five days, and never said a word" (57). Feeling as if one of the wood chips from the fire "must have entered her stretched dumb mouth [. . .]. Dorcas never let it out and never put it out. At first she thought if she spoke of it, it would leave her, or she would lose it through her mouth" (60–61). At last, she believes "that the glow would never leave her, that it would be waiting for and with her whenever she wanted to be touched by it" (61). Her unspoken trauma, the witnessed horror of her mother's demise and the end of her secure family and home, remains at the core of her identity.

Unfortunately, Dorcas never undergoes the retelling of the trauma that would allow her to reshape her experience. Dorcas's inner life is intolerable except for "lying down somewhere in a dimly lit place enclosed in arms, and supported by the core of the world" (63). In an echo of the cave and Wild's finding solace with Golden Gray, being held provides Dorcas succor. When unkind peers mock her, she feels that "[t]he body she inhabits is unworthy. Although it is young and all she has, it is as if it had decayed on the vine at budding time. [. . .] So by the time Joe Trace whispered to her through the crack of a closing door her life had become almost unbearable" (67). The "love appetite" that Joe unleashes in Dorcas has its source in her early parental loss.

Eventually, Dorcas seeks a peer to love her. To justify her shift from Joe to Acton, she claims that "Joe didn't care what kind of woman I was. He should have. I cared. I wanted to have a personality and with Acton I'm getting one" (190).[23] However, her deathbed need to reconcile, forgive, and acknowledge Joe's importance for her emerges in her last words to Felice: "There's only one apple. [. . .] Tell Joe" (213). This message will help Joe complete his mourning and begin to live again with Violet and Felice. After hearing it, he repeats, "'Felice. Felice.' With two syllables, not one like most people do, including my father" (214). Felice sees the life come back to Joe and welcomes him as a father figure for herself. When he says that "[t]his place needs birds," he verbalizes the beginnings of a new version of their prior life (214). Violet's birds once represented love and family life, something to take care of and nurture. With Felice's assistance, Joe and Violet remake themselves and their home. When Felice suggests to Joe that the house also needs "a Victrola," his retort, "Watch your mouth, girl," initiates the cycle of parenting, and a family unit is born (214). Felice promises to bring a record player and records, much to Violet's delight. Emerging from his mourning trance, Joe answers, "Then I best find me another job. [. . .] Felice. They named you right. Remember that" (215). He voices the hope for future work and family pleasure.

But Dorcas's kind words for Joe wound Felice, who is hurt that while dying in her arms, Dorcas is thinking of Joe and not of her. Feeling abandoned and betrayed by her best friend, Felice internalizes her own lack, being "not best enough for her to want to go to the emergency room and stay alive. She let herself die right out from under me with my ring and everything and I wasn't even on her mind" (213). Dorcas's dismissal of Felice mirrors that of Felice's parents, who work far away from the home where Felice's grandmother cares for her. When they are home, her parents want to relax together, and they leave Felice behind when they step out. Felice calculates the extent of their parenting: "Thirty-four days [a year]. I'm seventeen now and that works out to less than six hundred days. Less than two years out of seventeen. Dorcas said I was lucky because at least they were there, somewhere, and if I got sick I could [. . .] go see them" (200). But Felice feels their inaccessibility as a loss, as keenly as an orphan. Felice considers the ring that her mother stole while on an errand for her boss at Tiffany's: "A present taken from whitefolks, given to me when I was too young to say No thank you" (211). This token does not suffice to replace parental nurturing and daily care. Felice will resign herself to the loss of the ring—she loaned it to Dorcas the night she died, and it is buried with her—more easily than she will accept the loss of Dorcas, her friend and companion. Her death reenacts the bodily feeling of loss and betrayal of Felice's parents. Dorcas having abandoned her in a similar way, Felice thinks, "Some friend she turned out to be" (205).

To cope with her recent loss, Felice seeks the company of Joe and Violet, seeing strength and nurturing in them as individuals and as a couple. She senses that Joe will see her as a person in her own right, "as though the things I feel and think are important and different and . . . interesting" (206). His gaze reflects back a positive self. Felice admires his tenderness toward Violet, noticing how he touches her and listens to her. Felice thinks about how Violet says "'me.' [. . .] like somebody she favored and could count on. A secret somebody you didn't have to feel sorry for or have to fight for" (210).[24] She can learn how to come into her own following Violet's model of selfhood. She returns for a catfish supper even though Violet's catfish is not as good as Felice's mother's or her grandmother's. Felice's current need for nurturing wins out over her nostalgia for childhood cooking. Felice says of Violet, as a child says about her mother, "You'd never get tired [of] looking at her face" (206). Violet symbolically adopts Felice to replace the child she never had, which suggests that childlessness is not the proper way to end the cycle of loss. Mothering mutually assists both Violet and Felice; community parenting relies on one generation's teaching the next.[25]

Thus, the salve for abandonment trauma lies in the psychic safety of supportive couples and a united family unit. Violet, Joe, Felice, and Alice will work together to heal their psychic wounds. Philip Page writes that

> *Jazz* privileges fusion. Characters become whole again [. . .] in contrast to Morrison's earlier fragmented characters. [. . .] Joe and Violet are reunited as a couple, forming a new family with Felice and their new bird. Simultaneously, they find harmony with their community in New York, harmony and community that they did not even know they missed since leaving Vesper County. (*Dangerous* 176)

Violet captures the impact of generational trauma on subjectivity when she asks Alice, "Where the grown people? Is it us?" (110). She realizes that the time has come for her to be an adult and assume a parenting role. In turn, Joe has been seeking not just his mother but the comfort and safety of her home, "[t]hat home in the rock; [. . .] a place already made for me, both snug and wide open. With a doorway never needing to be closed" (221). He finds that home at last with Violet, where "they stay home figuring things out, telling each other those little personal stories they like to hear again and again" (223).[26]

Together, Joe and Violet build a psychic home and a safe space. They are content to hold each other, to

> whisper to each other under the covers. [. . .] They are remembering while they whisper the carnival dolls they won and the Baltimore boats they never

sailed on. [...] They are inward toward the other, bound and joined by carnival dolls and the steamers that sailed from ports they never saw. That is what
is beneath their undercover whispers. (228)

Through their sharing they recover a positive nostalgic memory, and it returns a
positive gaze. Together, they dare hope to build a future. Hovering over their protected space is the jazz music that the community shares. Collective rememory of
pain and possibility, generated by the music, soothes generations of trauma and
abuse. The narrator's desire—"Say make me, remake me"—becomes a cultural
invitation: "You are free to do it and I am free to let you because look, look. Look
where your hands are. Now" (229). Joe and Violet can name their desire to over-
throw the past in order to become subjects in the present. They can work within
their community, parenting Felice to reshape the master narrative and their future lives.

Like *Jazz, Tar Baby* depicts the damage white culture inflicts on black subjectivity, presenting various childhood personal traumas that compound cultural contexts. Just as relocation to the City does not erase personal or cultural
trauma, escapes to exotic places in *Tar Baby* do not bring relief.[27] The characters
in *Tar Baby* must confront their trauma, and in doing so they illustrate the difficult road to personal growth and responsibility. The novel opens with the line,
"He believed he was safe" (3). This idea of safety, crucial to the equilibrium of
home, is paramount for those who seek to escape trauma.[28] In this novel, William
Green, who goes by "Son," has wandered for eight years, having fled his home in
Eloe, Florida, after accidentally killing his cheating wife; Valerian has run from
his work and family responsibilities to retire in a remote setting and to keep his
wife, Margaret, away from their now-grown son, Michael; Ondine and Sydney,
Valerian's loyal employees, have followed him to escape the precarious American
job market for blacks; and Jadine, their niece, has sought a refuge from her highly
successful life as a model in Paris to sort out her future choices in the safety of the
only family she has known.

But memories invade their secluded paradise, so that they cannot elude their
past. They all must confront their conflicted identities in order to mature and
find peace. Ironically, this confrontation comes in the traditionally "safe" setting
of Christmas dinner, to which the blended family of employers and employees,
black and white, sit down together. The facade of camaraderie shatters when
decades-old trauma erupts, finally verbalized. While Valerian and Margaret are

removed from the institution of slavery itself, they act out the gaze of white culture, which needs to control its servants. They are subjects at the expense of their
black employees. How they handle their own traumas and their perpetuation of
hierarchies explains much of the black struggle for subjectivity.

At first glance, the patriarch Valerian should be free of trauma. As the rich,
white industrialist, with Ondine and Sydney to take care of his needs and those
of his beautiful wife, he appears smug and self-sufficient.[29] But as with those
around him, his childhood demons account for his often bizarre behavior. An
orphan raised by loving uncles and aunts, Valerian still carries the wounds from
his father's death. Even though as the only male grandchild he inherits the family
business and has his material needs met, other people create his identity. He duti-
fully complies with family expectations in regards to business, and even when he
marries "a teenager from a family of nobodies," he redeems himself by producing
a son (54). But his early "abandonment" by his mother and father plants the seed
of anxiety that Valerian will act out later in life.

Valerian exhibits insecurities when his environment does not reflect a positive gaze. His first wife, for example, was an "unlovable shrew," whom he only
misses in nostalgic recollection when he hears of her death (143). Yet with this
memory comes a reenactment of his earlier anxiety; her ghost comes to him in
the greenhouse, saying that she is glad she had the foresight to have two abor-
tions. By doing so, she denied him fatherhood, implying that he was not worthy
of being a father. This memory compounds his anxious feelings of having failed
to protect his son, Michael, exposing his own unprotected ego. His failure as a
father parallels the failure of the candy that bears his name: candy lovers do not
love Valerians. When he meets Margaret, "all red and white, like the Valerians,"
he will marry her out of sentimental attachment to his namesake candy, erasing
its failure with a positive reflection (51). But Margaret will disappoint him, failing
to adapt to her new class status and failing as a mother. She then reflects his own
sense of inadequacy when he ponders how she "made a perpetual loser of one
of the most beautiful, the brightest boy in the land" (75). To succeed in his business world, Valerian buries his personal fears and disappointments. But the childhood trauma of his father's death shapes his subjectivity and is always just below
the surface. When it erupts, Valerian retreats to nostalgic memory to restore his
sense of imaginary completeness.

Valerian's strongest memory, of the day he became an orphan, is a traumatic
one. He often thinks wistfully of the "back yard of the house of his childhood in
Philadelphia," where he went during his father's funeral, "out back to the shed

where a washerwoman did the family's laundry. [. . .] She was like a pet who would listen agreeably to him and not judge or give orders" (140). Like other servants, paid to cater to every whim of their employers, this washerwoman is perhaps the only person who mirrors a positive, independent self for Valerian. When he answers her daily question "What your daddy doin today?" with "He's dead today," he realizes that his loss is forever and enormous: "It was too big, too deep, a bottomless bucket of time into which his little boy legs were sinking and his little boy hands were floundering" (141). Perceiving his pain and helplessness, she makes him scrub pillowcases until he cries, his only verbalization of his traumatic pain. Valerian re-creates this childhood healing by having a separate wash house on the island; there is no "Octagon soap" now, but he has the nostalgic, fantasized, restorative space (142).

When Valerian escapes from Philadelphia and its traumatic associations, he brings the nostalgic trappings of his former home. The only things he misses from Philadelphia are "hydrangeas and the postman. [. . .] The rest of what he loved he brought with him: some records, garden shears, a sixty-four-bulb chandelier, a light blue tennis shirt and the Principal Beauty of Maine" (11). Valerian creates a home that contains what he needs to survive emotionally: the wash house, flowers, music, his wife, and his loyal workers. Yet even in his island paradise, trauma and anxiety, integral parts of his identity, surface. He worries that Ondine and Sydney, who have served as surrogate parents to him, will leave. Margaret's response to this concern assures him of their attachment when she says, "They won't leave you [. . .]. You couldn't pry them out of here" (30–31). The members of this group, bonded like family, cannot live without one another. Master and slave are mutually dependent.[30]

It is at this moment of reflection and need for positive reassurance that Son enters the scene. Son's presence reenergizes Valerian, sparking him to become the perfect host and father figure. He begins to look forward to dinner, appears happy, and sleeps with Margaret for the first time in ages. He invites Son to join them as a way to recapture his lost son, to reconcile with this version of Michael. He hopes even more than Margaret that Michael will come to dinner and that they will bond. Paralleling Michael's reaching out to the oppressed, Valerian reaches out to Son. In this way, he receives a positive reflection as a parent. Parents often get a positive mirroring from their children, but Michael and Valerian have never experienced this father-son mirroring, because of Valerian's passive parenting. Yet the hope for this reconciliation remains afloat.

Envisioning this ideal reunion, Valerian recalls his own childhood: "All that was needed was that holiday bread Grandmother Stadt used to make. Ollieballen" (187). When they sit down to dinner, Valerian beams, "It's good to have some plain Pennsylvania food for a change. This *is* an old-fashioned Christmas" (201). Nostalgic memory boosts his sense of self, which in turn allows him to hope that Michael has "turned out fine" (199). He recalls that Michael "was beautiful, wise and kind. That he loved people, was not selfish, [. . . and] wanted value in his life, not money" (199). Contrary to the ambitions of Valerian's forefathers, his son mirrors humane qualities that support Valerian's self-esteem. However, his opportunity to connect with Michael fails to materialize; instead of the longed-for visit, Valerian gains knowledge of Margaret's abuse of Michael. Valerian will dissociate from this pain, thinking "I have to cry about this" (234). While he verbalizes the need to express his grief in order to process it, he "achieved a kind of blank, whited-out, no-feeling-at-all that he hoped would sustain him until the blood tears came" (235). Without the washerwoman as a catalyst for his tears, Valerian lacks means to release his pain.

The past haunts both blacks and whites, as the core trauma of master and slave connects American culture. The encounter with Son, which initially energizes Valerian, ends up depleting him. Morrison's depiction of Valerian reinforces the mutual dependence created by the slave system and the master narrative. For Margaret, Son's arrival reopens old wounds. She feels invaded when Son hides in her things, a response that is perhaps a reenactment of her response to Michael's needing what she could not give him. Feeling anger and outrage, Margaret regresses to longing for her mother and the home of her youth, the trailer. Margaret's ego strength, always precarious, weakens to a point of unprotected helplessness. Son's invasion reactivates her prior bodily response to her childhood trauma. Stemming from her parents' lack of nurturing, Margaret has always felt vulnerable and incomplete. Because of her extraordinary beauty, Margaret's parents assume that "[s]he won't have to worry. And they stepped back and let her be. They gave her care, but they withdrew attention. Their strength they gave to the others who were not beautiful" (56–57). While they are not maltreating parents per se, they reject Margaret in subtle ways. For example, her presence emotionally upsets her father, and she senses that her mysterious red hair "caught his eye at the dinner table and ruined his meals" (55). Her internalized rejection compounds Margaret's feelings of isolation.

Margaret liked living in the trailer as a child because in that small space "the separateness she felt had less room to grow in" (57). Retreating to her room after

Son's intrusion, Margaret feels that she has "come full circle. The trailer had been like this room. All economy and parallel lines" (82). She sees her room as "a high-class duplication, minus the coziness, of the first" (83). Because memory reactivates bodily trauma, Margaret's first response is to seek the shelter of her own, enclosed space. Through nostalgic memory, she longs for home or a place that will supply her with the necessary, ideal imaginary self. But that self has been elusive; ostracized by her family, she experiences a loneliness that stems from "the inaccessibility of the minds (not the hearts) of Leonora and Joseph Lordi" (57). Unaware of the larger, middle-class culture, she is amazed to learn that trailers were looked down upon and that her town "was overwhelmed by her astonishing good looks" (82). Her beauty becomes a burden; she has to be "extra nice" so that people will not get mad at her, and teachers go "fuzzy in her presence" (82). But she found that Valerian "was never fuzzy," and the "safety she heard in his voice was in his nice square fingernails too" (83). He becomes a haven, having "comforted her and made her feel of consequence under the beauty" (83). Margaret marries him because he gives her the protective comfort of home and reflects an ideal self.

However, Valerian's large house is no home for a lonely seventeen-year-old, and Ondine provides comfort to her. Unfortunately for Margaret, "Valerian put a stop to it saying she should guide the servants, not consort with them" (59). He accuses her of "ignorance"; coming from a different class, Margaret must learn how to behave according to the middle-class master narrative of white culture (59). Fearing "the possibility of losing him" (59), Margaret gives up the company of Ondine, hoping that having a baby will secure her position. Unfortunately, "the afterboom" grows louder (60), and she cannot find peace in Valerian's world. Valerian's family's rejection of Margaret forces her to give up her past attachments: her Catholicism and her cross, a rare family gift. Telling her that "only whores wore crosses," Valerian's sister reinforces Margaret's negative self-worth (70). Thus, three factors contribute to Margaret's core identity and account for the recurring trauma that erupts: her rare and distancing beauty, her poverty, and her devout Catholic upbringing.

The birth of her son, Michael, while securing her place in Valerian's family, overwhelms Margaret's insecure ego and robs her of her strength. As a baby, Michael "seemed to want everything of her, and she didn't know what to give" (60). Not yet grown up herself, still in need of care and protection, Margaret cannot properly mother or give of herself to her own child.[31] Ondine differentiates between the "two" sons that Michael represents, Valerian's and Margaret's, describing Margaret's abuse as an attack on Valerian's baby because "[h]e kept her stupid; kept her idle," while "[h]er baby she loved" (279). Margaret's abuse of her son is an expression of her own pain or of the reactivated memory of dismissal by both her father and Valerian's relatives. She acts out her own trauma by inflicting pain on her child to provide psychic release.

Margaret will dissociate herself from the abuse, claiming, "I have always loved my son. [...] I am not one of those women in the *National Enquirer*" who abuse their children (209). Yet her trauma erupts in the form of forgetfulness, "the occasional forgetfulness that plagued her when she forgot the names and uses of things," and she "never knew when it would come back, a thin terror accompanied you always—except in sleep" (55). But after she finally tells of her abuse of Michael, she is more at peace. She talks about it in a dissociated way, "as though it were a case history, an operation, some surgery that had been performed on her that she had survived" (237–38). She tells Valerian "in bite-sized pieces [...] because she did not have the vocabulary to describe what she had come to know, remember" (236).[32] Justifying the abuse as a type of self-defense, Margaret recounts that "she was outraged by that infant needfulness. [... and] its implicit and explicit demand for her best and constant self. [... And] when she felt hostage to that massive insolence, that stupid trust, she could not help piercing it" (236). Voicing her sense of vulnerability, she describes the attack on her by Michael's needs; Son's later encounter gives rise to the return of her trauma.

In her verbalization, Margaret underscores her helplessness: "When it did happen, it was out of my control," she says, describing the intrusive nature of trauma (237). She also captures the act of splitting the self from the deed: "I would see the mark and hear him cry but somehow I didn't believe it hurt all that much" (232). Her inability to empathize with Michael's pain mirrors the slaveholders' treatment of slaves as less than human. She abuses Michael even though "I knew it was wrong, knew it was bad. But something about it was delicious too" (231). Her need to act out her own pain, to project her object status onto her son, controls her actions. Once she confesses, Margaret wakes with the "harmony that comes from the relieved discovery that the jig is up" (235). Her healing can begin now that she has confronted her past. She realizes her love for her son when she says, "I don't hate him. I love him," and confirms Valerian's earlier musings that "she wasn't ready for him. [...] Now, now she's ready. When it's over" (76). At the novel's close, Valerian's need after his stroke to be fed and cared for allows

Margaret to assume a mothering role. She cheerfully attends to Valerian, bathing him and supervising his care. When she tells Sydney, "God, is he stubborn. Worse than a child," she confirms that she is finally ready to be a mother (278). In a reversal of roles, she has control; Valerian is now at her mercy. By gaining control and independence, Margaret has gained a self, having articulated and come to terms with her past trauma so as to be able to act in the present.

Margaret's trauma of parental neglect and ostracism, as well as Valerian's treatment of her as an object, leads her to traumatize her son. Michael suffers on two accounts, through the firsthand trauma of abuse and through the absorption of his mother's injured psychic state. While he remains an underdeveloped character, Michael seems to have "escaped" the source of his trauma and its lingering effects by avoiding his parents and helping others. All we know about him is his unrest. Unsettled in his career, he moves frequently, working with Native Americans but considering environmental law. Perhaps by helping other victims, Michael relives and works through his own experiences, verbalizing through compassionate deeds.[33] As a child, he lacks the words to speak his trauma, and Valerian describes him "singing because he could not speak or cry—because he had no vocabulary for what was happening to him" (234). Through singing, Michael acts out his trauma as well as his attachment to his mother:

> [H]e'd be under the sink. Humming to himself. When I'd pull him out, ask him what he was doing there, he'd say he liked the soft. He was two, I think, two years old, looking in the dark for something—soft. [. . .] humming that little, I can't tell you how lonely, *lonely* song. [. . .] But he seemed to miss her so, need her so that when she was attentive he was like a slave to her. (76)

Valerian tries to understand Michael's needy state but cannot alleviate it, sensing that he is "[a]ll the time scared. And he wanted her to stop. [. . .] I'd see him curled up on his side, staring off. After a while—after a while he didn't even cry" (209). Reduced to a constant state of fear, Michael experiences the approach/avoidance of a child who seeks parental safety from the abuser, described by Hesse and Main. This unrelenting fear haunts trauma victims like Michael: "The not knowing when, the never knowing why, and never being able to shape the tongue to speak, let alone the mind to cogitate how the one person in the world upon whom he was totally, completely dependent—the one person he could not even choose not to love—could do that to him" (234). Like other abuse victims,

Michael concludes that somehow "he deserved it" (234). Yet the love bond for the maltreating parent remains, much to the puzzlement of Valerian, who asks, "Why does he love you?" (238).[34] Ondine knows Margaret's crime: "I didn't say he didn't love her; I said he don't want to be near her. Sure he love her. That's only natural. He's not the one who's not natural. She is" (36). When he grows up, Michael separates himself from his parents, protecting his adult subjectivity by his absence. Despite the hopes of Valerian and Margaret, Michael will not come to Christmas dinner. However, a surrogate son arrives and provides the vehicle for Valerian and Margaret to work out their own unresolved relationship with Michael.

Unlike Michael, who suffers from parental abuse, William Green, or "Son," recalls the love and protection of his life in Eloe, Florida. No matter how long or far he wanders, he retains his image of home: "the fat black ladies in white dresses minding the pie table in the basement of the church and white wet sheets flapping on a line, and the sound of a six-string guitar plucked after supper while children scooped walnuts up off the ground" (119). Church, food, music, and family harmonize in his memory. Although Son considers himself a man adrift, with no ties, he realizes the value he places on "fraternity" and that "he'd better go where he could never be deprived of it—home" (168). Home for Son is the small, all-black town of Eloe, Florida, a town of "[n]inety houses, three hundred and eighty-five people" who farm and fish (173).[35] Raised by his father after his mother's death, nursed by the churchwomen and encouraged by Miss Tyler, who teaches him to play the piano, Son nostalgically defends his unsophisticated town: "Nothing's better than Eloe" (173). Despite spending eight years as a fugitive, having fled Eloe after catching his wife with a thirteen-year-old, driving his car into their house, and losing his wife in the fire that followed the car's explosion, Son still finds comfort in the memory of his community. "[H]e'd had seven documented identities" in eight years, all "required to protect Son from harm and to secure" his sense of self (139). Son has managed to protect his core identity of a small-town boy with values rooted in his close community and family ties.

It is with these ties in mind that Son seeks refuge in Valerian's home, where the piano draws him like a magnet. He "looked again at the house lights—the home lights—beaming like a safe port in front of him" (135). Instinctively, Son picks Valerian's home as a place of safety and protection. Despite his filth from days of hiding, Son manages to provide a source of comfort to the household. His farming knowledge and acquaintance with country life allow him to cure

Valerian's nonblooming plants and to create a barrier with mirrors against invad-ing ants. He tells Ondine to put banana leaves in her shoes to cushion them, and her earlier skepticism about Son fades when Ondine sees "the orphan in him" (161). His need for attachment strikes a chord with her, and he reveals his de-sire for approval when he tells Ondine, "I didn't want to leave without making peace with you all. My own mama wouldn't forgive me for that" (161). He later reveals his sentimental side to Jadine, telling her of his devotion to his first em-ployer, Frisco, "who used to pay him to clean fish" and gave him his first dime (224). When a gas explosion kills Frisco, Son finally finds release for the trauma of Vietnam, his mother's loss, and his wife's death: he "cried like an infant for all the blowings up in Asia" (225). Years of repressed feelings finally emerge as tears "verbalize" his trauma.

This surge of physical emotion returns when Son, freshly bathed and in Valer-ian's clothing, looks at Yardman's [i.e., Gideon's] back as he toils in the backyard in contrast to his own new cleanliness: "he was as near to crying as he'd been since he'd fled from home. You would have thought something was leaving him and all he could see was its back" (140). Son's connection with his people and the injustices heaped upon the less fortunate by white society in general overrides the abundance of Valerian's hospitality. Although physically removed from his own culture and in Valerian's accepting environment, Son cannot separate him-self from the master narrative that has shaped him. He cannot control the intru-sion of cultural rejection that overwhelms him and destroys his comfort in Valer-ian's home when he sees the mistreatment of Gideon and Therese. Referred to as Yardman and Mary by Valerian's household and thus stripped of their individual identities, Gideon and Therese (like the slaves in *Beloved*) become nameless workers, hired to keep Valerian's world in order. "It bothered him that everybody called Gideon Yardman, as though he had not been mothered" (161). Son's core identity, molded by an exclusionary white culture, mirrors that of Gideon and creates the tension with which he will struggle in his relationship with Jadine.[36]

Having been adrift for eight years, Son gravitates to Valerian's home and the possible anchor that Jadine can provide. He begins to think of future possibili-ties: "this heavy, grown-up love made him feel fresh-born" (218). Thoughts of a future home and family with Jadine restore Son's sense of selfhood as the protec-tive function of love takes over. "The birdlike defenselessness he had loved while she slept and saw when she took his hand on the stairs was his to protect" (220). Love creates a reciprocal responsibility, causing Son to not want to love Jadine, "because he could not afford to lose her" (220). If he loses her, he will lose his positive mirroring. For example, when they flee to New York, Son loses himself whenever Jadine is away from him. He needs Jadine to ground him there amidst "a whole new race of people he was once familiar with" (217).

However, their love struggles when Son's trauma in white culture erupts. The cultural symbolic order stamps Son as other, perpetuating the division of races that stems from slavery's legacy. "There wasn't a permanent adult job in the whole of the city for him, so he did teenager's work on occasion and pieces of a grown man's work" (227). Eight years away have not changed the discrimination that denies him recognition as a man. He insists on taking Jadine to Eloe, his place of ego support and family. But in Eloe, Jadine rejects his family and background as too backward and restrictive in an ironic mirroring of Valerian's problem with Margaret's class. Jadine forces Son to choose, a choice he cannot make. Their fights revolve around Jadine's denial of her black heritage and white racism. Son articulates her lack of insight when he tells her that "until you know about me, you don't know nothing about yourself" (264). He wants her to realize that it was Ondine and Sydney, not Valerian, who put her through school and that she deserted them. Yet in his own escape from the law, Son deserted his family in a parallel way, and as he comes to terms with this part of his identity, he hopes to help Jadine touch base with her own. This principle of core identity divides them, and Jadine abandons Son rather than work through her conflicted identity. She follows the voices of white culture instead of identifying with her black heritage.

When he loses Jadine, Son relives his earlier abandonment at his mother's death, with one exception: the people of his hometown no longer provide a safety net. He gazes "at the photos one by one trying to find in them what it was that used to comfort him so, used to reside with him, in him like royalty in his veins" (294). His nostalgic vision of home no longer holds, and thus he experiences his bodily stored trauma of loss and abandonment. Son's love for Jadine competes with his love for his family and the community that raised him. He questions his stubbornness: "Let go the woman you had been looking for everywhere just because she was difficult?" (298). Following her to win her back, Son thinks that he will give up his devotion to fraternity, until he sees the poverty of Alma Estée's pathetic "wig the color of dried blood. [. . .] 'Oh, baby baby baby baby.' [. . .] It was all mixed up. He did not know what to think or feel" (299).[37] How can he choose between Jadine's loving protection and his core identity as abused other? How can he abandon his principles to protect his ego? In his chase, Son grapples with his conflict. Therese warns him, "Small boy [. . .] don't go to L'Arbe de la Croix. [. . .] Forget her. There is nothing in her parts for you. She has forgotten her ancient properties" (305). Infantilizing him, Therese points to his childlike neediness.

Which path will redeem Son or cause him to finally grow up, the one with a loving partner and future family or the one that has shaped him? Like Milkman in *Song of Solomon,* Son strips himself of his worldly possessions, leaving his bag with Therese. To reunite with Jadine, he must cross the hills in the pitch-black night to the other side of the island. In her parting words Therese advises him to join the blind men in the hills and free himself from Jadine. As Son gropes, then steadies himself, "[t]he mist lifted and the trees stepped back a bit as if to make the way easier for a certain kind of man" (306). What kind of man is Son at the novel's close? Which identity wins out? Morrison's ambiguous text captures an ever-conflicted identity between a new path that mirrors his ancestors and the one that white culture prescribes.[38]

Like Son's, Jadine's emotional growth has been stunted by identity conflicts. Her core trauma is twofold: being an orphan and being black in the white culture. As a result, she harbors a vulnerability and a sense of unworthiness. She thinks of her mother's death as an abandonment that reflects her own lack: "You left me you died you didn't care enough about me to stay alive you knew Daddy was gone and you went too" (261). Thus, Jadine knows and fears Lacan's Real, the gaze that erupts to threaten her equilibrium; she has learned to play a game in the rejecting white culture and to cover her "black self." Born into a white, racist, and capitalistic system, she learns how to succeed through modeling and playing a part. Jadine knows that to make it in a white world, blacks "played the game with house cards, each deck issued and dealt by the house. [. . .] She needed only to be stunning, and to convince them [white people] she was not as smart as they were. Say the obvious, ask stupid questions, laugh with abandon, look interested" (126). Modeling in Europe, she can obtain a positive gaze and identity; Jadine's modeling provides a home, a safe place of acceptance and admiration. Rather than articulate her desire, Jadine opts for the white master narrative, in which her beauty gives her access that most blacks lack. While her beauty initially masks her conflict with her black identity, it actually complicates it. In a mirror image of her own youth, Margaret sees Jadine as having "Everything. Europe. The future. The world" (29). Just as her own family mistakenly assumes that Margaret does not need their attention because she is beautiful, Margaret assumes that Jadine's life is an ideal one of money, beauty, and fame. But Jadine's life is a struggle that epitomizes racial conflict and low self-esteem.[39]

While Jadine's beauty provides her with access to white culture, she is never sure whether she is loved and accepted for herself or for what she represents. For example, she wonders whether her Parisian boyfriend, Ryk, wants to marry her "or a black girl" (48). In the end, she realizes that she will need to grow up to protect herself; the only question is how: "There were no shelters anyway; [...] Every orphan knew that" (288). The equation of orphans with blacks is an astute one, as we saw in *Jazz*. By depriving infants of their parents at birth, the slave culture renders blacks perpetual orphans without shelter. How does the orphaned black community grow up? How can it become independent in the gaze of white culture? The core trauma of slavery surfaces as each generation attempts to create a subjectivity out of a void. With no prior history to rely on, blacks adopt white culture, perpetuating their erasure. By playing with the white man's deck of cards, Jadine remains a dependent pawn. Like Fanon, she cannot escape the white gaze that strips her of true subjectivity. This gaze erupts throughout the novel, forcing Jadine to recognize her core identity.

At age twelve, when her mother dies, Jadine witnesses an assault by male dogs on a defenseless dog in heat. Acknowledging that the dog is blameless, "she decided then and there at the age of twelve in Baltimore never to be broken in the hands of any man" (124). Identifying with the defenseless dog, Jadine vows to be "always ready to rein in the dogs" (124). She must remain in control of her life to protect herself. Yet on one of her happiest days in Paris, while she is shopping for a celebratory party, a native woman in a yellow dress stops Jadine in her tracks and haunts her later. Jadine critiques her as "a woman much too tall. Under her long canary yellow dress Jadine knew there was too much hip, too much bust. The agency would laugh her out of the lobby, so why was she and everybody else in the store transfixed?" (45). Not in the Western mold of beauty, there was "something in her eyes so powerful it had burnt away the eyelashes" (45). With the native power of "eyes too beautiful for lashes" (45), this woman represents "that woman's woman—that mother/sister/she; that unphotographable beauty" (46). Jadine sees in this woman her own native beauty, which she has rejected.

By carrying out "three chalk-white eggs" (46), not a dozen or a half-dozen, the woman transgresses the law and convention. Her powerful gaze represents Lacan's gaze of the Other, stunning the storekeepers and shoppers alike. Her parting gesture is to make eye contact with Jadine and spit, leaving Jadine hard pressed to "figure out why the woman's insulting gesture had derailed her—shaken her

out of proportion to incident. Why she had wanted that woman to like and respect her" (47). The encounter makes her feel "[l]onely and inauthentic" (48).
Confronted with Lacan's gaze of the Other, Jadine senses that Western beauty is
a false home for her (despite her identification) and misrepresents an authentic
identity with the deidealization that bell hooks and Kaja Silverman describe. But
like Son, she does not know which path to choose.

The woman in the yellow dress haunts Jadine even when she escapes her life
in Paris to regroup at Valerian's island retreat, because psychologically, "seemingly
insignificant reminders can [. . .] evoke [. . .] memories, which often return with
all the vividness and emotional force of the original event" (Herman 37). Thus,
no environment is "safe." Jadine's encounter with Son will reactivate this image,
and when she sinks in the swamp, she reexperiences the feeling of orphaned
abandonment. She realizes that she can save herself from sinking by figuring
out what her ancestors would have done. By "edging up the tree that wanted to
dance," she clings to her "partner, the tree [. . .] like man and wife" (182–83). Her
sisterhood with the swamp "women hanging from the trees" enables her to save
herself (183). Here, her identification with her cultural past rescues her.

But such an identification is not Jadine's first course of action, and her instinctual flight from black identity resurfaces "in the form of vivid sensations and
images" (Herman 38) when she travels with Son to Eloe. The nightmare she has
there of being surrounded by women staring at her, showing her their breasts,
troubles her as she sees in their gaze a reflection of herself confined; she senses
that she has to flee Eloe to remain independent. She feels that they "were all out
to get her, tie her, bind her," in a way parallel to the way the white gaze confines
black subjectivity (262). However, despite her escape to New York City, where
she will wait for Son, "[o]n the fifth day, she was feeling orphaned again" (260).
Reliving her abandonment trauma, she realizes that New York is "not her home
after all. The dogs were leashed in the city but the reins were not always secure"
(288). New York turns out not to be the shelter she anticipated. When she first
arrives to meet Son, "[h]er legs were longer here, her neck really connected her
body to her head. [. . .] This is home, she thought with an orphan's delight; [. . .]
And now she would take it; take it and give it to Son. They would make it theirs"
(221–22). The positive gaze for blacks that New York provides Jadine evaporates
after her love connection to Son, a truer home for an orphan, falters.

As a consequence, she moves from an imaginary totalized image of herself to
a body in pieces. While the energy of New York and the white world of Valerian
—like the seal coat Ryk gives her—are "seductive," neither provides Jadine a psy-

chic home (112). Her nostalgic attachment to Valerian and Margaret stems from the safety they have provided, and "she had known them so long, and they were like family, almost, and had given her so much" (90). But Valerian's eyes reflect a false gaze for Jadine, "all reflection, like mirrors, chamber after chamber, corridor after corridor of mirrors, each one taking its shape from the other and giving it back as its own until the final effect was color where no color existed at all" (73–74). Her blackness remains, despite her comfort in that family. Her place there, like that of Sydney and Ondine, is a home circumscribed by white needs.

Sydney and Ondine choose life in the master narrative with Valerian over whatever family life they could have back in the States. In fact, they let Jadine know through their eyes that if forced to choose between Jadine's vision for them to "live together like a family at last" with a store in New York, on the one hand, and life with Valerian, on the other, their real home was their job with Valerian (49). Their home with Valerian, like Sethe's life at Sweet Home with the Garners, represents a nostalgic longing for a space that mirrors back an integrated self.

Even when Jadine joins Sydney and Ondine when she is twelve, they do not live together as a true family, but as appendages to their white employers: "After her mother died they were her people—but she never lived with them except summers at Valerian's house when she was very young" (49). While Valerian's financial and physical support eases her orphaned state, Jadine fails to develop emotionally. Her beauty enables her to escape the harsh reality of black life, and she fails to grow into an independent, responsible person. By the end of the novel, Jadine realizes that there is no escape from her conflicted identity. Gideon summarizes her dilemma as follows: "It's hard for them [high yellows] not to be white people. [. . .] Yallas don't come to being black natural-like. They have to choose it and most don't choose it" (155).[40] Yet Valerian's island retreat, as well as her charmed life in Paris, fail to erase Jadine's traumatized core identity. Only by verbalizing her emotional needs can she mature as an adult. Sydney and Ondine will soon need the parenting they have lavished on her: "They had been her parents since she was twelve and now she was required to parent them—guide them, do the small chores that put them in touch with the outside world, soothe them, allay their fears" (91). The thought of parenting them frightens her because she knows that she is not yet ready, and she thinks, "I cannot be needed now. Another time, please. I have spent it all" (280). In an echo of Margaret's burden of Michael's neediness, Jadine verbalizes her need to grow up in order to meet the needs of others.

Ondine has lectured Jadine about growing to become a proper daughter: "A daughter is a woman that cares about where she come from and takes care of them that took care of her. [. . .] I don't want you to care about me for my sake. I want you to care about me for yours" (281). The rawness of her orphan trauma remains on a bodily level. "When Ondine said, 'You didn't have a mother long enough,' blood rushed to Jadine's skin the way it always did when her mother-lessness was mentioned" (281). Her bodily response to Ondine's mentioning the loss of her mother occurs instantly, taking her unawares.[41] Losing her mother as a child makes her extremely vulnerable.[42] But Ondine's verbalization of Jadine's trauma helps her to focus on working through it. When Jadine returns to Paris, it will be to start over and to grow up. She declares, "No more dreams of safety. [. . .] A grown woman did not need safety or its dreams. She *was* the safety she longed for" (290). Like Sethe in *Beloved,* Jadine needs to be her own "best thing" if she is to fight her continuing orphan trauma. While her instincts are to be with Sydney and Ondine as a family, she needs to be independent first.[43]

Jadine's need to mature represents the struggle of black culture to be free of white paternalism. As long as blacks depend on white culture, as orphans depend on the charity of others, being free from the cycle of black trauma remains elusive. Jadine's experiences exemplify how the trauma of black oppression in the white culture cannot be easily separated from personal trauma. While we do not know much of the past personal trauma of Sydney and Ondine, their attachment to Valerian illustrates the perpetuation of slavery's legacy. Tied to Valerian like a master to his slaves, Sydney and Ondine, rather than being taken care of by Valerian, are victims of his control and manipulation. In their subservient roles, Sydney and Ondine totally rely on Valerian's employment. As insecure as he claims to be about losing them, they depend on their place in his home for their livelihood as well as their subjectivity.

Sydney and Ondine fear losing Valerian as a child fears losing a parent; his money and power perpetuate their fear of abandonment and dependence. "I want us to stay here. Like we have been. That old man loves you. Loves us both. Look what he gives us [stock certificates] at Christmas" (101). They have found their balance and peace with Valerian, who takes care of them as well as Jadine. However, trauma materializes in the form of Son's invasion and the truth of Margaret's abuse of Michael, creating anxiety for Sydney and Ondine when Lacan's Real threatens their stability. Valerian's invitation to Son to join his family at the table insults them for two reasons: Son's menacing presence threatens their secure family unit, and Valerian's inviting Son to dine at the white man's table transgresses the taboo of the color line. Sydney stays awake all night worrying about Jadine's safety and tells Ondine that Valerian does not realize that "[m]y family lives here—not just his" (99). In doing so, he voices his own desire rather than that of white culture: the black man's family is just as important as the white man's.

However, Sydney and Ondine resign themselves to living with minor reminders of their position as Valerian's pawns. For example, Margaret's demands for a traditional Christmas dinner in a tropical climate points to their displacement from the world they have escaped. Ondine complains that "everything I need to cook with is back in Philadelphia" (37). In addition, Ondine voices her annoyance at Margaret for taking over her kitchen and then abandoning the meal halfway through. But they cannot escape the truth of Valerian's lack of concern for their workload or their feelings when he fires Gideon and Therese without telling them first: "The sea spread around him and his wife. They were afloat in it and if removed from the island there was nowhere to land. They had no house, no place of their own" (233). When Ondine asks Sydney to face the fact that this is not his home, he says, "If this ain't my home, then nothing is but the grave" (284). Moreover, they realize that when death comes, they will have to bury themselves. Their home with Valerian is inadequate, a shell of what a real home should be. And yet, when Valerian's stroke weakens him, and he says, "I should leave this place and go back to Philadelphia," Sydney seizes the opportunity to take control (286). Drinking the wine of the helpless Valerian, Sydney tells him, "I figure we're going to be here a long time [. . .]. We'll give you the best of care. Just like we always done. That's something you ain't never got to worry about" (287). The safety of Sydney's family rests on the status quo of life in Valerian's island home. Valerian's illness gives Sydney the strength to voice his own desire and thus take charge of the household.

Without Valerian, Sydney and Ondine lack a secure physical home and economic means. However, as a couple they provide a positive gaze for each other to counter the traumatizing larger cultural gaze and their precarious economic situation. They draw emotional and spiritual comfort from their marriage, "a pair of married servants sleeping back to back. [. . .] There is safety in those backs. Each one feels it radiating from the other, knows that the steady, able spine of its partner is a hip turn away" (43). Unlike the rest of Valerian's house, which has "a hotel feel about it [. . . and] tentativeness" (12), their room "had a tacky permanence to it, but closed. Closed to outsiders" (160). Their protected space counters everyday worries, and at night Ondine finds succor from nightmares when "still asleep she turns over and touches her husband's back—the dream dissolves and with it the anxiety" (61). Sydney also sleeps peacefully in this space and dreams of his hometown of "Baltimore of 1921. The fish, the trees, the music, the horses' harnesses. It was a tiny dream he had each night that he would never recollect from morning to morning. So he never knew what it was exactly that refreshed him" (61). Family connections buffer assaults from the larger culture, and while they worry about their job stability, with no savings and just "a few stocks and Social Security" to fall back on, their home becomes a metaphor for safety (193). Jadine, a "'child' whom she could enjoy, indulge, protect" (96), completes Ondine's secure circle, and she reassures Sydney that "Jadine's here. Nothing can happen to us as long as she's here" (102). Although displaced, they have maintained their strength through family attachments.

With no children of their own, Sydney and Ondine have treated Jadine as their daughter, reveling in her affectionate nickname "Nanadine," "a child's effort to manage 'Aunt Ondine'" (38). When Jadine's face appears on the cover of all the Paris magazines, Ondine boasts that it was the "[p]rettiest thing I ever saw. Made those white girls disappear. Just disappear right off the page. [. . .] Your mother would have loved to see that" (40). She voices her pleasure at the erasure of white culture in the gaze of Jadine's black beauty. Ondine accepts Son's relationship with Jadine not only because she senses his having been raised correctly but also because of the home they provide for each other. Like Ondine and Sydney, Jadine and Son "told each other all of it. Or all they could" (224). With Son, Jadine "came to feel unorphaned. He cherished and safeguarded her. When she woke in the night from an uneasy dream she had only to turn and there was the stability of his shoulder and his limitless, eternal chest. [. . .] He unorphaned her completely. Gave her a brand-new childhood" (229). As in the protected sleep space of Sydney and Ondine, love and connecting with others rejuvenates subjectivity.

However, the balm of family life does not eradicate completely the stress of the larger culture. Blacks in a predominantly white culture remain under the control of people with power and money and cannot totally escape race and class restrictions. Eventually, the need for black verbalization of white abuse erupts at the Christmas dinner table, with everyone shouting like a family quarreling, saying things they would regret later. Despite living under the same roof, they are not a true family, and Son observes that "white folks and black folks should not sit down and eat together. [. . .] should not eat together or live together or sleep together. Do any of those personal things in life" (210). Cultural oppression eventually takes its toll, causing Ondine to finally snap, like the stars Son describes that "throb and throb and throb and sometimes, when they can't throb anymore, when they can't hold it anymore, they fall out of the sky" (214). She can no longer hold her silence and perform her job; she explodes. Although she knew of Margaret's child abuse, Ondine remained silent because she was a loyal employee and feared losing her job. Margaret's accusation that Ondine just wanted her to be "the mean white lady and you could be the good colored one" illustrates white society's perpetuation of black trauma through projection (240).

Although removed from U.S. soil, Valerian's island retreat reinforces these cultural hierarchies of race and class, and the hopeless position of Therese and Gideon mirrors the state of blacks in American white culture. Therese, once valued for her abundant milk, suffers economically when formula replaces her ample supply. With Therese, Morrison's text echoes Sethe's stolen milk and the plantation system's abuse of black women who were forced to nurse white babies as well as black ones. Left defenseless, Therese tricks her nephew Gideon into "coming back to Dominique to handle family property" (108). Since she is the only property left, she voices her need to have Gideon, her only remaining family, take care of her. Although he returns without the fortune in American dollars he had hoped for, Gideon finds contentment in Therese's devotion, and "the thought of being able to die in those coffee-growing hills rather than in those lonely Stateside places gave him so much happiness" (110). Valerian's firing of Gideon and Therese for stealing his apples angers Son, who recognizes that Valerian represents white masters. The clashing world-views of Valerian and Son—of men of "industry" and men of "fraternity," of "French Chevaliers" and "black men on [. . .] unshod horses"—represent both men's psychic tie to ancestral identity through cultural memory (205–6).

Valerian fails to see the humanity of Therese's desire for the pleasure of apples; he turns a blind eye to her subjectivity, just as he ignores his son's true plight. He realizes that he "had not known [of Michael's abuse] because he had not taken the trouble to know. [. . .] Knowing more was inconvenient and frightening. [. . .] What an awful thing she had done. And how much more awful not to have known it" (242). Valerian "had chosen not to know the real message that his son had mailed to him from underneath the sink," just as white culture ignores black suffering: it is inconvenient and uncomfortable to face the gaze of the Other (243).

Like Valerian, Sydney and Ondine also chose to look the other way in order to protect their place, perpetuating the status quo. As Vamik Volkan suggests, the larger culture molds subjectivity, causing Sydney and Ondine to seek Valerian's protection.

The explosive Christmas dinner unleashes a verbalization that is necessary to derail the cycle of black trauma. When Margaret seeks forgiveness, Ondine tells her, "You forgive you. Don't ask for more" (241). Recognition of one's own subjectivity is the first step to healing. The novel closes by asking whether the next generation, Jadine and Son, will make it as a couple in this racist culture: "Mama-spoiled black man, will you mature with me? Culture-bearing black woman, whose culture are you bearing?" (269). Both Jadine and Son realize their conflicted identities. She must face her denial of blackness to succeed in the white world and live in Paris on her own terms. Son acknowledges that his cherished "original dime" earned from Frisco was as tainted as Jadine's monetary support from Valerian when she explains to him that "some black woman like me fucked a white man for it and then *gave* it to Frisco who made you work your ass off for it" (272). Each must grow up and learn how to move from the yoke of white culture to self-love and life beyond cultural restrictions. Their stability as a couple will depend on their ability to nourish and parent each other. In addition, they must connect with the greater black community. Fultz writes that "no individual can live securely without some affective links to community" (42), and J. Brooks Bouson describes the "potentially healing power of the sense of safety and connection offered by the African-American community and in their antishaming and restitutive fantasies of what Morrison calls the African-American ancestors" (5). Only by articulating their own desire and rejecting that of the white master narrative can they establish subjectivity.

Together, the individual and the community can reshape the future. Such refashioning, based on connection with others, provides a more productive response to trauma than escape or relocation. Morrison shows us that as Paul D and Sethe discover in *Beloved*, hope lies in creating new families and homes that become part of a greater community. Processing black trauma through verbalization of black desire leads to healing relationships for the individual and the community. Morrison's theme of supportive love to combat the master narrative in *Jazz* and *Tar Baby* continues in *Love*, where she describes once again how people carry their personal and cultural pasts wherever they go.

FOUR

Bodies of Trauma
Memory, Home, and Subjectivity in *Love*

As we saw in the previous chapter, neither relocation nor total isolation alleviates the deeply rooted trauma carried over from slavery. Aggression, an alternative response that mirrors the master narrative, serves as an insufficient solution,
as we saw in chapter 2. As in Morrison's previous novels, in *Love* characters are
displaced from home, orphaned, and abandoned, and even Cosey himself, like
others, remains scarred by American culture. Cultural re-creation of slave trauma
indicates the deficiency of the white mirror for black culture, and despite movements of social progress, white culture's denial of black desire perpetuates the
black struggle for subjectivity. In *Love,* Cosey's Hotel and Resort serves both as a
physical and a psychic space, a site of personal and collective memory that boosts
the self-concept of Cosey's community and of his family. Yet the helplessness resulting from both communal and personal trauma overwhelms the characters,
and like Morrison's other novels, *Love* illustrates the reliance on the past and
memory for a sense of self.

Nostalgic memory, connected to home as a physical place and the people associated with it, protects the fragile ego. Both the past and possessions come to
represent home in their reflection of a positive self. *Love* suggests that despite
the historical distance from slavery, the black community remains vulnerable to
cultural forces. Characters rely solely on family members and a sheltered, small
community to reflect a self, with access to wealth and power shaping status and
thus subjectivity. The failure of Cosey's Hotel and Resort, like the failure of Ruby
in *Paradise* and Macon's summer homes at Honore in *Song of Solomon,* suggests
that despite shifts in social conditions, a core trauma remains. Healing requires
giving voice to black trauma so as to override the values of white culture and
name personal desire.

Love tells the story of Bill Cosey, the effect of his Hotel and Resort on his Florida community, and the family that survives him. Cosey uses the money his father makes as an informant to create a vacation escape for the greater black community. In addition, Cosey employs many blacks in the local vicinity and serves as a role model because of his generosity and success. His loyal cook, L, adds warmth to the hotel and helps to raise his son, Billy, when Cosey's wife dies. Billy marries May, the daughter of an impoverished minister, who makes it her mission to keep Billy and Cosey happy and the hotel in superlative condition. Unfortunately, Billy dies young, leaving May and their daughter, Christine, in Bill Cosey's care. After playing the field, Cosey chooses to marry Heed, Christine's eleven-year-old lower-class playmate. This action results in tensions and hostilities among the women in the household that escalate when Bill Cosey dies, leaving a questionable will.

The novel opens with an aging Christine and Heed at war over Cosey's property, with Heed hiring a young homeless waif, Junior, to assist her. For both Christine and Heed, Cosey's property represents a worthy self. By fighting over the estate, they express their need for personal recognition. Anissa Wardi writes that "beyond receiving Cosey's wealth, each woman vies to hold the position of Bill Cosey's sweet child" (210). Romen, the grandson of the former Cosey employees Sandler and Vida, helps the women out as gardener. While this black community should provide a safe space, bitterness, hierarchies, and unrest infiltrate the community (as in *Paradise*), and trauma erupts. Individual trauma reflects an urgency and an immediacy that indicate the bodily aspect of past experiences. The community's core identity, shaped by slavery, segregation, early integration, and civil rights efforts, signifies the generational inheritance of trauma. Christine, Heed, May, Junior, and Cosey search for a connection and bonding they never attain. As with characters in Morrison's other novels, their vulnerability points to weak parental attachments that originated with slavery. Despite a potentially supportive community, aggressive and competitive behavior prevails.

Morrison captures the essence of individual trauma, its causes, and ways to alleviate it in her foreword to *Love*, where she states that "among the things Christine, Heed, and Junior have already lost, besides their innocence and their faith, are a father and a mother, or, to be more precise, fathering and mothering. Emotionally unprotected by adults, they give themselves over to the most powerful one they know, the man who looms even larger in their imagination than in their lives" (xii). To counter the trauma of parental abandonment, these characters seek physical and psychic adult protection in Bill Cosey. In addition, Christine and Heed find solace from family deficits in a friendship love bond. Christine seeks to recover from the loss of her father when she was five, and Heed needs refuge from the mercenary parents who will oust her from home at age eleven when they barter her marriage to Cosey. The girls' love bond, along with the vocalization and sharing of pain, can address trauma. The parental manipulation that betrays this bond produces a lifetime of abandonment issues for these women. Only at the novel's close, when they face each other and combat their trauma, can the healing, albeit too late for Heed, begin.[1]

The vulnerability and sense of insignificance that Heed and Christine experience from their family structures magnify their need for support from the symbolic structure to ward off anxiety. *Love* portrays the insecure ego that stems from one's being defined negatively by the larger culture as well as from the lack of strong attachment and adequate parenting. On a social level, Cosey's Hotel and Resort represents a response to historical discrimination and segregation. Many of the characters' nostalgic views of Cosey and his resort derive from the need for a positive self-image in response to the negative gaze of the Other. Despite civil rights legislation, white cultural hierarchies and historical patterns of interaction continue to plague society. In response, as we saw in *Paradise*, the black community establishes a pecking order, complete with scapegoats and pariahs. Consequently, the community compounds the larger culture's cycle of trauma. For example, the "Rurals," who live in the Settlement, contend with poverty and ostracism similar to what Pecola and her family suffer in *The Bluest Eye*. Finally, the personal trauma of Christine, Heed, and Junior erupts from deficient family situations. Thus, these three levels of distress—cultural, communal, and personal—operate in *Love*, illustrating the complexity of working through trauma embedded in the social fabric.

Throughout *Love*, individual crisis plays out against a backdrop of larger social, civil rights issues. On the national level, as Cosey remarks, "every law in this country is made to keep us [blacks] back" (44). Nostalgia emerges to reinforce a positive black image in a segregated society, and Bill Cosey's success provides hope in an otherwise bleak scenario. Unlike his father, who "snitched" on his own kind to amass his fortune, Cosey creates a space to provide comfort to other blacks, a place where *"they could walk in the front door, not the service entrance"* (102). The community members take pride of ownership in Cosey's accomplishment because it represents the possibility of their own. The resort furnishes the community with a positive gaze, or an ideal imaginary self:

> It was enough to know Bill Cosey's Hotel and Resort was there. Otherwise, how to explain the comfort available nowhere else in the county, or the state, for that matter. Cannery workers and fishing families prized it. [...] all felt a tick of entitlement, of longing turned to belonging in the vicinity of the fabulous, successful resort controlled by one of their own. (41–42)

The aura of its glory days lives on through nostalgic reminiscence even after the hotel has closed and Cosey has been buried. The healing psychic function of a positive reflection continues to provide solace in the face of nationwide racial turmoil and economic uncertainty.

Fond memories cause the community to forgive "Cosey. Everything. Even to the point of blaming a child for a grown man's interest in her" (147). By ignoring the fact that "Cosey didn't mix with local people publicly" and that "none was truly welcome at the hotel's tables or on its dance floor" (41), the people reap a psychic benefit from Cosey's achievement. For his community members, Cosey's caretaking and success provide a reflection of their own Lacanian imaginary self that serves as a validation of themselves in the symbolic order. Later, as people branch out to enter the larger symbolic structure, *"folks who bragged about Cosey vacations in the forties boasted in the sixties about Hyatts, Hiltons, cruises to the Bahamas and Ocho Rios"* (8). The cachet of Cosey's Hotel and Resort diminishes when the ability to interact with the greater social structure becomes available. However, even in future times, Cosey's community will remember him and his heyday with fond nostalgia.

For example, Sandler Gibbons, who perhaps knew Cosey better than anyone else as a result of his fishing excursions on Cosey's boat, idealizes Cosey despite his factual knowledge:

> Each year Sandler became fonder of the neighborhood he and Vida had moved away from. She had been right, certainly, to leave Up Beach when they did, before the drought that ended in flood, and she never gave it another thought. [...] He couldn't forget the picture the moon turned those Up Beach cabins into. Here, in this government-improved and -approved housing with too much man-made light, the moon did nothing kind. (39)

Memories washed with moonlight reflect Cosey's ability to provide an imaginary self. Because Sandler's "own boyhood had been shaped by fear of vigilantes," he forecloses that trauma and the "dark blue uniforms [that] had taken over posse work now" (15) with positive memories. In order to maintain his equilibrium despite social forces, Sandler "was becoming more and more fixed on the past rather than the moment he stood in" (46). He clings nostalgically to a memory of time and place. Personal memory re-creates pleasant sensory-motor patterns, evoking comforts of home and blocking fearful cultural images.

Ironically, Sandler criticizes his wife Vida's rose-colored memories. Knowing the dark side of Cosey, Sandler thinks, "Vida believed a powerful, generous friend gazed out from the portrait hanging behind the reception desk. That was because she didn't know who he was looking at" (45). Her idealized picture of Cosey counters Sandler's true knowledge. Later, he will further fault Vida: "What was the point in remembering the good old days as though the past was pure? [. . .] She acted as though Heed had chased and seduced a fifty-two-year-old man, older than her father. That she had chosen to marry him rather than having been told to" (147). Underneath Vida's exaggerated vision of Cosey, Sandler encounters the Real of his community by acknowledging that Cosey has coerced the marriage of an eleven-year-old. Yet racial tensions and economic struggles diminish in Cosey's arena, which ultimately provides a respite for the black community. "Cosey's Resort was more than a playground; it was a school and a haven where people debated death in the cities, murder in Mississippi, and what they planned to do about it other than grieve and stare at their children" (35). This community, which mirrors its white counterparts, creates a sense of political power compounded by social well-being. *"No matter the outside loneliness, if you look inside, the hotel seems to promise you ecstasy and the company of all your best friends"* (7). Despite the trauma of the cultural structure, the resort provides imaginary relief.

Both Sandler and Vida recognize their precarious place in the larger social structure, as well as their need to stand up for principles and values. They use this knowledge to parent their grandson Romen with guidance and love. Together, they provide a steady presence of integrity and strength, observing his behavior and considering the causes of, and the influences on, his actions. Their concern for his welfare emerges in all of their discussions about him, and through their behavior they show how individuals can alter social patterns through good parenting. In times of crisis with his peers, Romen will think about how his grandparents would view his actions. For example, his ability to pity and thus to rescue

rather than abuse the girl his friends gang-rape stems from the teachings of Sandler and Vida. Likewise, at the novel's close, when Junior seduces him into making love in obscure places, Romen hears Sandler's voice telling him that he has
the ability to choose wisely: "'You not helpless, Romen. Don't ever think that.'
[. . .] He was trying to warn him, make him listen, tell him that the old Romen,
the sniveling one who couldn't help untying shoelaces from an unwilling girl's
wrist, was hipper than the one who couldn't help flinging a willing girl around an
attic" (195). This protective, nurturing, parental voice enables Romen to reject
Junior's bed and go to the assistance of Christine and Heed.

Good nurturing provides Romen with a sense of self and the individual integrity that serve to protect him as well as his community. On one level, Romen
carries on Cosey's legacy of caring for and rescuing others. Ironically, Cosey himself struggles to achieve inner peace. Having suffered as a child from his father's
stinginess, Cosey creates a persona of generosity and love. Yet even though Heed,
L, Vida, guests, and community women see him through idealizing eyes, Cosey
himself strives to find his own happiness. For example, although the community
and vacationers worship him, Cosey cannot find his imaginary reflection in his
first wife's eyes. "His adored first wife thought his interests tiresome, his appetite abusive. So he chose the view he saw in the eyes of local women, vacationers, slightly tipsy vocalists whose boyfriends had not joined them on the tour"
(110). Further, his boating parties and his paying off the local officials reinforce
the price of his position. As Heed comments to Christine, "He forgot what every
pickaninny knows. Whites don't throw pennies in your cup if you ain't dancing"
(186). The white community represents Lacan's Real, or the ever-present under-
cutting of Cosey's ideal identity. Perhaps the trauma of Cosey's own parenting
by his petty and withholding father leads to his insecurities and inappropriate
arousal by the innocence of Heed's youth. It is possible that his own issues of
abandonment and betrayal shape his behavior.

Cosey also welcomes unconditionally his son's wife, May. Confident in his
son's choices, he does not find fault, nor should he. May is a *"pretty, undercher-
ished girl in an overmended coat"* (137), someone who values the protection of the
Cosey family and needs their love. A motherless minister's daughter of barebones
means, May is dutiful and loyal. She works hard to keep the hotel running and all
the guests happy, carving her niche at the resort. Her past has made her all too
familiar with *"the live death of poverty, the Negro kind May was familiar with. Un-
housed, begging"* (136). Cosey's son rescues her, providing her with security. May

is more than grateful for the opportunity to work hard and share in their success. Unfortunately, her husband's untimely death and Cosey's choice of Heed for a wife upset her equilibrium. To preserve peace in the Cosey household and to secure her place in it, May will desert her daughter, Christine. Her own abandonment trauma prevents her from protecting Christine as a mother should. Her failure resembles that of Pauline in *The Bluest Eye,* Helene in *Sula,* Ruth in *Song of Solomon,* and Wild in *Jazz.*

The upset of her family balance mirrors that of the outer world. "The world May knew was always crumbling; her place in it never secure" (96). May's seemingly bizarre and erratic behavior stems from her need to preserve her place in the Cosey household and prevent a return to the earlier Real of her impoverishment. Like the "traumatized children [who] develop ways of mental functioning designed to prevent the return of the helpless or hopeless state of traumatization," May envisions the hotel as a "fortress" to protect her, and those that she relies on, from the violent reality of the social structure (McDougall 138). "She is frantic with worry that the hotel and everybody in it are in immediate danger. That city blacks have already invaded Up Beach, carrying lighter fluid, matches, Molotov cocktails; shouting, urging the locals to burn Cosey's Hotel and Resort to the ground and put the Uncle Toms, the sheriff's pal, the race traitor out of business" (80). Her identification with the violence that hopelessness begets gives rise to repressed fears and insecurities.[2]

May's father's position as a minister elevates them in the community despite their poverty. But the poorest segment of this community becomes other, neglected and scorned by middle-class society. Having empathy for this low element would point to the community's vulnerability, and so the black community members shun and mock those who live in the Settlement. This segment serves the same function as the Breedlove family does in *The Bluest Eye.* "'Rurals' is what these strange unteachable children are labeled. Although they infuriated ordinary students from decent farming families, Guidance Counselors had to choose some socially benign term to identify these children without antagonizing their parents" (53). The community needs to separate from this group without alienating its members. Like the all-black community in *Paradise,* Cosey's community mimics the hierarchy and exclusive structure of the greater white culture. By representing Lacan's Real for society, this impoverished group from the Settlement recognizes its position as other and gains a protective power. "Settlement people have it the way they want it: unevolved and reviled, they are also tolerated, left alone, and feared" (54). Their threat allows them to live by their own (often heartless) rules, albeit in their meager surroundings. Sula and Shadrack achieve a similar power over their community in *Sula,* and Pilate's otherness allows her to create her own rules and live on her own in *Song of Solomon.*

Junior, a victim of the misguided cruelty that results from society's abandonment of the Rurals, breaks away from the Settlement. First, she rebels by seeking education: "She was the first Rural to speak up and make a stab at homework" (56). Second, she makes friends with Peter Paul Fortas, a boy outside of the fold, who gives her a sense of worth. Like Heed and Christine, Junior and Peter share an innocent friendship and exchange gifts, reinforcing a positive sense of being. Finally, Junior escapes from her tormenting family members, who physically abuse her. She needs to get "away from people who chased her down, ran over her foot, lied about it, called her lucky, and who preferred the company of a snake to a girl" (59). Her mother "could not protect her from Vosh or the uncles" (58). Abandoned by her father, Junior lacks a protective mother. Her uncles, rather than providing a supportive family network, choose her as a target for their aggression. Treated like an animal, Junior survives through her own devices, failing to develop the capacity for empathy.

Her traumatic upbringing has foreclosed any nostalgic memories; the Settlement is in no way a Sweet Home. Once she left, "[s]he had no intention of going back to the Settlement. Correctional had saved her from them" (117). Despite its institutional structure, Correctional provides Junior with the sense of family and protection that she has lacked and needs to develop as an individual. By the time she answers Heed's ad, Junior "had the unnerving look of an underfed child. One you wanted to cuddle or slap for being needy" (23). That she raises conflicting impulses—both loving and aggressive—suggests the paradox of psychic identity. The need for the Other in order to be whole gives rise to the nurturing impulse. On the other hand, the need to reject one's own vulnerability—Lacan's Real— produces the desire to attack. Later, Romen will think of Junior as "like a gorgeous pet. Feed it or whip it—it lapped you anyway" (155). In Junior, as in Seneca in *Paradise,* who describes herself as a puppy to play with but not keep, the need for love predominates, causing her to love the caretaker, whether kind or cruel. Junior's early attachment figures mistreated her, desensitizing her to cruelty.[3]

Sharing Junior's background of Settlement life, Heed hires her without references. "Heed glanced at Junior's face in the mirror, thinking: That's what it is, what made me take her on. We're both out here, alone" (127). Their lack of parenting has rendered them homeless. While Heed never quite reflects Junior's homeless situation—the "bus station soap, other people's sandwiches, unwashed hair, slept-in clothes, no purse, mouth cleaned with chewing gum instead of toothpaste" (23)—she understands Junior's abandonment and her need for protection. They both appreciate tenderness and touch, which were deficient in their upbringing. As Junior bathes Heed, she considers how "soaping a body—any body—held a satisfaction only a Settlement child could know. Besides, it pleased him [Cosey] to see her taking care of his wife" (124). Human interaction via caretaking and physical contact protect against trauma, and Junior's bathing of Heed echoes how the bathing of Sethe by Baby Suggs and Paul D restores integrity to the body in pieces. The mutual pleasure of the caressing bath is compounded for Junior by a sense of approval from Cosey's portrait's gaze.

Junior intuitively understands that she receives a sense of self through the gaze of the Other. She knows all too well the debilitating effects of the rejecting gaze of her family and seeks the nurturing gaze she perceives in Cosey's portrait. She thinks about how "being looked at by her Good Man delighted her" (116). She dreams of Cosey as "[a] handsome man with a G.I. Joe chin and a reassuring smile that pledged endless days of hot, tasty food; kind eyes that promised to hold a girl steady on his shoulder while she robbed apples from the highest branch" (30). Junior envisions Cosey as a rescuer and a protector—physically, nutritionally, and emotionally. She considers what it might have been like to have had Cosey as a parental figure: "If you'd known me then, nobody would have messed with me. You'd have taken care of me because you understand me and everything and won't let anybody get me. Did you marry Heed to protect her? Was that the only way?" (156). Junior verbalizes the need for parenting and protection, as well as her desire to please her protector, to develop under his watchful gaze. Her talking to Cosey represents Junior's attempt to articulate her trauma.

While she voices her needs, Junior is still too focused on them to empathize with Heed and Christine. Thus, she fails to secure a place in the Cosey home, and she loses Romen as well. Junior does not understand her role in securing a home, because she has never had one. She had delighted in visualizing a home: "she was turning the space into Correctional's Rec Room. Well, why not? [. . .] Sitting there, Junior felt the kick of being, living, in a house, a real house, her first" (156). In contrast to the Settlement, Correctional provided a model of home and family. Now, at Cosey's, she feels that "[t]his was the right place and there he was, letting her know in every way it had been waiting for her all along. As soon as she saw the stranger's portrait she knew she was home" (60). Yet her one-sided vision, created by her neediness, ends when she perceives Cosey abandoning her: "Her Good Man hasn't shown up for some time" (171). Her behavior produces a repetition of her abandonment trauma. At the very moment that Junior experiences acceptance and love in the form of Romen's "lollipop lick" (196) of her deformed foot, her inability to show compassion and assist Christine and Heed deprives her of her newly discovered self. Like the Settlement dogs, having raised herself, Junior has become "adept at keeping outsiders out, but at [her] brilliant best when hunting" (55). She has protected her physical well-being at the expense of empathy for others. Romen, like Cosey's spirit and her family, "ran. Away from her. As fast as he could" (196).

Junior's lack of a nurturing home and the trauma that results illuminate the feelings of abandonment that Heed and Christine share. Heed and Christine meet and bond innocently, but from the beginning of their relationship adults try to separate them:

Once a little girl wandered too far—down to big water and along its edge where waves skidded and mud turned into clean sand. Ocean spray dampened the man's undershirt she wore. There on a red blanket another little girl with white ribbons in her hair sat eating ice cream. The water was very blue. Beyond, a crowd of people laughed. "Hi, want some?" asked the girl, holding out a spoon. They ate ice cream with peaches in it until a smiling woman came and said, "Go away now. This is private." (78)

Two girls share an ice cream moment until a parent defines one as other, lesser, and unwanted. L reminisces about how the innocence of youth defines Heed's and Christine's relationship: *"If such children find each other before they know their own sex, or which one of them is starving, which well fed; before they know color from no color, kin from stranger, then they have found a mix of surrender and mutiny they can never live without. Heed and Christine found such a one"* (199). The purity of their bond is sullied by adult intervention. L continues to describe the adult manipulation that destroys their lives and hope for peace: *"It was marrying Heed that laid the brickwork for ruination. See, he chose a girl already spoken for. Not promised to anyone by her parents. That trash gave her up like they would a puppy. No. The way I see it, she belonged to Christine and Christine belonged to her"* (104–5). Heed's parents sacrifice her youth for money through her arranged marriage to Cosey;

Cosey will disregard Christine's need for a playmate so that his own needs are met. Christine will later describe her trauma to Junior: "My grandfather married her when she was eleven. We were best friends. One day we built castles on the beach; next day he sat her in his lap. One day we were playing house under a quilt; next day she slept in his bed. [. . .] One day this house was mine; next day she owned it" (131–32). Both girls suffer from their forced separation.

Heed's state of confusion stems from several sources. First, she experiences guilt over her budding sexuality, evidenced by her wiggle to the music that seduces Cosey. Further, her parents reject her by handing her over to another's care. In addition, their increasing monetary demands after the transaction compound her confusion: "Her kinfolk so overreached, they forced the break that was never repaired" (77). Finally, her ultimate rejection by Christine when she returns from her honeymoon unsettles her. "Trembling, Heed looked to Christine for help. There wasn't any. [. . .] Wonderful as the honeymoon was, she could hardly wait to get back and tell Christine all about it. Hurt by her reception, she kept her stories to herself" (127–29). Thus, denial of her own needs through silence begins.

Over time, Heed will nostalgically focus on those positive elements that provide her with a sense of self. When she describes her attachment to Cosey's barber chair, she thinks about how much she "treasured it, because in the early days of their marriage it was in that very chair that he took pains to teach her how to manicure, pedicure, keep all his nails in perfect shape" (124). The chair creates a positive identity for Heed as it comes to represent Cosey's care for her juxtaposed with the neglect of her parents. That she calls Cosey "Papa" is apt indeed. The warmth she feels from his interest in teaching her provides her with a sense of self-worth. "Her insight was polished to blazing by a lifetime of being underestimated. Only Papa knew better, had picked her out of all he could have chosen. [. . .] she was what everybody but Papa assumed she was not: smart" (72–74).[4] Abandoned by her family and her friend, Heed relies on Cosey and the home he makes for her to protect her identity. "Although it turned out she had to fight for her place in it, Papa made it possible. When he was around everybody backed off" (127). Cosey provides her with the parenting and protection necessary for her to establish her sense of self.

Later, when she is twenty-eight and has an affair with a grieving hotel guest, Heed will sort out the difference between love and obligation, "the difference between being needed and being obliged. [. . .] She was stunned to be wanted by a man her own age who found her interesting, intelligent, desirable. So this is what happy feels like" (172). As she struggles to protect her right to Cosey's home, Heed reflects that had she had a child, "she wouldn't need to sneak off, driven by an untethered teenager to a collapsing hotel in order to secure her place" (174). Family provides the safety net that she lacks. It is this feeling of being protected that Heed remembers desiring as she lies dying in Christine's old room: "Drawing a ribbon of breath, she blocks any tears that may be lurking like memories behind her eyelids. But the forget-me-nots roaming the wallpaper are more vivid in this deliberate dark than they ever were in daylight and she wonders what it was that made her want it so. Home, she thinks. When I stepped in the door, I thought I was home" (183). Christine's home satisfied Heed's craving for protection, place, and self-esteem.

While Heed's trauma stems from parental rejection and displacement into a new family and a new sexual role, she does get reinforcement for her self-esteem from Cosey. In contrast, Christine experiences rejection from her mother, her friend, and her grandfather, as well as a loss of home. In some ways, Christine's trauma is more severe: she loses her seemingly secure place and reexperiences in her displacement the loss of her father when she was five. She remembers "huddling the porch steps [. . .] rigid with fear and the grief of abandonment. [. . .] Is she [Heed] afraid to go? Neither one understands. Why can't she go too? Why is he taking one to a honeymoon and leaving the other? They will come back, won't they?" (170).[5] Thus, Christine's separation from Heed reenacts the separation from her father. She cannot be sure that her grandfather and her friend will return to her, because her father did not. Their abandonment of her challenges her subjectivity.

Christine's mother further abandons her when she "chose to send her away rather than confront" Cosey (133). Christine perceives herself as innocent and forced to leave. "Even when she returned, a sixteen-year-old, poised and ready to take her place in the family, they threw her away" (133). Because of this lack of recognition, she cannot recapture her place in her family. She thinks, "It should have been different" (133). Christine says of Heed,

> That's been her whole life, don't you get it? Replacing me, getting rid of me. I'm always last; all the time the one being told to go, get out. [. . .] This is *my* place. I had my sixteenth-birthday party in that house. When I was away at school it was my *address*. It's where I belong and nobody is going to wave some liquor-splashed menu at me and put me out of it! (95)

Christine's claim on Cosey's property is a claim on her own subjectivity. At stake is nothing short of her very essence as a person. Christine's sense of abandonment is compounded by a sense of betrayal:

> This *was* important. Her struggle with Heed was neither mindless nor wasted. She would never forget how she had fought for her, defied her mother to protect her, to give her clothes: dresses, shorts, a bathing suit, sandals; to picnic alone on the beach. They shared stomachache laughter, a secret language, and knew as they slept together that one's dreaming was the same as the other one's. Then to have your best and only friend leave [. . .]. It changed her life. (132–33)

Abandonment and betrayal form Christine's core identity. In response, she makes poor choices in relationships. For example, seeking connection, she marries a soldier after one dinner together. Similarly, later in life, even though Dr. Rio is married and therefore unavailable to her, she thinks that "her kept-woman years [with him] were the best" (84). Essentially, the very fact that she cannot marry Dr. Rio mirrors her parental relationship with her grandfather. By living with someone who is not accessible to her full time, she replicates her abandonment trauma. She realizes that "after Dr. Rio threw her out there was no place like and no place but home. Hers. To hang on to and keep an insane viper from evicting her" (167). Christine intuits that she needs to fight for a home that will protect her; how to create that love and acceptance is her constant challenge.

Christine's struggle to establish her place in the Cosey household manifests itself in the multiple ways that she seeks recognition that will validate her. For example, when she returns from school, she tries to steal the spotlight from Heed, getting "lured into showing off about grammar" in her effort (134). Later, she attempts to use possessions as a means of validation, wearing "[t]welve rings, two on three fingers of each hand" (20). Likewise, she cherishes her childhood silver spoon: "It was tiny, a coffee spoon, but Christine ate every meal she could with it just to hold close the child it was given to, and hold also the pictures it summoned" (22). By using the spoon, Christine recaptures love through memory. Further, she fights with Heed "about whether the double C's engraved on the silver was one letter doubled or the pairing of Christine's initials" (73). Possessions equate with the recognition from the outside that Christine needs to feel whole and loved. As she hurries to her attorney to protect herself in the fight over Cosey's will, a former Cosey hotel worker tells Christine, "I remember you. Best legs on the beach. My, you used to be so cute. Your skin, your pretty hair. I see you still got those eyes, though. Lord, you was one foxy thing" (93). In contrast to Christine's poor self-image, this stranger verifies Christine's obvious beauty. Nevertheless, without validation of her inner worth, her outer beauty cannot protect her.

Her one healthy relationship, with Fruit, provides Christine with a worthy sense of self. "When she listened to him, everything was suddenly so clear she spent nine years in his company. [...] Pumped by seething exhilaration and purpose, Christine's personal vanity became racial legitimacy and her flair for acting out became courage" (163). With Fruit she was no longer "the disrupting wife, the surplus mistress, the unwanted nuisance daughter, the ignored granddaughter, the disposable friend. She was valuable" (164). Unfortunately, over time the "issues changed, spread, moved from streets and doorways to offices and conferences in elegant hotels. Nobody needed a street-worker-baby-sitter-cook-mimeographing-marching-nut-and-raisin-carrying woman who was too old anyway for the hip new students [...]. She was irrelevant" (167). As their historical world changes, Christine perceives herself of less value to Fruit. Sensing that he will abandon her if she cannot fulfill his needs, Christine, because of her low self-esteem, moves on, thus reenacting her abandonment trauma. She illustrates how "[s]tates of fear, anger, or shame can [...] reemerge as a characteristic trait of the individual's responses" (Siegel, "An Interpersonal" 9).

Christine's early trauma prevents her from establishing a positive sense of self, and the public aspect of her own life further complicates any recovery. "Her slide from spoiled girl child to tarnished homelessness had been neither slow nor hidden. Everybody knew. There was no homecoming for her in elegant auto driven by successful husband. [...] She was a flop. Disreputable. But she was also a Cosey" (87–88). The prominence of her grandfather's position denies Christine the privacy of a personal self. Overwhelmed by a sense of shame and blame, Christine struggles to find her way home. "Christine discovered a way to convert a return to Silk in shame and on borrowed money into an act of filial responsibility: taking care of her ailing mother, and a noble battle for justice—her lawful share of the Cosey estate" (86). Thus, Christine will revert to the notion of family that has heretofore eluded her as her means of returning. She thinks of home as "a familiar place that, when you left, kept changing behind your back. [...] The house had not shrunk; you had. The windows were not askew—you were" (86). Home for Christine is a concept that reflects her psychological state.

That Christine and Heed need each other in order to be emotionally whole explains their ability to coexist in Cosey's home. "Along with age, recognition that neither one could leave played a part in their unnegotiated cease-fire. More on the mark was their unspoken realization that the fights did nothing other than allow them to hold each other. [. . .] Like friendship, hatred needed more than physical intimacy; it wanted creativity and hard work to sustain itself" (73–74). By living together, the women sustain an emotional bond and connection that counter abandonment and loss. Unfortunately, they have not been able to heal, because they have not verbalized their trauma. Cathy Caruth explains that "one's own trauma is tied up with the trauma of another, [. . .] through the very possibility and surprise of listening to another's wound" (*Unclaimed* 8). Christine and Heed's shared trauma is finally verbalized in the painful wounds of their final encounter. Morrison describes this vocalization: "Language, when it finally comes, has the vigor of a felon pardoned after twenty-one years on hold. Sudden, raw, stripped to its underwear" (184). Language unleashes the burden of living with pain. Caruth finds that trauma is "a kind of double telling, [. . .] between the story of the unbearable nature of an event and the story of the unbearable nature of its survival" (*Unclaimed* 7) and that "the dreams and flashbacks of the traumatized [. . .] bear witness to a survival that exceeds the very claims and consciousness of the one who endures it" (60). Heed's need to talk is suggested earlier in the novel when Junior muses that "Heed didn't want to write a book; she wanted to talk, although why she had to pay somebody to talk to, Junior hadn't figured out yet" (61). She articulates the need to give voice to her trauma.[6]

Love's ending suggests that aggressive behavior stimulated by trauma is an inadequate response because it fails to provide relief. Impoverished and politically disempowered, Junior's family members release their aggression onto Junior in their physical attacks and psychological bruising. They make her their scapegoat when they drive over her foot, causing "unbearable" pain and "a hurt so stunning she could not fill her lungs" (59). Junior suffers in silence, as she "watched her toes swell, redden, turn blue, then black, then marble, then merge" (59). In response to this aggressive attack, Junior fails to develop empathy and will leave Heed and Christine for dead rather than summon help. Her aggressive sexual manipulation of Romen, along with her desertion of the women in need, causes him to leave her, just as he left the group of boys that gang-raped the helpless girl. Such aggression simmers in other black characters, as Christine's lovers mistreat her and Cosey steals the innocence of his child bride Heed. The wounds of slavery still have their bite for blacks in white culture, but aggression proves to be an ineffective response, as it mirrors the master narrative.

As they confront each other at the novel's close, Christine and Heed abandon their aggression and rekindle their childhood bond. They experience their former selves in each other's gaze: "The eyes of each are enslaved by the other's. Opening pangs of guilt, rage, fatigue, despair are replaced by a hatred so pure, so solemn, it feels beautiful, almost holy" (177). What begins as hatred reverts back to their initial love: "In light sifting from above each searches the face of the other. The holy feeling is still alive, as is its purity, but it is altered now, overwhelmed by desire. [. . .] There in a little girl's bedroom an obstinate skeleton stirs, clacks, refreshes itself" (177). Their desire for their earlier innocent friendship conquers years of active hatred, and they recognize the need to heal old wounds. As they regress, their dialogue reflects their former closeness: "Hey, Celestial" (187). "Aw, girl. When did we first start that?" (187). Memory has not forgotten their secret code. In an echo of Nel's "girl, girl, girlgirlgirl" in *Sula,* they realize that they should have lived differently. "We could have been living our lives hand in hand instead of looking for Big Daddy everywhere" (189).

If they had had adequate attachment and love at home or in the greater culture, they would not have had to seek reassurance elsewhere. Christine and Heed reconstruct:

May wasn't much of a mother to me.
At least she didn't sell you.
No, she gave me away. (184)

They can admit the nature of the trauma that has plagued them.

I wanted to be with you. Married to him, I thought I would be.
I wanted to go on your honeymoon. (193)

This realization releases their pent-up emotion and the core of their trauma:

You're crying.
So are you. [. . .] He took all my childhood away from me, girl.
He took all of you away from me. (194)

They finally can articulate the pain of Cosey's disruption of their childhood and friendship, as well as their need to be together.[7] Although their healing comes too late to help Heed, Christine can now peacefully live with Heed's ghost as confidante and adviser.[8] For example, when deciding what to do about Junior, she discusses the situation with Heed's spirit:

> She knows how to make trouble.
> So do we.
> Hey, Celestial. (198)

Left unexpressed is the shame each has internalized from Cosey's inappropriate touching and arousal. For both girls, this memory "lack[s] verbal narrative and context" (Herman 38) and connects to the sense of disgrace embedded in their psyches. Without words to articulate trauma, abuse victims blame themselves, as do Pecola in *The Bluest Eye* and Seneca in *Paradise*. Even at death's door neither can discuss the "thing that made each believe, without knowing why, that this particular shame was different and could not tolerate speech—not even in the language they had invented for secrets" (192). The trauma of their own lack, while recognized by both, defies language.

Hovering throughout the novel is the voice of L, who by doctoring Cosey's will and administering foxglove to his food protects the girls at his death as she tried to do while they lived together. She explains, *"I wasn't going to let him put his family out in the street"* (201).[9] L is the one person who has attempted to provide parenting for them in the wake of their own parents' failure to do so. Thus, memories of L resurface nostalgically for Christine and Heed. Her room was always a haven, and as Christine approaches her final encounter with Heed at the hotel, she remembers L's room as a sanctuary. She "was five when her father died. [...] That was the first time she took refuge under L's bed, and if she had her druthers, she would be there now instead of climbing toward the place that rocked her with fear and, and—what was the other thing? Oh, yes. Sorrow" (170). L's comforting presence explains why Christine takes L's apartment as her home in the house she shares with Heed: "the apartment looked much the same as it had some fifty years ago when she hid there under L's bed" (89). For her part, Heed realizes that "[s]he could never have navigated those treacherous waters [of life with Cosey] if L hadn't been the current" (76).

Despite their repressed trauma, both girls have warm memories of L to protect them in their loneliness.[10] Once together again, they verbalize how much she meant to them:

Jesus, I miss her.
Me too. Always have. (189)

They share the memory of L as their one nurturing, parenting figure. Christine fondly recalls L's food and the picnic lunches she packed when they played. At the close of the novel, the hotel, L, and her cooking merge to envelop Heed and Christine with a sense of home as they finally verbalize their trauma. When Junior tells Heed that she "smells baking bread, something with cinnamon," Heed replies, "Smells like L" (175). Releasing the memory of their childhood bond in the wake of trauma, the smell of L's cinnamon bread serves as a catalyst for healing.[11] L's humming—her response to violence, modern chaos, and the loss of the past—resembles a parent's soothing lullaby.

The titles of *Love*'s chapters—"Love," "Portrait," "Friend," "Stranger," "Benefactor," "Lover," "Husband," "Guardian," "Father," "Phantom"—suggest the roles that caretakers perform, for the helpless infant and the separating adolescent as well as for the maturing adult and the aging orphan who re-create the parent in fantasy. Parental attachment, family nurturing, and community support serve to counter individual and collective trauma by building self-esteem and providing a safe, protected environment.[12] This secure place, or home, creates memories that maintain identity. In her foreword to this novel, Morrison says, "People tell me that I am always writing about love. [. . .] I nod, yes, but it isn't true—not exactly. In fact, I am always writing about betrayal. Love is the weather. Betrayal is a lightning that cleaves and reveals it" (x). Concepts of home, reconstructed through memory to provide a sense of self, counteract the repressed trauma that betrayal begets.

At the heart of betrayal in Morrison's novels is the specter of slavery and white culture's denial that blacks are human beings. The bodily reenactment of abandonment that commodification produces compounds the lack that threatens all subjectivity. Creating a self despite this lack remains a challenge for black identity. Morrison's novels trace this strife through America's history—from the physical and psychological abuse of slavery; to the rejection as citizens, as well as the terrorizing that accompanied lynching, false arrests, and riots during Reconstruction; to the discrimination that remains after the civil rights movement; to the ongoing othering by America's master narrative. In *Playing in the Dark,* Morrison claims that she investigates "the ways in which a nonwhite, Africanlike (or Africanist) presence or persona was constructed in the United States, and the imaginative uses this fabricated presence served" (6). She examines "the impact of notions of racial hierarchy, racial exclusion, and racial vulnerability and availability on nonblacks who held, resisted, explored, or altered those notions" in order to create "a serious intellectual effort to see what racial ideology does to the mind, imagination, and behavior of masters" (11–12). Her novels illustrate the multiple ways that white culture damages and circumscribes black subjectivity. In the absence of positive cultural mirroring, nostalgic memory remains the route to a positive imaginary self.

FIVE

Echoes of "The Foreigner's Home" in *A Mercy*

Morrison's steady examination of home as a palliative response to trauma appeared in her exhibition "The Foreigner's Home (Corps Étrangers: Danse, Dessin, Film)" at the Louvre Museum, in Paris, in the fall of 2006. In the exhibition she considered how throughout history, social, cultural, and political displacement has put a sense of self in jeopardy, resulting in a reflection on the idea of home, belonging, and coming of age in each culture and generation. Morrison's title, "The Foreigner's Home," has two meanings: the possessive, where the foreigner's home is not a home; and a contraction, where the foreigner *is* home, creating a home out of otherness (Morrison, "'The Foreigner's Home': Introduction"). This creation of home as a response to dispossession and its trauma suggests that a selfhood built on knowledge of cultural rejection reflects how one can move past the gaze of the master narrative to create a life based on personal (instead of cultural) desire. Morrison's exhibition at the Louvre and her ninth novel, *A Mercy,* show her continuing concern with home, subjectivity, and recovery from trauma.

In the inaugural lecture for the exhibition at the Louvre, on 6 November 2006, Morrison stated that she had been analyzing

> certain themes of cultural orphanage and shame that inform so much American literature. The promise and dread of displacement are major themes of early American literature. Along with the satisfactions of being reborn in a new country was the peril of somehow not belonging. The articulation of foreignness and dispossession, of utopianism and rootlessness, and claims of an infinite border, infinite frontier, became representations of the exiled's yearning, the isolate's despair. ("'The Foreigner's Home': Introduction")

These conflicting emotions of the displaced—the yearning for acceptance by the dominant culture and the regret about one's place as other—point to a Lacanian vacillation between an imaginary wholeness and the Real of one's existence in the symbolic structure. Both emotions underline the necessity of finding a positive reflection and self-esteem in the adopted culture. The themes in Morrison's novels—from the cultural oppression of slavery and its aftermath in *Beloved* and *Paradise* to the realization of the self's otherness in *The Bluest Eye, Sula,* and *Song of Solomon,* the search for subjectivity in exile in *Jazz* and *Tar Baby,* the social unrest in *Love,* and the black communities' hierarchical structures of other and projection in all of these works—serve as a foundation for her project at the Louvre.

Whether a person in exile finds acceptance or rejection depends on both the host culture and each individual's determination. For Morrison, "how individuals resist or become complicit in the process of demonization, a process that can infect the foreigner's geographical sanctuary with the host country's xenophobia," as well as the "question of cultural apartheid and/or cultural integration," is at the core of her exhibition ("'The Foreigner's Home': Introduction"). According to Vamik Volkan, a country's xenophobia surfaces because "[m]inor differences become the last frontier separating a regressed group's identity from the 'other,' and members must therefore maintain that difference in order to maintain their separate identity" (73). Volkan contends that people adamantly maintain these differences because they perceive them to be "their very existence" (73). Similarly, Paul Connerton writes that "our experiences of the present largely depend upon our knowledge of the past, and [. . .] our images of the past commonly serve to legitimate a present social order" (3). Further, "Every recollection [. . .] exists in relationship with a whole ensemble of notions which many others possess: with persons, places, dates, words, forms of language, that is to say the whole material and moral life of the societies of which we are part or of which we have been part" (36). Thus, the host culture stubbornly resists change or accommodation that would dislodge the status quo. For their part, displaced people carry with them the residues of their own cultural practice that resist acculturation. Even those newcomers who embrace assimilation retain a prior cultural memory to sustain their subjectivity.

The resistance of receiving cultures explains the dual function of the apostrophe in Morrison's title "The Foreigner's Home":

The foreigner's *own* home—memory and ancestry—and the foreigner *is* home—citizenship and belonging. The theme therefore requires us to come to terms with being, fearing, or accommodating the stranger. Traveling between these two connotations offers the scope and reach needed to comprehend the means by which art enlightens and history informs. ("'The Foreigner's Home': Introduction")

The past that the exile carries, filled with supportive familial links and a reservoir of nostalgic memory, collides with qualified acceptance. Marginal citizenship and conditional belonging undercut a safe haven. Consequently, as Morrison contends, "[t]he relocation of peoples has ignited and disrupted the idea of home and expanded the focus of identity beyond definitions of citizens to clarifications of foreignness" ("'The Foreigner's Home': Introduction"). In this way, exaggeration of otherness derails subjectivity. Frantz Fanon writes of this phenomenon in *Black Skin, White Masks* when he describes how in his own country "the Antillean does not think of himself as a black man"; however, "he will learn once he goes to Europe" that the word *black* "includes himself as well as the Senegalese" (148). His displacement coincides with the new culture's classification of the self as lesser. In the perception of the dominant culture, "[f]oreign is the designation of the curious, the 'not us,' the rupture between self and society" ("'The Foreigner's Home': Introduction"). Morrison summarizes how the visibly foreign perform a scapegoat function for society: "For an assumed safety, hegemony, or pure land grabs, foreigners were constructed as the sum total of the putative nation's ills" ("'The Foreigner's Home': Introduction").

Morrison tied the exhibition to one of the Louvre's most striking and impressive paintings, Theodore Gericault's *The Raft of the Medusa*. She observed that this painting, in which "abandoned crew members afloat without oars [...] wander like nomads between despair and hope, between breath and death," epitomizes her theme of home: "The plight of Gericault's abandoned figures suggests that the idea of home is not confined to rescue, shelter or motherland." While rescue offers possible sanctuary, unknown hosts threaten continued distress. The painting thus examines "national purity, or contamination, [and] deliberate annihilation in search of the illusion of empire stability." Finally, "because Gericault's painting focuses rapt attention on bodies, we may suddenly realize that the most obvious and fundamental location of home is the human body—the final frontier of identity" ("'The Foreigner's Home': Introduction"). Gericault's work depicts how bodily and racial identity physically accompanies those who seek new beginnings, forming a paramount obstacle to acceptance and therefore to safety.

Just as our bodies mark our identity, they also house our memories, which shape our subjectivity. Marianne Leuzinger-Bohleber and Rolf Pfeifer define memory as both subjective and objective, with the "subjective side [. . . dictated] by the individual's history, [and] the objective side by the neural pattern generated by the sensory motor interactions with the environment" (3). That is, in addition to physical and genetic attributes, biological and neurological components of memory resurface in interactions with current behavior, unconsciously repeating memories as "pathogenic or traumatic object relations and experiences" (3). In this present social interface, "[o]ur memories are located within the mental and material spaces of the group" or in our interactions with culture (Connerton 37). This research on the bodily and communal aspects of memory supports Morrison's definition of home as a space of security and comfort lodged in memory. Ultimately, Morrison defines home as embedded in the unconscious: "one's mother tongue, the language one dreams in, is home" ("'The Foreigner's Home': Introduction").

For Morrison, "[h]ome is where the memory of the self dwells. Whether those memories spawn or shrivel determines who we are and determines what we may become" ("'The Foreigner's Home': Introduction"). Thus, cultural memory plays a role in shaping emerging cultures. Accommodations to the existing culture depend on the processing of both personal and collective memory. Morrison asserts that the institution of slavery destroyed such memory through the breakup of families and tribes:

> [Slaves] were not able to maintain tribal and language separations, because the worst thing you could have if you were going to have slavery is people who knew each other, and spoke the same language from before, so you mix that all up and people who had nothing to do with each other originally from the areas and tribes they came from were suddenly lumped and called black folks. ("'The Foreigner's Home': Introduction")

Slavery systematically disrupted personal subjectivity through the conflation of an individual's cultural identity with those of others, and the severing of personal connections, language, and cultural practice compounded the dislocation from one's physical home. Morrison's trilogy considers the trauma that this arrangement bequeathed: *Beloved* vividly depicts the damaging effects of slavery's uprooting and separation of families; *Jazz* further presents the emotional and psychic toll that parental abandonment takes, as well as the cycle of familial separation that slavery and economic deprivation beget; and *Paradise* explores the reaction to slavery's legacy of separation in an all-black community's insistence on remaining intact by excluding outsiders. Also, in *Song of Solomon,* characters struggle to trace their lineage and create their subjectivity through familial and personal names. Cultural and personal memory create the self, and the stability of one's personal memory and sense of self is a key factor in psychic survival. All of Morrison's novels examine how memory is written on and stored in the body, to be generationally passed on to descendants who cannot escape social discrimination.

In her response to questions from the audience, Morrison explained that blacks hoped that emancipation would allow them to integrate into the social structure. "After 1865, black people just tried everything they could to assimilate. They didn't want a black identity." But the white culture persisted in claiming that

[y]ou all are different for all sorts of reasons and even whenever you say you're not, well we can look at you and tell you are [. . .] it's a visible difference. So then eventually there rose a black culture that was the result of the creativity and sensibilities of the black people who said well, ok, we're going to sing this music, we're going to make jazz, so out of that came a cultural identity that exists. ("'The Foreigner's Home': Introduction")

Consequently, black rejection by white society spawned an international black identity called jazz. Morrison emphasized in her discussion that in responding to cultural othering, people need to reject an either/or position: "You can have a powerful singular black identity and a universal one. They don't conflict, as the artists have proven over and over and over again" ("'The Foreigner's Home': Introduction"). Thus, Morrison reinforces Siegel's theory that how people make sense of their situation and trauma determines how they and future generations survive and move forward. Describing her own writing stance, Morrison claims to write from the edge, an observation point that becomes "the place of genuine insight and power" ("'The Foreigner's Home': Introduction"). She exposes the gaze that erases subjectivity so as to empower those outside of the master narrative.

One value of Morrison's novels and the artworks of others is their function as "reservoirs of cultural memory and/or a source of community integration." Art reshapes and reimagines national identity; in this way "the erstwhile stranger enriches all of our homes" ("Harlem"). Music is a prime example, with today's musicians having achieved a state Morrison calls "post-black," describing music that is "out of black culture, it's black, but we recognize no boundaries, we recognize no label, no confines, no gate" ("Writing"). This concept echoes her essay "Home," in which she speaks of "contemporary searches and yearnings for social space that is psychically and physically safe" (10). According to Morrison, such a space is "[b]eyond the dichotomous double consciousness," where "one can imagine safety without walls, can iterate difference that is prized but unprivileged [. . . a] world 'already made for me, both snug and wide open, with a doorway never needing to be closed.' Home" (12). By rejecting the contempt of society, artists illustrate how to rise above it.

In her Louvre lectures Morrison introduced the themes present in the varying art forms of the exhibition, from ancient artifacts to modern film, dance, literature, and painting. While the Louvre houses works of art through 1865, Morrison updated the collection by pairing existing pieces with contemporary theory and art genres. For example, working with a co-curator at the Louvre, Morrison meticulously cataloged the Louvre's collection of Egyptian, Greek, and Assyrian antiquities in order to examine how women were portrayed in those societies. Morrison's angle of vision deconstructs the artistic rendering of the subordinate position of women. In another example, she organized an evening of "slam poets," who performed in front of Gericault's pivotal piece, *The Raft of the Medusa,* to illustrate contemporary marginalized voices of pain and suffering.

Other installations in the exhibition revolved around themes, such as "Battlefields," and illustrated how an artist like Degas subverted traditional historical battle scenes by, as one of the curatorial descriptions in the exhibition states, "depicting conflict and confrontation between male and female forces [. . .]. By subverting the idea of heroism that is inherent in historical paintings, these works [selected works] are an experiment in looking at female identity in a different way, not as a figure of seduction for the male eye, but as something more precarious where otherness is seen as threatening." The exhibition paired Degas's rendering of sexual battle with the work of the Brazilian artist Sonia Andrade, whose 1977 video *Untitled* graphically violates the female body. As the accompanying curatorial description states, the artist "inserts a nylon thread through her pierced ear, then binds up her whole head [. . .]. A face where a line is used, not to delineate the features, but to invade and deform it. The graphic violence of the mutilated subject is conveyed as much by what is done to the face as by the impassive way the action is filmed." Similarly unsettling, within the theme "Erasures," Samuel Beckett's *Film* (starring Buster Keaton, with no dialogue) explores failed attempts to erase the self. Beckett's notes, the curatorial description tells us, describe the film as portraying the "[s]earch of non-being in flight from extraneous perception breaking down in inescapability of self-perception." His film captures the essence of Lacan's gaze and the inescapable trauma of the Real, exploring "the precariousness of [our] presence in the world." By depicting the struggle for recognition, these installations reinforced the connection between having a presence in the world and being home.

Morrison's novel *A Mercy* elaborates her concern with home, safety, and identity prevalent in "The Foreigner's Home." The book jacket describes *A Mercy* as revealing "what lies beneath the surface of slavery. But at its heart it is the ambivalent, disturbing story of a mother who casts off her daughter in order to save her, and of a daughter who may never exorcise that abandonment." In addition, the characters are "all men and women inventing themselves in the wilderness." These two themes, the parental betrayal that begets trauma and the creation of self, highlight the need to create a home. Like Morrison's other novels, *A Mercy* probes the psychic scars of ownership, as well as the search for a positive reflection in an evolving American culture. Morrison has said that she wanted to write a novel about slavery before it was associated with race, setting *A Mercy* in America in the years 1682–90, when ownership of others was prevalent. According to Morrison, the book is "pre-racial in that it happens before it became institutionalized. [. . .] a period before racism was inextricably related to slavery" (Brophy-Warren). Most of the characters in the novel are owned by someone. All four of the women in *A Mercy* belong to Jacob Vaark, a trader with Dutch roots: Lina, the Native American forced to convert but later rejected by the Baptists and sold to Vaark; the orphaned Sorrow, shunned as useless and taken in by Vaark out of charity and in exchange for a supply of lumber; the young Florens, given to Vaark in payment of a debt; and his wife, Rebekka, sold by her father to Vaark to be his bride. Even the two indentured men, Willard and Scully, work for Vaark in "exchange for land under lease" (7). Although Vaark is a kind master and husband, without him the women are vulnerable and subject to decisions made by their community. Their need for Vaark's protection parallels that of the orphans and children in Morrison's other novels. While Morrison's earlier works investigate how the original core trauma of slavery persists in American culture, *A Mercy* reveals the seeds of slave trauma in the orphaned and dispossessed settlers.

Thus, colonial America represents a quintessential "Foreigner's Home," a nation of transplanted populations. A mirror image of stratified European cultures, the America of 1682–90 contains a landowning and moneyed class that depends on others to survive both physically and psychologically. The physical need for a labor force to cultivate a wild terrain couples with the psychological need for scapegoats, and Morrison artfully depicts the capacity for cruelty of "free" people of means. Class, family connections, and occasionally luck determine power and ownership. Over time, slavery will equate with race, but Morrison's developing America focuses on the personal trauma of individuals rather than on collective memory or group suffering. As we have seen in Morrison's other novels, nostalgic memory soothes trauma, and verbalizing trauma enables characters to name their own desire despite community voices. Morrison closes *A Mercy* with the words that minha mãe longs to have shared with her misguided daughter, Florens: "to be given dominion over another is a hard thing; to wrest dominion over another is a wrong thing; to give dominion of yourself to another is a wicked thing" (167). In an interview with Bob Thompson, of the *Washington Post,* Morrison claims that Florens needs to find inside herself "the beloved—the part of the self that is you, and loves you, and is always there for you" (Thompson C4). To be able to name one's own desire, separate from the social constructions that surround one, constitutes the true "mercy" one can attain. It is a mercy one earns for oneself by surviving trauma through creation of the self out of loss and lack.

Minha mãe understands that in the plantation culture women have no protection from men. "To be female in this place is to be an open wound that cannot heal. Even if scars form, the festering is ever below" (163). Her daughter's vulnerability exists simply because she is a woman living in a culture without laws of God or man to protect her. Unfortunately, minha mãe has never told Florens about the danger of men or that she herself was raped by a crew of men and therefore does not know which one is Florens's father. She also does not share her family history prior to D'Ortega's plantation—forced to flee her burning village, moved four times, and sold into slavery. When she arrives in Barbados as a victim of the slave trade, minha mãe learns that she is not human but "negrita" (165). That one word wipes out all of her heritage and past: "Language, dress, gods, dance, habits, decoration, song—all of it cooked together in the color of my skin"

(165). Life on D'Ortega's plantation confirms her position as object, which robs her of the ability to protect her children.

Florens's last memory of her mother before being given away was her singing about the inability of a mother bird to protect her unborn children: "A song about the green bird fighting then dying when the monkey steals her eggs" (166). Her mother will live with the regret of all she was unable to teach her daughter about life and her culture, just as Florens will wrestle with how parental teaching could have saved her much heartache. Believing that "[t]here is no protection but there is difference" (166), minha mãe sees in Vaark the one chance she may have to help Florens. She perceives Vaark's kindness, that he has "no animal in his heart" (163) and thus can see Florens "as a human child, not pieces of eight" (166). Minha mãe protects Florens the only way she can, by begging Vaark to take her daughter to cancel D'Ortega's debt.[1]

Vaark, himself "a ratty orphan become landowner, making a place out of no place, a temperate living from raw life," realizes that ownership of the land is arbitrary but that he is owner of himself, creating a self out of no self (12). He travels the land successfully as a native would, following signs of nature. "Recognizing the slope of certain hills, a copse of oak, an abandoned den, the sudden odor of pine sap—all of that was more than valuable; it was essential" (13). His instincts are geared toward helping disadvantaged others, as we see when he frees the trapped raccoon, "perhaps to the mother forced to abandon it or more likely into other claws" (11). He disdains the vanity and greed that divide people. But American society is taking shape in less than equitable ways. For example, an uprising in Virginia, where an army of "blacks, natives, whites, mulattoes—freedmen, slaves and indentured—had waged war against local gentry," leads to the legalization of othering in the new laws that arise to suppress nonwhites (10). These laws tie slavery to race: by "eliminating manumission, gatherings, travel and bearing arms for black people only; by granting license to any white to kill any black for any reason; by compensating owners for a slave's maiming or death, they separated and protected all whites from all others forever" (10). Vaark must preserve his place in the social structure as a free man of means. Despite his charitable and humane instincts, in the end his social environment lures him into its web of greed. Ultimately, Vaark becomes a victim of society's voices and vanities. His kindness and sense of moral superiority no longer give him a positive reflection, because his encounters with D'Ortega leave him victim to the gaze of the wealthy Other.

Believing that "[f]lesh was not his commodity" (22), Vaark accepts Florens because he acknowledges that "there was no good place in the world for waifs and whelps other than the generosity of strangers. Even if bartered, given away, apprenticed, sold, swapped, seduced, tricked for food, labored for shelter or stolen, they were less doomed under adult control" (32). Vaark acknowledges that the commodification of people is a "most wretched business" (26). In the New World culture, Florens is not a human but rather goods to be traded: "the girl was worth twenty pieces of eight, considering the number of years ahead of her and reducing the balance by three hogsheads of tobacco or fifteen English pounds" (27). Previously Vaark had purchased Lina "outright and deliberately" to work his farm (34). In the case of minha mãe, it is the desperate "terror in her eyes" (26) as she begs him to take her daughter, Florens, that touches Vaark, although he misunderstands the mother's motive, thinking that she simply "had no use for her" (96). Vaark perceives Florens as an "ill-shod child that the mother was throwing away" (34), and having been himself "misborn and disowned" (33) until he inherited land unexpectedly from an uncle, he rescues her just as he had taken in the woeful Sorrow, a "sullen, curly-headed girl" that a sawyer "had found half dead on a riverbank" (33). That charity was also financially based, with Vaark asking that the "sawyer forgive the cost of the lumber he was buying" (33). In accepting Florens from D'Ortega, Vaark moves one step closer to D'Ortega's values in that his visit leads him into the rum trade, a trade that involves slave labor—"a remote labor force in Barbados"—for profit (35).

In addition, this visit threatens Vaark's balance and perspective of his own place in the social structure. Keenly aware of class differences, Vaark realizes that a gentleman like D'Ortega would not be dining with a trader unless he needed help. Despite Vaark's assessment of D'Ortega as a "sloven man, stubborn in his wrongheadedness like all of the Roman faith," he still feels inferior because of class (17). Even though Vaark criticizes D'Ortega for his lack of values, he envies his "house, the gate, the fence" (27). Although Vaark knows that he has "gone head to head with rich gentry" by confronting D'Ortega in their negotiation, he ultimately abandons this sense of a worthy self for the very terms he has rejected: "only things, not bloodlines or character, separated them" (27). To feel equal to D'Ortega, Vaark seeks a positive self from the reflection in a grand house and expensive, "whimsical" gifts, "useless on a farm" (88). In coveting D'Ortega's acquisitions, he loses everything he has—his wife's respect and his legacy of a good name. Thus, his third, unnecessary house becomes not a home but a mausoleum, a sterile legacy that boosts his ego but destroys all that he has built and loves. He leaves his wife and dependents unprotected in a travesty of grandeur.

While Vaark's acceptance of Florens represents a charitable act that can give her a more hopeful future, this event actually damages her sense of self-worth. Florens experiences erasure when her mother, while holding on to her nursing son, offers Florens to Vaark. In her new life, Florens learns from her interactions with Vaark, Mistress Rebekka, Lina, Sorrow, Willard, Scully, Widow Ealing, Daughter Jane, and the blacksmith. Florens radiates the helplessness of an unprotected child, and everyone she meets senses her need for approval. Florens's vulnerability stems from her mother's abandonment, leaving her "grateful for every shred of affection, any pat on the head, any smile of approval" (61). In all of her encounters she seeks validation of her being. Florens's core trauma of abandonment develops when her mother chooses to keep the still-nursing boy instead of her: "mothers nursing greedy babies scare me" (8). She does not understand the message she knows was in her mother's eyes, "saying something I cannot hear. Saying something important to me, but holding the little boy's hand" (8).

This traumatic separation scene recurs in nightmares, as well as when she is in danger. On her journey, Florens relives the bodily fear of abandonment when the young girl at Widow Ealing's house screams from behind her mother's skirts. Likewise, when Florens sees the little boy at the blacksmith's peering at her, she conflates the scene with her own hiding behind her mother just before being sent away. In both instances Florens is in danger and outcast. Florens chooses to fight for the blacksmith rather than be rejected. Her fear of being thrown away, as if she were discarded property or garbage, repeats her mother's trauma of being "cargo" on the slave ship, where much of the "cargo" is lost, thrown into the sea during the journey. Minha mãe recalls that "[e]ach water, river or sea, has sharks under. [. . .] Who lives who dies? Who could tell in that moaning and bellowing in the dark, in the awfulness" (164). While Florens does not know details of her mother's crossing, she repeats the trauma when she feels cast off.

Florens does not yet comprehend slavery and ownership, only the loss of a loved one, and in her needy state she wonders why the people on the Ney brothers' wagon want to be free from their indentured state: "Everyone has to work. I ask are you leaving someone dear behind?" (40). But Florens knows on some level that the blacksmith "cannot steal [. . .] nor wedding" her because "[n]either one is lawful" (105). But she pursues him, thinking "I choose you" (41). Unfortunately, she is also a slave to her love for the blacksmith, as he tells her: "Your head is empty and your body is wild. [. . .] Own yourself, woman, and leave us be. [. . .] You are nothing but wilderness. No constraint. No mind. [. . .] a slave by choice" (141). Florens will not be free until she verbalizes her underlying need for his protective love. Seeking protection even in "stories of mothers fighting to save their children from wolves and natural disasters" (61), Florens thinks of the blacksmith in these terms: "You are my protection. Only you. You can be it because you say you are a free man from New Amsterdam [. . .]. I don't know the feeling of or what it means, free and not free" (69). She fears freedom because its "looseness" reenacts her lack of maternal protection (70). Her love affair with the blacksmith gives Florens a mirrored self she does not get from her mother or her culture. In her nostalgic memory of their love Florens finds a safe haven where "[n]o one steals my warmth and shoes because I am small. No one handles my backside. No one whinnies like sheep or goat because I drop in fear and weakness. No one screams at the sight of me. No one watches my body for how it is unseemly. With you my body is pleasure is safe is belonging. I can never not have you have me" (137). Her bodily need to be loved by the blacksmith motivates her to overcome obstacles on her journey to get him to help save Rebekka's life.

Florens begins to confront her orphaned and abandoned core at Widow Ealing's when she claims that she has no father and that her mother is dead. Seeing Daughter Jane with her mother makes her realize that she misses having a mother to teach her things that can protect her. For example, when Widow Ealing tells her daughter that demons do not bleed and that cutting herself can save her from being punished for being the devil, Florens thinks: "If my mother is not dead she can be teaching me these things" (109). When the villagers examine her, Florens realizes her designation as other: "they are looking at me my body across distances without recognition. Swine look at me with more connection when they raise their heads from the trough" (113). The villagers' examination leaves her reeling from her status as nonhuman object.[2] Florens attempts to verbalize what she feels, thinking,

> Inside I am shrinking. [. . .] I am losing something with every step I take. I can feel the drain. Something precious is leaving me. I am a thing apart. With the letter I belong and am lawful. Without it I am a weak calf abandon by the herd, a turtle without shell [. . .] a darkness I am born with, outside, yes, but inside as well and the inside dark is small, feathered and toothy. Is that what my mother knows? Why she chooses me to live without? (115)

Florens internalizes the community's projection of evil onto her, feeling that it must be inside her and that this evil may explain her mother's abandonment.

With this realization, she is "not afraid of anything now. The sun's going leaves darkness behind and the dark is me. Is we. Is my home" (115). Accepting her fundamental nothingness and her dark core, she embodies Lacan's Real; this recognition now protects her from fear.

Lina has tried to teach Florens that she needs to rely only on herself, telling her, "We never shape the world [. . .]. The world shapes us" (71). As an example, Lina explains that Mistress Rebekka runs to Vaark for protection when a moose threatens her "[b]ecause she can" (71). Mistress has a culturally sanctioned support system in a husband and provider. But Florens does not yet understand Lina's message, thinking about how the blacksmith both shapes and is her world. She feels no "need to choose," because her heart makes the choice for her (71). But when she finds the blacksmith, she sees that the hate in the eyes of his adopted boy, Malaik, "is loud. He wants my leaving. This cannot happen. I feel the clutch inside. This expel can never happen again" (137). Once again she suffers erasure by another's choosing to reject her. Her dream reflects her situation: when she looks into water, her "face is not there. Where my face should be is nothing" (138). There is no reflection for her in the mirror, no self to return a gaze. She imagines that Daughter Jane will find her face, connecting her inner self with the devil. In her confusion, Florens sees Malaik's doll in the corner and wonders whether it is hiding from her evil or is a "precious child no person wants" (139). Either interpretation points to her lack of a worthy self. Once the blacksmith assumes her guilt, hits her, and chooses Malaik over her, Florens feels lost and abandoned, without comfort.

Only when she realizes, in a repetition of her mother's desertion, that the blacksmith has chosen the orphaned boy over her will she fight back for recognition: "No. Not again. Not ever. Feathers lifting, I unfold. The claws scratch and scratch until the hammer is in my hand" (142). Like Sethe in *Beloved,* who strikes Schoolteacher to assert her position as subject and mother of her children, Florens resorts to physical violence to assert her subjectivity. Her violent eruption and physical attack on the blacksmith, who has been her refuge, bodily enacts her rage at the repeated trauma of not being chosen. The fierceness with which she fights to protect herself causes Willard and Scully to describe her as having "turned feral" (146). They comment that while previously she had been a "combination of defenselessness, eagerness to please and, most of all, a willingness to blame herself for the meanness of others," now "she had become untouchable" (152). She has come a long way from the girl so eager "for approval" that "any kindness shown her she munched like a rabbit" (96). She alone can save herself "from any who look closely at me only to throw me away. From all those who believe they have claim and rule over me" (157). In her new isolation Florens develops a dangerous freedom reminiscent of Cholly's in *The Bluest Eye*, feeling like "[a]n ice floe cut away from the riverbank in deep winter. [...] I have no kicking heart no home no tomorrow. [...] The feathers close. For now" (158).

After this bodily verbalization of her trauma, Florens writes her own story in order to claim a lovable self. Vaark's ghost and his doomed house, along with the imagined returning blacksmith, serve as witnesses to Florens's trauma. Florens begins her transformation by writing her story at night on the floor, walls, and ceiling of a room in Vaark's unfinished house: "the telling will give me the tears I never have," allowing her to verbalize her trauma (158). She realizes that the blacksmith may not be able to read but that the writing will free her: "I am become wilderness but I am also Florens. In full. Unforgiven. Unforgiving. [...] Slave. Free. I last" (161). Standing up for herself frees the words. Her feet have hardened, so that her body has accepted physical pain as part of the trauma involved in overcoming the weak, vulnerable self. The "soles of my feet are hard as cypress" (161). She transforms the "Portuguese lady" (4) who cannot live in a culture that defines black as a subhuman commodity into a woman who can stand on her own two feet. The contrast between her ladylike feet and her hardened soles, developed from being on her own, portends her ability to take care of herself by relying on her own inner resources.

For Florens, experience has been a hard teacher, but she learns the lessons that both her mother and Lina have been longing to teach her about surviving in an alien culture. Like minha mãe, Lina understands her object status and claims herself as subject, naming her own desire when the Anabaptists fail her. Having witnessed her tribe's erasure, Lina is one of three survivors who undergo a harrowing night listening to birds and wolves devour the pox-infested dead. "They stayed there all night listening to gnawing, baying, growling, fighting and worst of all the quiet of animals sated at last" (46). Recognizing herself as mere carrion, Lina seeks protection as the converted heathen, a "praying savage" who "dances in secret at first light when the moon is small" (5). But even though she has converted to their religion, members of her new society reject her when her lover beats her; they refuse to help her in her battered state or to tend to her wounds. She will turn to her native culture when Christian society lets her down. In her progression to self-ownership Lina moves from terror to gratitude to objectivity toward the invading Europeans: "Once they terrified her, then they rescued her. Now they simply puzzled her" (44). Nostalgic memory of her tribe supports a worthy self in a hostile environment.

Lina cannot adopt the invaders' values and so goes her own way, even if it means a loss of community. The "Europes could calmly cut mothers down, blast old men in the face with muskets louder than moose calls, but were enraged if a not-Europe looked a Europe in the eye" (46), and Lina rejects their capacity for inflicting pain on others. When her village dies of smallpox, the Europeans rescue her and two boys, taking her to "live among kindly Presbyterians," and these settlers admire her work ethic (47). "Afraid of once more losing shelter, terrified of being alone in the world without family, Lina acknowledged her status as heathen and let herself be purified by these worthies" (47). But after cutting Lina's hair and indoctrinating her, they abandon her as other, leaving a "bowl [...] for her on the porch. Like a dog" (105). Finally, they put her up for sale in order to expel her from their community. Although she had accepted the "Europes" to ease her fear of abandonment, Lina, "without clan and under a Europe's rule," will call upon her ancestry to save her from their ostracism (104). In doing so, she names her own desire.

Turning to her mother's ancient ways, native medicine, and tribal lore, Lina "recalled or invented the hidden meaning of things. Found, in other words, a way to be in the world" (48). She becomes "one more thing that moved in the natural world"; by naming her own desire, she survives in a hostile social environment, remaining loyal to Vaark, who treats her like a human and not other (48). She relies on positive ancestral memory to create a self: "She sorted and stored what she dared to recall and eliminated the rest, an activity which shaped her inside and out. By the time Mistress came, her self-invention was almost perfected. Soon it was irresistible" (50). Having survived her drunken lover's beatings and society's ostracism, she becomes self-sufficient. In this new state Lina chooses to love and care for Florens as a mother would, trying to guide her with the lessons she has learned from her experiences. "Mother hunger—to be one or have one— both of them were reeling from that longing which, Lina knew, remained alive, traveling the bone" (63). In an echo of minha mãe's parting song to Florens about the green bird's inability to protect her eggs, Lina tells Florens a story about an eagle mother thrust out of her nest by a human traveler. But in her supportive story the eggs "hatch alone," and the orphaned birds, like Lina and Florens, survive (63).

Lina keenly comprehends the precarious state created by Vaark's death, for if Mistress Rebekka dies, the community will sell Florens, Sorrow, and herself— "three unmastered women and an infant out here, alone, belonging to no one, became wild game for anyone" (58). They cannot inherit Vaark's land or live there as squatters, because they are "[f]emale and illegal" (58). In this community, the defiance that Vaark and Rebekka thought would insulate them in fact will not protect their goods from being auctioned off or their human property from being sold. Lina realizes that "[t]hey were orphans, each and all" and that "her own life, everything, depended on Mistress' survival, which depended on Florens' success" (59–60). Therefore, she fears "the shattering a free black man would cause" and that Florens's enslavement to her love for the blacksmith will interfere with her mission to bring the blacksmith back to save Rebekka's life (61).

As Rebekka waits for the blacksmith's cure, she thinks about the irony of having left a pox-filled England to die in the clean air of the New World: "So to have sailed to this clean world, this fresh and new England, marry a stout, robust man and then, on the heels of his death, to lie festering on a perfect spring night felt like a jest" (90). Rebekka's abandonment trauma, like Florens's, stems from parental rejection. At sixteen she "knew her father would have shipped her off to anyone who would book her passage and relieve him of feeding her" (74). While her mother mildly protests that Vaark must be "a heathen living among savages," she nonetheless does not protect her daughter (74). The religious fervor her mother shares with her husband makes them treat "each other and their children with glazed indifference" (74). Rebekka's family background allows her to bond with Lina despite their different origins, as "both were alone without family [. . . and] both had to please one man. [. . .] they became what was for each a companion" (75). Likewise, the women on Rebekka's boat over bond through the common experience of the crossing, during which they are housed below with the animals. All of the women but Rebekka have transgressed society's moral boundaries. These "exiled, thrown-away women" perform perhaps their last cultural act—having tea—with a formality and parodic ritual that enacts their desire to be recognized as human and not powerless objects: "Breathing quietly, they sipped warm, spirited water and munched stale biscuits, daintily brushing away the flakes. [. . .] Rebekka recalled how each of them, including the ten-year-old, lifted her little finger and angled it out" (82, 85).[3]

Rebekka arrives in America hoping that her new society will be less violent than her English home, where "execution was a festivity as exciting as a king's parade" (75). Nightmares of public hangings, drawing and quartering, and routine "[b]rawls, knifings and kidnaps" remind Rebekka of the horrors of torture and public shaming that she has escaped (75). In her class-bound British society, where she lived in "reeking streets, spat on by lords and prostitutes, curtseying, [. . .] her prospects were servant, prostitute, wife" (77–78). Whatever America has to offer, her position as wife in a classless society is her best alternative: "Whatever the danger, how could it possibly be worse?" (78). In the end, her new community in America contains the same religious zeal as her parents, and Rebekka resigns herself to her community because she is dependent on them to protect her when Vaark dies. They will produce a new husband for her if she follows their rules. While her desire is to survive without the church and thereby avoid the fervor that caused her parents to fail her, her choices are limited. In contrast to the nostalgic memory of her balanced and joyful life with Vaark, her traumatic memories replay English life, where the upper classes take pleasure in the suffering of others. Having witnessed these public atrocities, Rebekka stores this secondhand trauma as if this violence had been done to her. Memory traces have been burned into her psyche, written bodily into her consciousness to compound the trauma of her unloving parents.

The Baptists Rebekka must live among have "even narrower definitions of God's preferences than her parents. Other than themselves (and those of their kind who agreed), no one was saved" (92). She wishes that her family and home had been protective; in her new, hostile environment Rebekka will wonder somewhat nostalgically about her family and how they might have aged. Her abandonment by them is complete when she attempts to contact them, only to find that they have moved, leaving no traceable address. Even if she should want to find them, that door is closed to her. The light in her goes out as she mirrors the Christian women around her, becoming harsh and demanding of Lina, Florens, and Sorrow. When she thinks she will die from her sickness, Rebekka studies her face in the mirror, "gently apologizing. 'Eyes, dear eyes, forgive me. Nose, poor mouth. [. . .] skin I do apologize'" (95). She is reduced to the body in pieces, and her only recourse for salvation is to accept the social structure of her community, for here, as in England, women are at the mercy of men, no matter what their station or circumstances may be. Lonely without Vaark, she gradually turns to her village for acceptance and support.

In contrast, Sorrow, rejected by the village, turns to her child for support, embracing a self by naming herself "Complete" when she gives birth (134). At her core is the loss of her father and their life at sea. The sole survivor of a shipwreck, Sorrow undergoes a psychotic break, speaking only to "Twin" (118). This supportive imagined double enables her to survive the accident at sea. Only Twin calls her by the name her father gave her, and Twin is her only link to her past self, before the shipwreck. Twin becomes "her safety, her entertainment, her guide" (119). Sorrow is only eleven when the sawyer's family, who had rescued her and named her "Sorrow because she was abandoned" (120), gives her to Vaark because she is incompetent and the mother does not want her around to tempt her husband and sons. In Twin's company Sorrow closes herself off from the assaults of the sawyer and his sons, as well as the Deacon. These rapes are seen as encounters, and Sorrow later perceives a difference in the coupling of the blacksmith and Florens, a passionate exchange she never had in her own sexual encounters: "What Sorrow saw yonder in the grass under a hickory tree was not the silent submission to the slow goings behind a pile of wood or a hurried one in a church pew that Sorrow knew. [...] It was a dancing" (128). While the blacksmith's love affair gives a self to Florens, Sorrow has no self until her child is born.

Sorrow's first pregnancy makes her feel "flushed with pleasure at the thought of a real person, a person of her own, growing inside her" (123). Motherhood gives her purpose and a job she can do well. In this circumscribed culture women have limited options, and motherhood appeals to most of them. Lina wants to mother Florens, Rebekka begins to decline when her last child dies, and Sorrow is Complete with her baby. Florens alone does not covet children, because a nursing baby lies at the root of her abandonment trauma; she still seeks a mother. Fearing that Lina will drown her second baby as Sorrow suspects she did her first one, Sorrow goes to Willard and Scully when her water breaks. Giving birth provides her with a sense that "she had done something, something important, by herself" (133).[4] With Sorrow's new agency, Twin disappears, "gone, traceless and unmissed by the only person who knew her" (134). Sorrow "had looked into her daughter's eyes; saw in them the gray glisten of a winter sea while a ship sailed by-the-lee. 'I am your mother,' she said. 'My name is Complete'" (134). Her daughter's eyes mirror back a complete self. As Willard and Scully describe it, she cares for her baby "out of a need to trust herself" (146). She gains a self in her daughter's gaze.

In their constrained village, Lina and Sorrow survive best because their memories of home provide them with a positive self. Like Lina's tribal lore and customs, Sorrow's memories of her father and their sailing life together prop her up in the face of mourning, loneliness, and ostracism. Her pregnancy gives her subject status as mother. Unlike Sorrow and Lina, Florens and Rebekka lack a nostalgic positive parental home, but they have supportive memories of the blacksmith and Vaark, respectively. Willard and Scully, also betrayed by their families, rely on memories of Vaark's kindness and the supportive community of his farm. Their talk about life with Vaark echoes reminiscences of Sweet Home in *Beloved* in that the group functioned like family. However, Scully sees that death and betrayal have torn the familylike group apart, and he concludes that he "once thought they were a kind of family because together they had carved companionship out of isolation. But the family they imagined they had become was false" (155–56). They know Mistress will have to marry to keep the farm and that "[t]he village will provide" a partner (146).

Scully worries that Rebekka will no longer pay them for their work on the farm if she remarries, because a "new husband handling the farm could make very different arrangements, arrangements that did not include him" (155). Money is the only way out of his life of servitude. Thus, Willard resents the free blacksmith's ability to earn coin, but when the blacksmith calls him Mr. Bond, Willard likes being recognized as a worthy self and enjoys "the lift that small courtesy allowed him" (151). This lift provides the possibility that even though "their wages were not as much as the blacksmith's, [. . .] for Scully and Mr. Bond it was enough to imagine a future" (156). Together they can provide the home that each needs to stave off loneliness and have hope for a future as free men.

In Morrison's struggling colonial society, the insecurity of the settlers breeds aggression in white communities. One religion distrusts another, with varying sects of Catholics, Anabaptists, Baptists, and Presbyterians all vying for recognition and power. *A Mercy*, along with the insights and selections from her Louvre exhibition and lectures, manifests Morrison's continued development of the concepts of trauma, home, and subjectivity that I trace in her other novels. She continues to explore themes of being other, being an orphan, and being vulnerable. The search for a safe community, family, and subjectivity in order to survive echoes her previous works. Subservient groups and their individual members process trauma to survive; reconstructed memory becomes a vehicle to protect the ego. Thus, home as a positive mirror, created by nostalgic memory and the desire for a lovable and worthy self, fulfills Lacanian lack and allows for the formation of selfhood. Displacement and marginalization necessitate a reconstruction of home and consequently a rebuilding of subjectivity.[5] Morrison's characters search for a positive identity; it is a search made more difficult by their marginalized conditions and the bodily component of stored memory. One route to self-discovery is through a memory of an idealized self, whether created by people, relationships, a physical place, or concept. Such a home, reconstructed through memory, is essential to establishing subjectivity in Morrison's novels.

NOTES

INTRODUCTION

1. Recent works by Keith Byerman, J. Brooks Bouson, Jill Matus, and Lucille P. Fultz focus on Morrison's telling of historical and cultural trauma stories, as well as trauma's connection to shame and racial difference. Keith Byerman discusses Morrison's telling trauma stories of survivors and her "rewriting of the American grand narrative" in order to "begin to forge relationships that can become communities that can make a difference" (*Remembering* 3, 10), while J. Brooks Bouson discusses "the painful sense of exposure that accompanies the single shame event and also the devastating effect of chronic shame on [Morrison's] characters' sense of individual and social identity" (3–4). With the idea of shame as the focus of her work, Bouson explores the "protective power of the black folk community and the timeless ancestor figures" (5). Jill Matus depicts Morrison's novels as "a form of cultural memory" and shows "how, in their engagement with the African American past, they testify to historical trauma" (1). She focuses on both the witnessing function of literature and the reader's participation "in the testimony," concluding that there are no easy cures for trauma. Lucille P. Fultz traces Morrison's narrative process and its deconstruction of race, focusing on the trauma of racial difference in women in particular.

2. Andrea O'Reilly's work looks at trauma in terms of a severed "motherline" and the loss of healing patterns in African mothering that provided a safe homeplace and developed self-love (*Toni Morrison*). I explore the psychological and social repercussions of this loss of ancient properties and ancestral memories, focusing on the role of both the rejecting gaze of Western culture and generationally inherited trauma in re-creating a selfhood.

3. In addition to works by Bouson, Byerman, Fultz, Matus, and O'Reilly, eight recent dissertations consider trauma from various viewpoints: Sylviane Finck analyzes how Morrison's novels testify to silenced voices; Kathleen MacArthur considers the aesthetic re-creation of trauma; Matthew L. Miller discusses how witnessing (through the aesthetic witnessing of literature) restores agency by a working through of trauma; Melissa Ann Ruisz considers America's failure as a nation to incorporate black trauma; Jonathan Daniel Sabol claims that both remembering and forgetting are necessary in order to heal from trauma; Eva Tettenhorm considers avenues of black resistance to trauma; Ellen Timothy looks at how loving contexts can heal trauma aimed at dismantling the self; and Lynette Marie Ubois confirms the function of novels in witnessing. My multidisciplinary discussion enlarges these studies with a multifaceted definition of trauma and its social, psychological, and biological components.

4. Marc Conner describes Morrison's communities as "predatory, vampiric, sterile, cowardly, threatening; and the individual must struggle desperately to survive in the midst of this damaging community—a struggle that is often a losing one, resulting in the fragmentation and destruction of

these desperate selves" ("From the Sublime" 49). He concludes that the aesthetic and ethical progression of Morrison's work "is defined by a cohesive and nurturing sense of love" and that her work "is an ongoing and passionate effort at healing the divisions that quite literally haunt the scarred individuals and fractured communities of later twentieth-century America" (74).

5. Kathleen Marks argues that "the very blackness of African Americans is somehow always 'other' despite attempts to bring about racial integration" (128).

6. The psychologist Janice Gump discusses how "[s]lavery evoked the core intrapsychic experiences of helplessness, shame, and rage" and how "[t]o a large extent, conditions enabling the integration of slavery's trauma have been absent" in American culture. She discusses dominance as one relational pattern derived from slavery and uses clinical material to describe its operation in an African American family.

7. Matthew Miller adds that *Beloved* "shows slavery to be traumatic, something so shattering and profound that the very telling disrupts narrative flow, form, and comprehension" (60).

8. Double-consciousness bars an effective imagined completeness. Edward Guerrero calls this gaze "'the look' [...] the controlling gaze of a dominant, racially oppressive society which constructs whiteness as the norm while viewing African Americans as 'Other'" (762). bell hooks describes how oppressive social structures maintain dominance and strip blacks of agency by controlling the gaze: "white control of the black gaze [. . .] den[ies] the subjectivity of blacks [. . . by] relegating them to the realm of the invisible. [. . .] To look directly was an assertion of subjectivity, equality. Safety [for blacks] resided in the pretense of invisibility" (*Killing* 35–36). Patricia Hill Collins states that although black women occupied central roles in white households, they remained "outsiders." She argues that this "outsider within" status provided black women insight into their position in society (S14). For more on race and double-consciousness in Morrison's novels see Adell; Awkward; Butler-Evans; Harding and Martin; Heinze; Mobley; and Weinstein.

9. Annamarie Christiansen shows how Morrison's novels redefine the stereotype of the "tragic mulatto [. . .] envision[ing] a complex and vibrant African American community" and "refashion[ing] master narratives about African American life" so as to turn "a figure of despair [...] into one of hope and change" (95).

10. Dean Franco discusses the different meanings of the word *claim*, concluding that when Sethe breaks the law by destroying Schoolteacher's "property," she creates trauma for "the one who would claim her, at the same time that it is a trauma to her" (423).

11. I am grateful for the work of Claudia Tate, who meaningfully brought psychoanalytic theory to bear on criticism of African American literature even though many "would contend that the imposition of psychoanalytic theory on African American literature advances Western hegemony over the cultural production of black Americans, indeed over black subjectivity" (192).

12. Dean Franco questions the adequacy of a psychoanalytic model of "working-through [. . .] when the experience of loss is mediated through the discourse of property" (427). I argue that it is because this loss, whether emotional or material, is lodged in bodily circuits as well as psychological ones that the working through needs to be understood on levels besides the psychic, including bodily reenactment and cultural performance. The "political redress" he advocates necessitates a change in cultural ritual connected to the master narrative.

13. Sylviane Finck claims that Morrison's novels investigate silenced voices and historical trauma in such a way as to testify, while Lynette Ubois writes that her novels represent "a special kind of witnessing to historical trauma" (6).

14. Miller writes that "[w]itnessing's basic function—to return agency to a traumatized and virtually *inactive* self—awards the survivor with some control over memory and the trauma" (9). LaCapra attributes the failure to work through trauma to "scenes in which the past returns and the future is blocked or fatalistically caught up in a melancholic feedback loop" (21).

15. Melissa Ruisz claims that Sethe cannot heal because she cannot narrate her story to a listener who will testify. According to Miller, Morrison's novels provide an "aesthetic witness [that] not only represents trauma but promotes a working through" (24).

16. For more on community in Morrison's work see Bjork; Christian; Harding and Martin; Holloway; and Demetrakopoulos.

17. Daniel Siegel presents D. N. Stern's (*The Interpersonal World of the Infant*) stages of self-development from birth to age two: the "emerging self," which "takes in sensory data"; the "core self," constituted by a sense of "agency" and "coherence"; the "subjective self," comprising "a sense of self and self-with-other that involves the shared attention, intention, and emotion between caregiver and child"; the "verbal self," in which words form communication "between self and other"; and finally the "narrative self," in which "autobiographical narratives play a major role in defining the self" ("An Interpersonal" 34–35).

18. Jean Wyatt's adept and clear work *Risking Difference: Identification, Race, and Community in Contemporary Fiction and Feminism* uses Lacanian theory to focus on issues of identification, the "confusion of self and other, impelled by the (usually) unconscious desire to be the other" (1). Her discussion of *Beloved* includes how race "complicates a similar structure of primary identification," asking "what is the identification mechanism that enables someone to suffer the symptoms of collective trauma, of a traumatic past experienced by a whole group but not by the sufferer herself?" (15, 66). She focuses on Denver's acting out of Sethe's desire. Wyatt also analyzes *Tar Baby* in terms of how Jadine "is fixated on the ideal ego and is prone to identifications with idealized figures" (16). Rebecca Ferguson describes how the "self—always questing, provisional and in process—is for Morrison necessarily relational, depending not only on a complex, shifting dialogical awareness of its affinity with and difference from others, but also on a consciousness of heritage [. . . and] 'traces' of the past. [. . .] The physical and emotional trauma that many of her fictional characters experience may indeed entail a radical fragmentation or fracturing of the self" (15–16).

19. Here the biological compounds the psychological, as the addiction to the "endorphins and to the memories that release these chemicals" that trauma produces reinforces the psychic need to repress the anxiety of lack (Young 95).

20. On the function of the past and memory in identity in Morrison's work see the works of Eleanor Branch, Genevieve Fabre, Robert Grant, Deborah Guth, Jennifer Holden-Kirwan, Karla Holloway, Linda Krumholz, Kathleen Marks, Barbara Mathieson, Deborah McDowell, Marilyn Mobley, Barbara Rigney, Ashraf Rushdy, Justine Tally, and Margaret Wilkerson.

21. Petar Ramadanovic suggests that "trauma (traumatic memory) does not concern a past event but rather a becoming form, not something that has finished but a certain kind of futurity. The subject of/in trauma is not a fragmented subject but a subject which is not whole because it is not yet to come" (6).

22. In *The Identifying Fictions of Toni Morrison: Modernist Authenticity and Postmodern Blackness* John N. Duvall discusses how Morrison's writing moves from fictionalized biography to African American historiography, reflecting modern and postmodern identity. Justine Tally, in *Toni Morrison's (Hi)stories and Truths,* discusses the "cultural production of History/history and its unsta-

ble relationship to both memory and story" in *Paradise* (14), focusing on how Morrison's "artistic concerns with language, discourse, voice and narrative strategy are intimately linked with her
commitment to social issues and her understanding of her own position as 'othered' in both the
academy and in society at large" (11). Sam Durrant's work on Morrison focuses on Freud's distinc-
tion between mourning and melancholy to describe the differences between what he calls "cultural
memory" and "racial memory," claiming that "[c]ultural memory constitutes a healthy mode of
mourning, which has as its aim the recovery of an African American subject," while racial memory
is "a collective memory of negation that threatens to overwhelm the individual with the consciousness of 'disproportionate' loss" (20–21). Racial memory "takes on a bodily form precisely because it
exceeds both the individual's and the community's capacity for verbalization and mourning" (80).
Eva Tettenhorn claims that this black exclusion from historiography leads to melancholia.

23. For a discussion of the libidinal aspect of ideology and discourse see Alcorn.

24. Joel Williamson writes that "[t]he sudden and dramatic rise in the lynching of black men in
and after 1889 stands out like some giant volcanic eruption on the landscape of Southern race relations. There was, indeed, something new and horribly palpable on the earth" (117).

25. Jennings writes that "semblances of African medicine (wo)men and priest(esse)s present
themselves in contemporary life in unassuming ways. Morrison's composites of Soaphead Church,
Shadrack, Pilate Dead, M'Dear, Circe, Baby Suggs, and Consolata Sosa emphasize that these social
roles are by no means extinct but have only been distorted from their origins or morphed into figu-
rations more pliable for twentieth-century survival" (177).

26. For discussions of class in Morrison's work see Mbalia; and Patell.

CHAPTER 1

1. James Berger, J. Brooks Bouson, Kathleen Brogan, Kate Cummings, Kimberly Davis, Mary
Jane Elliott, Jan Furman, Nancy Jesser, Lynda Koolish, Iyunolu Osagie, Emma Parker, and Caroline
Rody discuss *Beloved* regarding the importance of coming to terms with the past in the healing pro-
cess. For a discussion of the various interpretations of the character Beloved see below, n. 31.

2. For discussions regarding *Paradise* and the restrictions connected to strictly following an inherited master narrative see Davidson; Page, "Furrowing"; and Yukins.

3. In *Playing in the Dark,* Morrison describes this erasure of black identity in the service of white
subjectivity: "Africanism is the vehicle by which the American self knows itself as not enslaved, but
free; not repulsive, but desirable; not helpless, but licensed and powerful; not history-less but historical; not damned, but innocent; not a blind accident of evolution, but a progressive fulfillment of
destiny" (52).

4. Lynette Ubois writes that "losses and incomplete knowledge—particularly in terms of origins
—are a central part of the legacy of slavery" (170).

5. These blurred positions compound the identification and *méconnaissance* with white culture
that bell hooks and Kaja Silverman discuss.

6. Allan Schore reports that "the early social environment, mediated by the primary caregiver,
directly influences the final wiring of the circuits in the infant brain that are responsible for the future social and emotional coping capacities of the individual" (112).

7. Unfortunately, infanticide was not an uncommon response to the separation of mother and
child in the oppressive slave system. In *Within the Plantation Household* Elizabeth Fox-Genovese

explains that because children were the "master's property," some slave women felt that "by killing an infant they loved, they would be in some way reclaiming it as their own" (324). Jacqueline Jones writes that a woman's role as mother was cut off by the slave system, but some women managed to gain power through subversion of the system. This bodily defilement of women—their rape as well as their commodification of the reproductive act—remains as a kernel of the slave trauma. It represents one of the ways the trauma is written on the body.

8. Hesse et al. found that "a traumatized but nonabusive parent [. . .] might sporadically but repeatedly alarm the infant via (often *involuntary* or unconscious) exhibition of frightened or dissociative behavior" (59).

9. Lucille P. Fultz describes *Beloved* as an expression of maternal pain, noting that "Sethe and her children are denied the fundamental human rights of freedom and familial bonds" (65).

10. For more on Morrison's novels and narrative strategies, the oral tradition, and Morrison's use of folklore see Billingslea-Brown; Byerman, *Fingering*; Conner, "Wild Women"; Duvall, *Identifying Fictions*; Furman; C. Hall; Heinze; G. Jones; Smith; and Tally, *Story of Jazz*.

11. Mary Carden writes that under Mr. Garner, Paul D "lived as the precocious child of benevolent white parents" (405).

12. Many trauma theorists discuss the phenomenon of dissociation. Specifically, Bessel Van der Kolk and Onno Van der Hart relate that "trauma survivors report that they automatically are removed from the scene; they look at it from a distance or disappear altogether" (168). Janice Haaken writes that "in order to survive emotionally overwhelming experiences, the individual splits off the memory of the traumatic experience from consciousness. The dissociated memories are preserved in an alter ego state, or alter personality, through an amnesic barrier protecting one part of the personality from knowledge of the abuse" (1075). Judith Herman notes that "traumatized people alternate between feeling numb and reliving the event" and that "[d]enial, repression, and dissociation operate on a social as well as an individual level" (1, 2). Through dissociation, "[p]erceptions may be numbed or distorted, with partial anesthesia or the loss of particular sensations" (43).

13. In Kentucky "the greatest number of lynchings occurred during the period immediately after the Civil War, from 1865–1874" (Wright 71). According to a Freedman's Bureau monthly report, "It cannot be denied, that if a Negroe commits a wrong, there is a strong disposition on the part of the whites to take the law into their own hands and inflict summary punishment" (qtd. in Wright 43).

14. The community in *Paradise* also carries the memory of the white man's charge to Coffee and Tea to "dance" or be shot in the foot, as well as the segregation that prevents blacks from receiving urgent medical care from the white community.

15. Kate Cummings discusses the extreme commodification of black women, "forced to feed the slave system, not simply as field hands, cooks, or domestic workers [. . .] but also as the (re) producers of two raw materials[: . . .] the milk mothers produce goes first to feed white mouths immediately and then, if any is left, to keep alive slave children, potential laborers and commodities" (560).

16. Lacan theorizes that the act of repressing a sense of lack gives rise to desire, which can drive subjects to repeat obsolete behavior. Thus, desire as a response to lack is expressed in culture as the discourse inherited and passed on in each generation. For Lacan, the repetition of cultural ideology represents the drive's circuit as an expression of desire. The voices of one's culture dictate one's desire.

17. Sethe's nostalgia represents how "actual memories may [. . .] continue to exert their influence on current experience by means of the process of dissociation" (Van der Kolk and Van der Hart 159).

18. Daniel Siegel describes the neurobiology of this healing through memory as follows: "Memory is based on this process of integration [of neurons firing together in the future]" ("An Interpersonal" 5). Community connections promote healing because "the therapeutic interpersonal experience enables integrative fibers to actually grow and thus enable new abilities to be attained" (3).

19. Much has been written about Morrison's "rememory" in *Beloved*. James Berger defines rememory as a "[h]istorical trauma [that] returns as somatic-social symptom. [. . . It is] not the undoing of repetition [. . . but] rather, that repetition that cannot yet be worked through" (201). Mary Carden claims that "'Rememory' differs from 'memory' in its active force independent of the rememberer" (409). Rememory occurs as "violent eruptions of the past" (412). Emma Parker concurs, defining rememory as "the continued presence of that which has disappeared or been forgotten, as when Sethe 'remember[s] something she had forgotten she knew' (*Beloved* 61)" ("New Hystery" 2). Kathleen Brogan sees rememory as "memory as an external reality that can take possession of [Sethe]" (153). Sethe resists rememory because it "resurrects buried anguish and disrupts peace of mind" (Furman 262). This "uncontrolled remembering and reliving of emotionally painful experiences[, . . .] spontaneous recurrences of her traumatic and humiliating past" (Bouson 135, 149), connects with community trauma. Sam Durrant claims that "it is only by recognizing the excessive nature of collective history, by assigning a limit to the work of mourning, that the racially marked are able to come to terms with their personal histories" (101).

20. Steven Daniels writes that the "choices in *Beloved* that slavery is shown to allow, even oblige, are inevitably and necessarily unthinkable choices between bad alternatives" but that by partially "accepting a burden of responsibility for their impossible choices[, . . . Morrison's characters], in the midst of their victimization, achieve and maintain the dignity that most defies what slavery would have them be" (363).

21. As James Berger points out, "Only if traumas are remembered can they lose, gradually but never entirely, their traumatic effects" (212).

22. Much has been written about the healing power of storytelling and narration on both a personal and a communal level in Morrison's work. James Berger describes Beloved as "the sign of a society—both white and black—that cannot narrate its past and thus is trapped in an ever escalating circle of trauma and symptom" (201). Emma Parker claims that "[n]arrative [. . .] allows a subject to exercise a degree of control over her story rather than being physically controlled by it" ("New Hystery" 15). According to Iyunolu Osagie, "Psychic trauma [. . .] can be resisted through the oral transfer of (historical) information, through storytelling, dancing, and exorcism" (424). Caroline Rody outlines "the function of communal 'talking cure': its characters, author, and readers delve into the past, repeating painful stories to work toward the health of fuller awareness" (99). Further, the "storytelling exchange is a model for the intergenerational transmission of African-American oral culture" (103). Nancy Bate discusses how "dialogic storytelling" in *Beloved* can "heal and unify the community" (27), and Ritashona Simpson notes that the "dialogue between Beloved and Sethe is the goal of the text. It represents a kind of freedom for Sethe who is finally able to tell her story (about slavery) and find an audience in Beloved. It represents a discursive site where a community of slaves and their memories reside" (95). Finally, Nada Elia addresses how women inherit the trauma of slavery through a "history passed down orally and through the body" (1).

23. For trauma victims, "each process of recalling is changing the memory although, at the same time, this process is not an arbitrary construction but a complex process approaching the historical truth of the earlier developmental experiences" (Leuzinger-Bohleber and Pfeifer 16).

24. Mary Jane Elliott also claims that "self-liberation" comes "through communal support" (182). Emma Parker sees "the possibility of healing through access to communal narratives that construct a commemorative history of the victims of slavery" ("New Hystery" 16). Kimberly Davis articulates "the crucial importance of deep cultural memory, of keeping the past alive in order to construct a better future" (242).

25. Nicole Coonradt writes about "Amy's human need to love and be loved" (170) and how the interactions between Amy Denver and Sethe show "the possibility of mutual understanding and love" (182).

26. Daniel Siegel attributes the successful resolution of trauma to the sense of coherence in individuals that allows them to "reflect on the past, live fully in the present, and have an active sense of the self in the future" ("An Interpersonal" 52). Personal memory and communal rememory facilitate this process.

27. Siegel reports that community remembering and verbalization provide the "sense of safety and the emotional 'holding environment' of a secure attachment" similar to what happens "within a therapeutic relationship" that allows for "integrative processes to (finally) occur" ("An Interpersonal" 29).

28. Andrea O'Reilly outlines how some "adults finally acquire self-love and achieve selfhood by being remothered as adults. This remothering is achieved by way of a spiritual or psychic reconnection with a lost mother. [...] This reconnection [...] is achieved through what Morrison has termed rememory. Healing occurs when the son or daughter is able to remember the mother, mourn her loss, reconnect with her and recreate for themselves an identity as a mothered child" (*Toni Morrison* 40–41).

29. Judylyn Ryan discusses Baby Suggs's spiritual leadership as well as her role as ancestor, connecting her agency to African cosmology and claiming that her sermon confirms the "self-hatred oppression generates" (53–54). Baby Suggs allows her community to experience and embrace "the many dimensions of their full humanity" (55), with her spiritual authority "informed by an ethos of (inter) connectedness and derived from an African cosmology [...that] engendered a connectedness and commitment to cultural/spiritual kin" (60). Similarly, Carol Henderson writes that "[i]n re-membering the body one part at a time, Baby Suggs calls forth a complete being that counters the dismembered self created in chattel bondage. In this way, she creates a shared communal experience for the healing of personal pain" (158). Further, the novel points to "a reclaimed spiritual past that stands on the edge of time, healing the disfigurements of a tortured soul shaped by the vestiges of history" (162).

30. Jean Wyatt describes Denver's deafness as a "substitution of the body for language [that] expresses an identification with the trauma of her enslaved ancestors, who were likewise denied access to language and reduced to bodies" (67). Denver acts out a generationally inherited trauma.

31. Critical discussion of Beloved's identity covers a wide range of interpretation—Beloved as the returned, now living, murdered daughter of Sethe; as this daughter's ghost; or as a traumatic representation of the Middle Passage and the slave experience. Iyunolu Osagie sees Beloved as the returned daughter (429), while Jennifer Holden-Kirwan proposes that "Beloved possesses the identity of Sethe's slave mother [...] before she reaches America and gives birth to Sethe" (419). Kathleen Brogan claims that Beloved also represents how "[g]hosts [...] figure prominently wherever people must reconceive a fragmented, partially obliterated history" (164); and Petar Ramadanovic writes that this ghost re-creates trauma for the community because "the self emerges together with a trauma, that is, a ghost" (135). According to Kathleen MacArthur, "Beloved is a physical and/or

spiritual embodiment of the trauma of the Misery" (138). Lynda Koolish claims that "Beloved exists as the repository of unresolved feelings [. . . . She is] a figure of absence, loss, and powerlessness" (175–77). She "ceases to exist as a projection of other characters' interior lives, as she becomes an integrated part of each character's life" (190). For James Berger, Beloved is "a conflation of all the social, personal, and familial traumas of American race relations that continue to persist and return to this day," "a conflation of traumatic returns," "all the unresolved traumas of slavery" (198–99). Beloved also "embodies a fearful claim of the past upon the present, the past's desire to be recognized by, and even possess, the living" (Rody 104). Jean Wyatt claims that "Beloved is the real, in Lacan's terms," escaping symbolization (83).

32. J. Brooks Bouson describes their voices as "driven by collective memories of trauma and shame" (157).

33. Barbara Mathieson states that Morrison's text "affirms the regenerative power of two nurturant adult relationships: a heterosexual union and the support of the black community" (229). Both groups provide the positive imaginary mirroring of home. Michelle Phillips agrees, saying that Morrison is "attracted to love as a foundation for change because of its capacity to open the mind and the heart. [Her] goal is less didactic than it is emotional—[hers] is a desire to engender desire" (79). Further, in Morrison's Beloved "love produces the intersubjective recognition and commitment necessary for a promising future" (79). It is the "sharing of [their] stories [that] finally force[s] the characters each to contend with their history and, literally, move beyond their home and into the world" (MacArthur 102).

34. Sharon Jessee adds that "neither forgetting and repressing the past, nor the total immersion and retreat into it, will do" ("Tell me" 209). Jonathan Sabol concurs that the message of Beloved is that we need to remember as well as forget (47).

35. Jill Matus considers Beloved "the novel that demonstrates most obviously Morrison's concern to bear witness to the forgotten or erased past of African Americans" (103). Matus states that "novels can also be seen as ceremonies of proper burial, an opportunity to put painful events of the past in a place where they no longer haunt successive generations" (2). Lucille P. Fultz adds that "Morrison's fiction mirrors her search for metaphorical forms that assist African Americans in recovering their lost or diminished selves" (16). Claudine Raynaud claims that Sethe "is eaten up by [the] past, consumed by her memory, a psychological state that translates into a refusal to let Beloved leave" (50) but says that by the novel's end "[t]he characters move from a refusal to acknowledge the past to confrontation and to reconciliation with the pain made bearable through retelling" (48).

36. Holly Flint connects the exclusionary actions of the townsmen to westward expansion, in which "homesteading" was "a euphemism for settler colonialism" (585). She claims that "[b]y turning their backs on the American empire (so that they could build an empire of their own), the townsmen 'become exactly what they hate and fear.' As a group, they subscribe to a survivalist ideology that calls for a combined strategy of isolationism and violence" (599).

37. According to Holly Flint, at the novel's close "each woman is to a greater or lesser extent empowered, residing on the edge of society yet able to intervene, to communicate their love and support to their families." Further, they have shed "their racial identities" (606).

38. This town provides a subjectivity reminiscent of Frantz Fanon's description in Black Skin, White Masks of his life in the Antilles before his life in France.

39. Hesse et al. describe how "overwhelming events experienced by some patient's parents have indirectly become associated with the patient's symptomatology" (59). Generationally inherited trauma powerfully influences the community.

40. See Jenkins for an intriguing discussion of the false premise of 8-rock purity in contrast to racial tampering. She discusses the irony of the ancestors' idealization of the "creamy, sunlit skin" of the ladies they meet on their journey (Morrison, *Paradise* 110), as their light skin represents the impure blood that the 8-rocks disdain. She concludes that "the 'black' American is impure because on her own she is never ideologically black enough, never that ultimate, pure black thing that can exclude, once and for all, the feared and despised 'white' (biological or cultural) ancestor" (290–91).

41. Daniel Siegel's research reveals that "patterns of communication that have been found to be the most effective in secure attachments are those that involve reciprocal, contingent, collaborative communication" ("An Interpersonal" 44). By worshipping the previous generations, the current leaders of Ruby have failed their own children.

42. Holly Flint puts the plight of Ruby's citizens in a larger context, claiming that "[i]n the same way that postcolonial subjects around the world must constantly reinvent themselves in order to remain viable participants in an era marked by globalization and continued practices of imperialism, so too will Ruby's residents have to meet new demands and overcome old obstacles so that they can determine what new identity, what new place in the world, they wish to occupy" (608). Magali Cornier Michael describes the need for a "nonpatriarchal social structure," claiming that through the women, "the novel's gestures toward hope are all grounded in its reimagining of agency in terms of a reconceptualization of coalition and community as inter-related, emphasizing the need for constructing dynamic coalitions [. . .] that envision and enact power as power *with* rather than power *over,* and that work to ensure survival and a form of justice that embraces care and nurturing and is no longer grounded in hierarchical structures that depend on violence or the threat of violence" (*New Visions* 183).

43. Magali Cornier Michael explains how the women heal each other: "By willingly sharing and experiencing each other's painful stories, histories, and dreams with their bodies and psyches simultaneously, they provide for each other unmatched nurturing support" ("Re-Imagining" 654). Philip Page similarly describes how the templates allow the women to "see themselves, to interpret themselves, and thereby to begin to cure themselves. The templates are analogous to fictional selves, doubling the self and thereby allowing each woman to 'see in' to herself, to interpret herself, and thus to find a viable identity" ("Furrowing" 642). Carola Hilfrich claims that the "work with the templates allows the women to reinscribe their histories, while shifting attention from the historical reality of their moving bodies to the 'real life' of their erotically embodied templates" (330–31).

44. According to Joan Woodward, abuse victims feel that "they are to blame for what has been done to them and [. . .] that they are of no value" (16).

45. Pallas acts out her self-erasure: "[S]he drew her name in the dirt with her toe. Then slowly, imitating the girl's [Billie Delia's] earlier erasure with the vomit, she kicked her name away, covering it completely with red dirt" (175). For a discussion of how these women create identities with the help of Connie's gaze, see my earlier work *Subversive Voices: Eroticizing the Other in the Work of William Faulkner and Toni Morrison.*

46. Candice Jenkins argues that Consolata has a "clear self-identification with blackness in the text. Yet because of their preoccupation with biological purity, Morrison's 8-rocks seem simply unable to fit her identification into their racial schema" (287). Further, she has an "overwhelming feeling of kinship with Deacon" because of black roots in Brazil (286).

47. The women illustrate Daniel Siegel's claim that an "individual moves from being the passive victim of trauma to the active author of the ongoing story of his or her life" through "meaningful and invigorating connections with others" ("An Interpersonal" 53). Further, "[h]ealing is achieved

as overwhelming events and suboptimal developmental experiences, encoded in various forms of memory, become freed from their restrictive or chaotic patterns" (7). Connie's guidance and a home at the Convent perform this function.

CHAPTER 2

1. Justine Baille discusses Morrison's contribution to "the debates about notions of black beauty and the pathology of the black family prevalent among proponents of the Black Aesthetic and of Black Power in the late 1960s" (25). Elisabeth Mermann-Jozwiak also describes the "novel's ideological critique of discursive constructions of the body," noting that "Pecola's body is also the text upon which a racist society has written the story of *black* womanhood" (189, 191). Phyllis Klotman writes that Pecola learns "from school, from her peers, from her family and the world around her [...] that she is black, poor, and ugly, the antithesis of all that the society values" (124). Malin LaVon Walther concludes that "Pecola's self, her presence as a subject, remains unrecognized by those who have absorbed white standards of visual attractiveness" (777), and J. Brooks Bouson argues that Morrison exposes "the racial wounds and shame-humiliations suffered by black Americans in the race-conscious and race-divided American society" (45).

2. Attachment research indicates that early "[e]xperiences shape the brain connections that create the mind and enable an emerging sense of a 'self' in the world" (Siegel, "An Interpersonal" 10).

3. According to Jacob Arlow, the three theories of aggression include "Biological-instinctual theory," "Frustration theory," and "Social learning theory" (180–81). Further, aggression is "linked to the idea of danger: inner or outer danger, real or imaginary danger, conscious or unconscious danger. The various ways one learns to cope with danger modify the quality and the form of aggressive behavior" (181). Finally, "aggressive behavior in children [...] is] a form of defense against fear" (183). In "Studies of Aggression in Early Childhood," Rosalind Gould states that aggressive behavior may be seen "as *a* type of response, [...] one among other possibilities in objectively similar circumstances" (51). Her research finds that "early qualities of the child-parent interactions and the child's related inner experience of care and attachment have a singular catalytic influence on modes and frequency of recourse to aggressive feelings or action" (51). Daniel S. Jaffe concludes that "aggression in both the constructive and destructive aspects would not be considered a 'primal' instinct in the sense of a class of functions, but an instinct that is inevitable, innate, and constantly operative. As a drive, it is subject to modification and variability with learning experiences, but it is not extinguishable. In terms of behavior, its variable manifestations are subject to scaling. That is, a wide range of behavior [...] becomes genetically fixed by natural selection" (92).

4. Naomi Rokotnitz differentiates Claudia's development from Pecola's by saying that Claudia "possesses a powerful drive to self-determination" that is "fed by her receptiveness to external stimuli, a receptiveness that enables her to learn from her environment" (389). Using cognitive-scaffolding theory, Rokotnitz explains that "Pecola is disabled, mentally, physically, and socially, by being entirely cut off from all forms of human interaction, while Claudia is exposed to a wide variety of inputs that enable her to expand and develop her personal capabilities: to construct complex cognitive scaffolding" (390).

5. Katherine McKittrick writes that "[c]onsumerism bolsters and upholds the meaning of nation for the girls in the text—it is something they can purchase, consume, and put in their homes and bodies" (132).

6. Laurie Vickroy describes how "Morrison depicts an imposing white culture whose values are enforced through a variety of means" and "how the traumatic experience of social powerlessness and devalued racial identity prevents the African American community from joining together and truthfully evaluating the similarity of their circumstances, much less finding ways to oppose dominant forces" (92–93). Debra Werrlein concurs, writing that "self-abstraction offers nothing more than a false promise to black Americans" (68).

7. Christopher Douglas claims that "funk" has been lost by white people: "The funk is embodied and racialized through the various phenotypic differences that mark the social construction of race and that threaten to overwhelm the whitening process" (141). For blacks, "funk" points to the loss of culture with integration and the need for separatism and racial authenticity. Douglas suggests that the Black Arts/Aesthetic's project is to work on presence rather than absence (161). He concludes that Morrison's text exemplifies how social-science ideas invade literature.

8. In their study of children's play with dolls, Kenneth and Mamie Clark found that "a third of the children effectively 'misidentified' themselves as white when demonstrating a marked preference for the white doll" (Marriott 424). Their findings explain the attachment of Claudia's elders to the white doll.

9. For a more complete discussion of the psychic mechanism of eroticization in Morrison's novels, see my *Subversive Voices*.

10. Pecola's body illustrates how "the abusive and/or neglecting caregiver [...] induces traumatic states of enduring negative affect in the child" (Schore 124).

11. Doyle further states that Morrison "tracks the chain reactions that follow from this seizure, the force of its digressionary currents branching through bodies over time and into the future. She reveals the dangerous mingling of race, sex, and hatred as they move within these historical currents, especially as they shape Cholly's relations with the women in his family" (203).

12. Susan Mayberry claims that "Morrison deliberately places her black male characters into situations where their behavior becomes virtually unredeemable, yet she simultaneously urges us to forgive them" (*Can't I Love* 15). Because both Cholly and Pecola have been "[d]eprived of a self-constituting interior space, [...] they can occupy no place" (Doyle 205).

13. According to Doyle, "The impulses of reaching, touching, and holding each other that arise within the open of our-bodies-in-the-world merge here with the pressured need to invade, collapse, and violate" (205).

14. Ruth Rosenberg states that the "socialization patterns thoughtlessly transmitted from mother to daughter, from Pauline Breedlove to Pecola, are fatal to that child's self-esteem" (440), and Patrice Cormier-Hamilton writes, "Not only is Pauline's awful sense of self-worth passed on to her child, her impossible dream of blond blue-eyed beauty is passed on as well" (120). Laurie Vickroy finds that both Cholly and Pauline experienced trauma by being "physically or emotionally abandoned by their families [...]. Traumatized children themselves, they continue the trauma by denying their own weakness in their abuse of parental power" (93).

15. Judith Herman finds that traumatized and abused children "must find a way to preserve a sense of trust in people who are untrustworthy, safety in a situation that is unsafe, control in a situation that is terrifyingly unpredictable" (96). Pecola cannot do this; as Agnes Suranyi claims, Morrison illustrates in *The Bluest Eye* "that for a child the language needed to describe the traumatic effect of violence and abuse is not available" (17).

16. Maureen Peal's light skin allows her to act white. She and the other children aggressively taunt Pecola about her blackness with their chant of "Black e mo" (65).

17. *Beloved* chronicles Baby Suggs's desperate search for her children, who were sold to various owners, when she receives her freedom. Other characters share a similar plight of never knowing where family members ended up.

18. According to Andrew Eisen and Charles Schaefer, "[T]he bulk of the literature supports maternal responsiveness as a key determinant of secure attachment relationships" (19). Patrice Cormier-Hamilton finds that "Claudia has been equipped with the shield of self-love to combat negative influences from black and white society—Pecola has not" (121). Further, Laurie Vickroy states that through the love of her parents, Claudia "possesses the strength to have her own desires" (104).

19. Laura Doyle explains, "Morrison powerfully traces the communal and corporeal effects of sexual violation for both men and women; and at the same time, in the very act of story-telling, she reengages a resistant, communal, and chiasmatic intercorporeality" (184).

20. In *The Bluest Eye,* the three whores survive through their ability to laugh.

21. Eva adopts three orphans and names all three Dewey. They become interchangeable cast-offs, merging to form one personality. Like Paul D and his brothers in *Beloved,* they function like blacks in white culture, as interchangeable, unmanageable bodies. The Deweys respond by becoming "inseparable, loving nothing and no one but themselves" (38). They "spoke with one voice" (39), would never grow up, and "remained boys in mind" (84). The Deweys exemplify the struggling orphaned black culture that we shall see in the discussion of *Jazz* and *Tar Baby.* Susan Mayberry suggests that the Deweys represent "the value of community to insure human survival. Individually each Dewey is a lost boy; collectively as the deweys or Lost Boys, they find an identity" ("Something" 525).

22. Maia Boswell, in her Lacanian study of *Sula,* describes how black characters "have found themselves shut out from the doors labeled 'Ladies' and 'Gentlemen'; many have occupied spaces, if not outside of, at least on the margins of the official signifying system" (119). For a discussion of Morrison's framing of this novel, see Burrows 114–28.

23. According to Daniel Siegel, "Trauma during the early years may have lasting effects on deep brain structures responsible for such processes as the response to stress, the integration of information, and the encoding of memory. [. . .] States of fear, anger, or shame can then reemerge as a characteristic trait of the individual's responses" ("An Interpersonal" 9).

24. Jane Bakerman claims that Helene's "rigid attitude about sex" causes her to fail Nel (549).

25. Nel tolerates her mother's deference to white culture much as Claudia tolerates the "hateful bath" in *The Bluest Eye* (22).

26. According to Seshadri-Crooks, "The signifier that constitutes the subject's body emerges from the Other as the expression of recognition or ratification of the mirror image, thereby enabling the image to be introjected. The imaginary body has a symbolic status" (34).

27. Southern white violence to blacks continues in cultural patterns that once included lynching. Chuck Jackson examines the legacy of lynching, concluding that "Shadrack, Plum, and the two soldiers on the train to New Orleans have much to say about black men's struggle to keep from passing out of the national public sphere" and that "the final image of African-American shop workers handling money and with keys around their necks suggests that the lynching metaphor continues into the postmodern moment" (388).

28. In *Jazz,* True Belle abandons Rose Dear and her sister for eighteen years, much longer than Eva's eighteen months. However, both abandonments result in trauma for the children left behind. Felice also feels abandoned by her parents, who leave her with her grandmother while they work far from home to financially support the family.

29. Siegel writes that "the early years—when the basic circuits of the brain are becoming established that mediate such processes as emotional and behavioral regulation, interpersonal relatedness, language and memory—are the most crucial for the individual to receive the experience that enables proper development to occur" ("An Interpersonal" 12).

30. The latest research on the biological roots of trauma suggests that if "the caregiver does not participate in reparative functions that reduce stress and reestablish psychobiological equilibrium, the limbic connections that are in the process of developing are exposed to a toxic chemistry that negatively impacts a developing brain" (Schore 132). Further, "due to poor orbitofrontal organization, the achievement of emotional control, including aggression control, is precluded in these infants" (134). Post-traumatic stress disorder may compound earlier infant trauma.

31. According to Dayle B. DeLancey, "motherlove" can be "economically and mentally lethal" (15). She claims that the "struggle for survival has given Eva's love for her children a hard edge which has nearly destroyed her relationship with them" (17). Michele Pessoni states that "Eva's act is one of mercy and strength, albeit a terrifying strength. Unable to accept him back into her own womb and rebirth him, Eva sends Plum instead to a preferable place" (445).

32. The ultimate test of Eva's love for Hannah occurs when Hannah catches fire while burning trash and Eva jumps out the window in an attempt to save her.

33. When a caregiver "provides no interactive repair," writes Allan Schore, "the infant's intense negative states last for long periods of time" (124).

34. In her 1976 interview with Robert Stepto, Morrison described Hannah as "slack. She had no concept of love or possession. [...] Her relationship to her daughter is almost one of uninterest" (16).

35. According to Siegel, for "those with suboptimal attachment experiences, restrictive adaptations may have been required for survival and leaving them behind may feel overwhelming and dangerous. With the courage to connect and create a new pathway, patients often become conscious of their sense of belonging to a 'self' that is defined as connected to *community*" ("An Interpersonal" 7). Maggie Galehouse claims that Nel and Sula turn to "peer-parenting in the absence of balanced parenting and local role models" (351). She adds that Sula "believes in self-nurture as an end in and of itself, whereas for Eva, Nel, and the other women in town, mothering, care-taking and running a household are non-negotiable women's work" (353–54).

36. Agnes Suranyi claims that a "hallmark of Morrison's fiction is death-watch: the characters—as willing or enforced spectators—often witness violent (natural or unnatural) deaths," and she connects this witnessing to the "inexorable white gaze" (23).

37. Attachment to parental figures regulates aggression and empathy, which Sula lacks (Schore 112).

38. The acts of aggression toward the self may represent cultural self-hatred or a turning against the self. Severing a body part protects both Sula and Eva from further harm.

39. According to Morrison, "[O]ne terrible thing [. . .] was to put her grandmother in an old folks' home, which was outrageous, you know. You take care of people!" (Stepto 16).

40. Jude's desertion of Nel represents his circumscribed place in white culture. When he marries Nel, he is a waiter at the Hotel Medallion, but he would prefer to work on the road crew. However, the white bosses bar Jude and other blacks in his community from this work. In response to this lack of agency—as black and male in a white world—Jude marries Nel so as to be the initiator in their relationship. Jude needs to love and shelter Nel to be whole: "Without that someone he was a waiter hanging around a kitchen like a woman. With her he was head of a household pinned to an unsatisfactory job out of necessity" (83). Nel gives his life meaning to counter the trauma of being a

black man in white culture. Jude falls victim to the white gaze and complains of his life, "White man running it—nothing good" (102). He is attracted to Sula because of the positive gaze she gives back to him, the same reason that he was initially attracted to Nel.

41. Nel's own trauma on the train adds to her absorption of Helene's early painful experiences. Victoria Burrows discusses Nel's articulation of trauma and her ability to finally mourn the loss of Sula.

42. Children need proper attachment for both physical survival and psychological security (J. Woodward 8). Thus, children with "'insecure attachments' [...] can feel themselves deeply alienated from the rest of society. Such feelings make them highly vulnerable to further abuse, inflicted either by themselves, or by others" (16).

43. In *The Bluest Eye*, Pecola's need for such a friend is so great that she imagines one and splits from reality.

44. As Susan Mayberry writes about Shadrack's parallel function, "Like Sula, who is buried as a witch, Shadrack's gift to the Community is to provide a scapegoat for their destructive fear and lead them to freedom from it" ("Something" 531).

45. Theodore Mason Jr. claims that *Song of Solomon* "insists on the significance of shared history communicated by shared stories, shared traditions, and shared experience" (577). Catherine Carr Lee explains that the novel "addresses the need for the contemporary African American psyche to embrace community, the community that comes from a shared culture and history" (120). She further sees that Milkman must connect to "the community of his ancestors, and that requires, literally, the discovery of their names" (111). As Dolan Hubbard states, "To not own your name is tantamount to not owning your history" (301).

46. Pilate's "Aunt Jemima Act" in *Song of Solomon* resembles Helene's actions on the train in *Sula*. Both women act to protect their children; nonetheless, the children experience the trauma of discrimination.

47. Michael Rothberg claims that "the novel suggests that conspiratorial politics, which [take] their impetus from traumas rendered to the black community, end by repeating those traumas in ever more ghastly scenarios of acting out. The task that the novel sets itself might then be seen as the fashioning of a non-paranoid response to trauma that nevertheless takes its inspiration from the same social energies present in the Seven Days" (507). Likewise, Dana Medoro remarks that the "text makes it increasingly clear, though, that the Seven Days fundamentally resembles or mirrors the Klan [. . .]. Unlike X, Guitar has no vision of justice beyond vengeance, no sense of a system beyond a balanced coffin" (7).

48. Joan Woodward cites the research of John Bowlby to explain "the part that *unwilling* separation and loss of attachment plays in creating our deepest emotional distress and feelings of anger and violence" (15). Some of these children become "very aggressive; having felt themselves uncared for they will, in turn, care for no one" (15). However, Guitar claims that his violent activity with the Seven Days stems from love: "What I'm doing ain't about hating white people. It's about loving us. About loving you. My whole life is love" (Morrison, *Song of Solomon* 159).

49. Frantz Fanon describes this identification in which blacks adopt "a white man's attitude" (147), saying that "intellectually, the Antillean conducts himself like a white man" (148).

50. Brenda Boudreau explains that identity is "historically mediated" and says that Milkman comes "to understand his own identity within a larger 'American' history that includes his slave grandfather and the legacy that racism has left his family" (49–50).

51. Macon's numbness resembles Sula's when she watches her mother's body twitching as she burns to death.

52. Macon's comment here echoes Sethe's thoughts about Sweet Home and the intrusive nature of trauma.

53. Macon's experience illustrates Kai Erikson's research on trauma: "the hardest earned and most fragile accomplishment of childhood, basic trust, can be damaged beyond repair by trauma" (197).

54. Rolland Murray describes the irony of Macon Dead I's situation: he views "the accumulation of individual land ownership rather than political and legal enfranchisement as a central category in black liberation" (125), yet it is his "disenfranchisement [that] leaves him as vulnerable to white aggression as the most dispossessed black citizen" (126).

55. Jane Bakerman attributes Pilate's failure to the fact that she "does not really understand her father's messages at all: she cannot because she does not know her family history. The self-definition she builds, the world view she constructs based upon his advice keeps her sane and active, but it further isolates her, cuts her off from her community" (556).

56. The accidental death of the stranger in the cave and its aftermath are reminiscent of the accidental death of Chicken Little and its aftermath in *Sula*.

57. Gerry Brenner says that Pilate's "heroism resides in her self-acceptance and self-content, the heroism of performing routine responsibilities without fretting about whether she is 'macon' something of her life" (123). However, Gary Storhoff claims that "Pilate can reproduce her original family no more successfully than can Macon. Her family exposes her imbalanced character just as Macon's family reflects his" (295–96). Finally, Dolan Hubbard describes how Milkman sifts "between memory (Pilate) and forgetting (Macon)" (289) and "gains an appreciation for his culture as well as a grounding in the soil that produced the blues, spirituals, and folklore" (291).

58. Daniel Siegel's research provides hope for traumatized people. Pilate exemplifies his findings that "autobiographical narratives" can "'make sense' of past experiences" and can have an "impact on present functioning as well as allowing the mind to create a sense of hope for the future" ("An Interpersonal" 52).

59. According to Eleanor Branch, "Ruth's smallness is not a personal appraisal of stature [. . .] but a tragic assessment of self-worth that is subsequently reinforced by an oppressive marriage, empty social obligations and a marked isolation from meaningful relationships" (58).

60. Lena's realization about her circumscribed position resembles that of Nel and Sula.

61. Jane Bakerman writes that for "both Hagar and Corinthians, life *has* no worth without the men they love; they have no identity save the reflection of themselves in the eyes of those men" (563). She adds that the "overwhelming love of [Hagar's] immediate family will not be enough" (557).

62. Daniel Siegel lists what he calls the "'C's' of psychotherapy," including "connection, compassion, contingency, coherence, continuity, clarity, co-construction, complexity, consciousness, creativity, and community" ("An Interpersonal" 6). Interpersonal relationships, families, and nurturing communities can provide a healing environment.

63. Sula also struggles with the traumatic knowledge that her mother loves her but does not like her.

64. Before his journey, Milkman dreams that he stands by and watches his mother being choked by tulips in the garden, a scene reminiscent of the one in which Sula and Nel stand by and watch Chicken Little disappear, as well as the one in which Sula watches her mother burn. By the end of his search, Milkman has learned that responsible action is the proper response.

65. Marilyn Sanders Mobley comments that *Song of Solomon* suggests "that a viable sense of African American identity comes from responding to alternative constructions of self and community other than those received from mainstream American culture" ("Call and Response" 42–43). She further describes how, for Morrison, "male individuation [. . .] requires the recognition of one's inscription into patriarchal discourse as well as one's connection to the female voices that that discourse represses in our culture. Jessica Benjamin refers to this form of mutual recognition as intersubjectivity, a recognition of other speaking subjects as both like and different from oneself" (55).

CHAPTER 3

1. Nina Mikkelsen states that in "Morrison's fiction, characters must at times find a personal, familial, or communal voice to respond to visions that appear to be choosing, or finding, them, and they can only find such a voice if they revisit, through rememories, historical, legendary, or imaginative moments in time, no matter how [. . .] frightening nor painful" (99). See my discussion of rememory in chapter 1.

2. Black migrations north, beginning in the 1870s, peaked between 1910 and 1930; "by 1914 the largest exodus began. Masses of Negroes began to move to the Northern industrial centers such as Chicago, Detroit, New York" (L. Jones 95).

3. J. Brooks Bouson asserts that "Morrison lays stress on the psychic damage caused not only by family trauma—in particular, maternal abandonment or rejection—but also by inter- and intraracial shaming and violence" (167) and that "the search for family and cultural roots involves the recovery of painful and shaming memories of racial domination and white supremacist terrorism" (170). The damage by the larger culture to self-esteem and ego development remains. Anne-Marie Paquet-Deyris elaborates: "Traces of loss resurface and inscribe themselves in the characters' lives and bodies. The organic traces left by history on someone's skin and the stories enslaved and broken bodies tell form a major topos in Morrison's novels" (225). Karin Luisa Badt concludes that this history creates characters that "lack a true sense of centeredness—a core self—and they are drawn to the body of the (m)other in order to restore the integrity of their own," claiming that Morrison's novels have a political "project to repair the black mother—to restore her dignity and value in the 'hostile white environment'" (568, 569).

4. Andrea O'Reilly examines how "[c]hildren who are orphaned, abandoned, or denied nurturant mothering are psychologically wounded as adults. Never having been loved by their mothers, the unmothered children never learn how to love themselves. [. . . *Jazz*] tells the story of unmothered children who never take this journey from mother-love to self-love, and thus never come to know their own selves" ("In Search" 367–68). Michael Nowlin concurs that "the lost maternal imago [. . .] drives virtually all of the characters in *Jazz*" (166).

5. The development in music from blues to jazz parallels the shift from individual pain to social expression and action. "The blues is formed out of the same social and musical fabric that the spiritual issued from, but with blues the social emphasis becomes more personal" (L. Jones 63). Further, the blues "was the most plaintive and melancholy music imaginable" (78). As jazz develops out of the blues, it "becomes synonymous with spontaneous innovation and extemporaneous musical comment, as collective improvisation interrogates swing's practice of solo improvisation" (Jimoh 5).

6. Lucille P. Fultz explains that "the African American usable past is situated in 'rememory'—a remembrance fraught with abhorrent images at times too painful and frightening to face, at other

times poignant and memorable" (75). These "memories are freighted with the trauma of what it means to be black and female in America" (76). Marc Conner concludes, "*This* is the desire of Violet, and of Joe, and of Dorcas: that reuniting with the lost parent will heal their wounds and make them whole" ("Wild Women" 349). He goes on to state that the "method of reconciliation, then, is the method of memory, or what Morrison calls in *Beloved* 'rememory,' the process of recalling something and thereby making it live once more. [. . . Recollection] of the ancestor [. . .] is the key to their redemption. [. . .] The final reconciliation and regeneration offered by *Jazz* reaches toward a broad community" (361–63).

7. Much has been written about the elusive and indeterminate narrator. Roberta Rubenstein describes how "the narrating voice of *Jazz* paradoxically both observes (as if from inside) and invents (as if from outside) the 'action' of the narrative: straddling modernist and postmodernist modes, it imagines/records what it purports to 'know' or overhear, even as it authorizes its relation to the narrative to which it gives voice" (156). Nowlin calls the narrator "another orphan in search of a mother" (167), while Martha J. Cutter discusses the ambiguity of the narrator. For a summary of the debate about the narrator, see Conner, "Wild Women," where Conner concludes that the "narrator is not individual but rather is communal," like a Greek chorus (360). Morrison claimed in a 1995 interview that the narrator's voice is "one of assumed knowledge, the voice that says 'I know everything.' [. . .] Because the voice has to actually imagine the story it's telling[, . . .] the story [. . .] turns out to be entirely different from what it predicted because the characters will be evolving [. . . like] a jazz performance" (Carabi, "Toni Morrison" 41–42).

8. Jill Matus notes that "characters in this novel repeat the traumatic aspects of their past lives in relation to a current and tragic situation" (122).

9. According to Susan Mayberry, in *Jazz* "African Americans make love, music, or war with one another to counteract being controlled by some outside thing" (*Can't I Love* 215).

10. Rubenstein defines "the imagery of dismemberment as a trope for the incalculable damages inflicted on African-Americans by slavery and its devastating aftermath; remembering—'re-membering' —is understood as a compensatory act that might begin to heal the grievous personal and cultural dismemberments of that history" (158). Rubenstein states that the text describes a type of "*mourning*, whether for the 'phantom limb,' the phantom parent, or the phantom beloved: mourning for lost possibilities, lost selves" (159).

11. In a 1995 interview, Morrison suggested that the character Wild could be Beloved, saying that time frame and geography would enable the pregnant Beloved to turn up and give birth at the same time and place as Wild (Carabi, "Interview" 42). Whoever Wild is and whatever the cause of her wildness remain ambiguous. If she is the embodiment of slavery, perhaps she cannot live freely in white culture. In *Beloved*, Sethe comments that learning how to live once freed is problematic. Did Wild reject her baby because it was the result of a rape? Did she, like Sethe's mother, throw away all of the babies not fathered by her loved one? Although we do not have enough information to decipher the source and precise nature of Wild's trauma, her baby most likely inherits its residue. Joe, Wild's baby or not, lives a life controlled by the abandonment of his mother, as do countless others in similar circumstances. Philip M. Weinstein claims that "Wild seems to figure forth the priceless African mother that Morrison's twentieth-century orphans have lost, the Mama they therefore half remember, half invent in their damaged and indestructible lives" (155). Nowlin asserts that Wild represents "the trauma of a division into racially and sexually marked subjectivity" (168).

12. O'Reilly explains, "Only those daughters who have received maternal love as daughters are capable of giving maternal love when they become mothers. Rose Dear's despair and later death

prevent her from giving maternal love and being a mother to and for her daughter. [. . .] Not having been a daughter, Violet is unable to become a mother" ("In Search" 370).

13. Daniel Siegel writes that "[p]arental behavior that produces disorganization within the child's mind thus may create not only an impairment in functioning in the moment, but, if repeated, a tendency to dis-integrate in the future" ("An Interpersonal" 33). Allan Schore's research might explain Rose Dear's early dissociation when she ignores the eviction from her home and her later suicide; he finds that "severe traumatic attachments result in [. . .] a fundamental inability to regulate emotional states under stress" (108).

14. O'Reilly describes how Violet can grow after identifying with her mother's despair. She explains that her hairdressing and tending of parrots exemplify Violet's "attempts to find her lost self through mothering. [. . .] Through such projections, the adult Violet mothers the child Violet. She mothers herself. Through her mothering, Violet can be both the mother she lost and the daughter she once was" ("In Search" 370).

15. According to O'Reilly, "Joe does not seem ever to have had an original self because at birth he was abandoned by his mother" ("In Search" 375). Like Jadine, Son, Margaret, and Valerian in *Tar Baby*, Joe, Violet, Wild, and Rose Dear act out trauma in their own particular ways.

16. Weinstein elaborates the process: "Orphans meeting though thirty-five years apart, he mothers this girl, fathers her, loves her as the Violet he has lost, as the woman for whom Violet was the substitute. The roles blend into each other, all of them related under the sign of loss represented by the missing Mama" (155).

17. Grieving is a necessary part of the articulation of trauma. O'Reilly claims that "[w]ith the death of Dorcas, Joe is, at last, able to grieve the loss of his mother and move beyond the grief toward forgiveness and acceptance" ("In Search" 376). Philip Page asserts that Joe "has to work through his grief for his missing mother, has to renegotiate his own past" (*Dangerous* 162).

18. Joe echoes Cholly's comment in *The Bluest Eye* when Cholly realizes that "having never watched any parent raise himself, he could not even comprehend what such a relationship should be" (160). Feeling inadequate as a parent and a breadwinner, he thinks, "How dare she love him? Hadn't she any sense at all? What was he supposed to do about that? Return it? How?" (161). Not knowing how to love, Cholly responds with violence.

19. Acton and the woman in whose bed Dorcas dies talk about the "blood. What a mess it made" (210). Their concern about the condition of the mattress and sheets rather than about Dorcas's physical state parallels Golden Gray's worry about Wild's blood on his clothes.

20. Jadine experiences a parallel loss of subjectivity when she confronts the tar-black woman in the yellow dress.

21. Alice and Violet react aggressively toward the women and not their husbands, much as Cholly aims his hatred at Darlene rather than the hunters.

22. According to Elliott Rudwick, "[B]y far the most serious [race riot] was the violence in East St. Louis, Illinois, on July 2, 1917, when nine whites and about thirty-nine Negroes were killed" (4). In that riot, fires "destroyed over two hundred houses [. . .]. While hosemen were trying to extinguish one blaze, mobs were starting others" (48–49). Just as Ondine and Sydney take in Jadine, Alice tries to mother Dorcas. Both girls need to learn how to be a daughter, attached to a mother figure, before they can grow up enough to take care of themselves and their aging caregivers.

23. Jean Wyatt describes the process of idealization as follows: "The tell-tale mark of idealization —and of the imaginary identification that necessarily accompanies it—is the perception of the

other as a seamless whole, self-complete and self-possessed" (88). Dorcas seeks a Lacanian gaze that will make her whole rather than strip her of her unique subjectivity.

24. Like Sethe in *Beloved* and Jadine in *Tar Baby*, Violet and Felice must learn how to be their own "best thing."

25. The restorative relationships here illustrate Siegel's research on the healing ability of experience at any age. His neurobiological research explains that "experience leads to neural firing that can activate genes that then lead to the production of proteins that enable the formation of new synaptic connections" ("Attachment" 29–30). These neural firings enable empathetic attachments and personal connections.

26. Emma Parker writes that at the novel's close "Joe and Violet have regained a sense of the importance of black cultural values—community, sharing, support—as opposed to the values upon which capitalism thrives—individualism, competition, alienation—and that these values have become the basis of their renewed relationship" ("Apple Pie" 637–38).

27. For discussions of the Tar Baby story and its forms in Morrison's novel, see Werner; and Paquet.

28. In her essay "Unspeakable Things Unspoken" Morrison comments that she changed the opening line from "He thought he was safe" to "He believed he was safe" to show the precariousness of Son's situation: "'thought' did not contain the doubt I wanted to plant in the reader's mind about whether or not he really was—safe" (29–30). Craig Werner discusses how myths emerge to provide a false sense of safety, and John N. Duvall considers how women perceive a false sense of safety from men. Fultz claims that Jadine's return to Paris provides a "safety" that is "delusional" (41), while Ann Rayson notes that Jadine looks for a safe environment when she "determines to depend only on herself" (94).

29. Several critics describe Valerian as representing destructive white values and white culture. According to Page, he represents "control," "hierarchy," and "authority," and his "household resembles a stereotypical antebellum plantation" (*Dangerous* 120, 112). Evelyn Hawthorne writes that his "disruptive presence [...] breeds social problems" and that his "treatment of the land is exploitative and wasteful" (102). Valerian comes to represent the white patron (Paquet), "the highest authority in his world" (Lepow 368). Malin Pereira explains the need to combat this white control and says that "[r]ejecting that internalization of the (white) outside gaze was part of the project of the Black Arts Movement" (73).

30. Hawthorne says of Sydney and Ondine: "Like slaves interred with dead masters, the two servants must keep Valerian company to the end" (102). Fultz writes that they represent the "intersection of race and need—the elder servant's dependence on his master for employment, despite his frailty, and the old master's reliance on his servant to care for him, despite his economic wealth" (44–45). Yet in Rayson's view, "Sydney and Ondine, the black bourgeoisie in the novel, may finally have the last word as they become masters of their master Valerian, a helpless dependent at the end" (94).

31. Weinstein notes that "Morrison shows that forsaken children who grow up as 'absent' adults become parents who 'absent' their own offspring" (24).

32. Margaret's telling the history in small pieces echoes Sethe's telling Paul D about killing Beloved.

33. Matus claims that "Morrison is more interested in Michael's trauma as a way of exposing power relations in the Street household—and in the larger culture—than she is in probing the nature of childhood trauma itself" (86).

34. Judith Herman explains that children "develop pathological attachments to those who abuse and neglect them. [. . .] Unable to develop an inner sense of safety, the abused child remains more dependent than other children on external sources of comfort and solace" (98–107).

35. This all-black town parallels Ruby in *Paradise*, created to protect black subjectivity outside of the white gaze.

36. Many have written about the conflicting values at work in *Tar Baby*. Bouson describes how "Morrison points to the cultural ailment that comes out of the deep legacy of racial shame and the color-caste hierarchy" (105), causing Son and Therese to "become sites of racial shame and rage in the text" (107). Hawthorne claims that "Morrison is deeply concerned about contemporary black culture, which she feels has replicated all the faulty values of the dominant Western culture and disregarded what it had that was truly valuable" (103). Duvall describes this tension when he categorizes Jadine's subjectivity as "split between a desire to assimilate to the values of the white middle class and the voices that urge them to acknowledge a black racial identity" ("Descent" 325). According to Eleanor Traylor, Jadine, "disconnected from the life potential of her origins, has lost the crucial is-ness of her tribe" (145). Page depicts her choices "as mutually exclusive" between "white materialism and her maternal and racial instincts" (*Dangerous* 116). Rayson raises the question, "How long can the woman in yellow maintain the authenticity that Morrison imbues her with? As a colonial refugee in Paris, she has already lost her authenticity or traded it in for an even more powerful exoticism" (100). See also Paquet; and Werner.

37. The use of the word *baby* here echoes its use in *Beloved* and *Paradise* to move both Denver and Seneca to join a community.

38. Whether Son succeeds or fails has been given much consideration. Terry Otten concludes that "[n]either Jadine nor Son achieves a full victory in defeat" (78), and Page concurs that "Son's 'quest' thus becomes unheroic and passive, in some ways a retreat comparable to Jadine's two retreats" (*Dangerous* 129). Hawthorne points out that despite the notion that Son "can be led by ancestral wisdom (of the blind Therese) to make a beginning" (104), the "ending is problematic" (105). However, Paquet finds that "Son [. . .] may be running blind, but Brer Rabbit is a survivor and he is on home turf in the briar patch that is Isle de Chevaliers" (513).

39. Pereira explains that "Jadine represents the cultural costs to the African American community of blacks who identify with white culture to the extent that they reject their own. Jadine is not absorbed only by white culture's definition of beauty, she fully identifies with European cultural values about art, nature, family, and money" (75). In psychological terms, "the ideal ego is always on the lookout for a visual form that it can idealize and incorporate. [. . .] The woman in yellow reincarnates the gestalt unity perceived in the mirror" (Wyatt 96). However, "[h]er idealization of the woman in yellow is unstable and fraught with conflict; to sustain the idealizing identification, she would have to give up the material advantages gained by her long identification with the specularized model of herself as (white-defined) beauty" (111). Malin LaVon Walther concludes that "Morrison removes black beauty from the specular system" (786) and that this "redefined beauty [. . .] is available to everyone: useful, real, and embodying a self not to be objectified, represented, or appropriated" (789).

40. In *Jazz*, Golden Gray's father tells his son that since he can "pass," he has to consciously and consistently choose to be black.

41. Jadine illustrates how "people relive the event as though it were continually recurring in the present. [. . .] Adults as well as children often feel impelled to re-create the moment of terror, either in literal or disguised form" (Herman 37–39).

42. Jadine, along with Margaret, Valerian, Michael, and Son, indicates that the "need for feeling protected by attachment figures and for using them as secure bases for explorations is particularly intense during early development." Erratic behavior, the inability to feel secure, lack of confidence, and impulse control are "other basic functions regulated directly or indirectly through attachment relationships" (Cortina and Liotti 3). Morrison's characters exhibit a variety of attachment behaviors.

43. Whether Jadine succeeds or fails in the novel has been the subject of much discussion. Duvall suggests that "[i]t is precisely this recognition of her lack that suggests it may be possible for Jadine to forge a new identity as she returns to Paris" and that "the novel implies that, despite her pain, Jadine will be able to retain that which has been nurturing in her relationship with Son" ("Descent" 341, 346). Lauren Lepow states that "she has fully accepted her responsibility to mother herself" and "must be alone in her act of self-redemption" (375, 376). On the other hand, Fultz holds that "a black woman inadequately grounded in black culture or totally immersed in Western culture may not necessarily live securely in either" (42); Hawthorne describes Jadine as "an orphan from the values of womanhood possessed by the African woman in the grocery store" (104); Wyatt claims that "Jadine's revised self-image is culturally alienated, cut off from the African-American tradition of the tar woman who holds people together" (101); Page observes that "she does not realize the need for community, for telling one's story, for listening to others, for continual reconstitution of the past and the self" (*Dangerous* 127); and Rayson concludes that Jadine "does not have her 'ancient properties,' but she does survive on her own terms, still an orphan rejecting the magic breasts of Therese" (97). Mayberry writes that both Jadine and Son "must sacrifice their dream of past or future safety to gain their present freedom. [...] Each must leave off the safety of the other to become the safety for which the other longs" (*Can't I Love* 148).

CHAPTER 4

1. At the end of the novel, Heed is severely injured, immobilized, with Christine ministering to her needs and injuries. When Romen arrives, one of them is not breathing. I assume that it is Christine who survives and is strong enough to ride with Romen and lock Junior in L's room. I interpret the text as suggesting that Heed is dead and that Christine talks to her spirit.

2. Despite her repression, May's fears and insecurities resurface, especially as triggered by bodily sensations. May's early loss of her mother mirrors the weak mother attachments of Heed, Christine, and Junior, illustrating how "[d]eficiencies in the early sensory stimulation—as for example in the early interactions with a depressive mother—therefore have a detrimental effect on development" (Leuzinger-Bohleber and Pfeifer 23).

3. Junior's responses reflect Judith Herman's finding that "[t]raumatic events produce profound and lasting changes in physiological arousal, emotion, cognition, and memory" (34).

4. The text echoes Joe's wish in *Jazz* for his parents to "pick me out. From all of you all, they got to pick me" (124). Heed receives her subjectivity through the special attention paid to her by Cosey, special attention that her own family did not supply.

5. Andrew Eisen and Charles Schaefer define a key feature of separation anxiety disorder as "unrealistic and excessive anxiety upon separation or anticipation of separation from major attachment figures" (4).

6. According to Mar Gallego, the decay of Cosey's Hotel and Resort "epitomizes the sense of loss that runs throughout the whole novel and effectively questions the actual 'gains' of the Civil

Rights movement. Reflecting on the ambiguous legacy of the movement, Morrison emphasizes once more the manifold ways in which the past determines the present and future of the black community, and how important it is to retell African American history from their own vantage point" (93).

7. Gallego discusses the need to "nurture the 'right' kind of love, especially an untarnished friendship like Heed and Christine's, which can in turn pave the way for a hopeful future in community" (99).

8. Herman explains that recognition and restitution "are necessary to rebuild the survivor's sense of order and justice" (70). Further, the "survivor needs to mourn for the loss of her moral integrity and to find her own way to atone for what cannot be undone" (192–93).

9. L succeeds in protecting the girls here as Cholly and Pauline do not in *The Bluest Eye*, where they end up "Outdoors," where "there is no place to go. [. . .] outdoors bred [. . .] a hunger for property, for ownership" (17–18). The battle over Cosey's will represents the need for armor against "Outdoors."

10. Their memories of L reflect Mauricio Cortina and Giovanni Liotti's finding that "[d]istress signals mobilize attachment behaviors that reestablish proximity to attachment figures" (3).

11. A similar smell permeates Milkman's encounter with Circe in *Song of Solomon*.

12. In her discussion of Morrison's work, Anissa Wardi writes that "Morrison examines love's work, work that reviews, recovers, and heals" (215). Gallego concludes that Cosey never properly fulfilled his roles as father and husband, and "he represents the far-reaching effects of African Americans' adoption of a dominant value system that systematically calls into question the very foundations of the black family and community" (99).

CHAPTER 5

1. Here, the non-maltreating parent tries to protect the child, but the child is unaware of that love and care.

2. In *Beloved*, Sethe's parallel moment of realization of self as object comes when she hears Schoolteacher instructing his nephews to "put her human characteristics on the left; her animal ones on the right" (193).

3. This description echoes the one of Amy Denver and Sethe's parting on the riverbank: "They never expected to see each other again in this world and at the moment couldn't care less. But there on a summer night surrounded by bluefern they did something together appropriately and well. [. . .] two throw-away people, two lawless outlaws" (84).

4. In *Beloved*, Sethe expresses a similar sense of accomplishment: "I did it. I got us all out. Without Halle too. Up till then it was the only thing I ever did on my own. Decided. And it came off right, like it was supposed to. [. . .] I birthed them and I got em out and it wasn't no accident. I did that" (162).

5. In her paper "Imagining a 'Third Thing': Morrison's View of Black Modernity," delivered at the Fifth Biennial Conference of the Toni Morrison Society in July 2008, Carolyn Denard discusses how Morrison's novels involve a regeneration of the self in three different phases: the reclaiming of the self (in *Beloved*), the engagement with another (in *Jazz*), and the engagement with community (in *Paradise*). She describes how Morrison moves toward creating something new without forgetting the past.

WORKS CITED

Adell, Sandra. *Double-Consciousness/Double Bind: Theoretical Issues in Twentieth-Century Black Literature.* Urbana: U of Illinois P, 1994.

Akhtar, Salman. *Broken Structures: Severe Personality Disorders and Their Treatment.* Northvale, NJ: Jason Aronson, 1992.

Alcorn, Marshall W., Jr. *Changing the Subject in English Class: Discourse and the Constructions of Desire.* Carbondale: Southern Illinois UP, 2002.

Alexander, Jeffrey C. "Toward a Theory of Cultural Trauma." Alexander et al. 1–29.

Alexander, Jeffrey C., Ron Eyerman, Bernhard Giesen, Neil J. Smelser, and Piotr Sztompka, eds. *Cultural Trauma and Collective Identity.* Berkeley and Los Angeles: U of California P, 2004.

Allen, Walter R. "The Dilemma Persists: Race, Class and Inequality in American Life." *"Race," Ethnicity and Nation: International Perspectives on Social Conflict.* Ed. Peter Ratcliffe. London: UCL, 1994. 48–67.

Antze, Paul, and Michael Lambek, eds. *Tense Past: Cultural Essays in Trauma and Memory.* New York: Routledge, 1996.

Arlow, Jacob A., MD. "Perspectives on Aggression in Human Adaptation." *Psychoanalytic Quarterly* 62.2 (1973): 178–84.

Awkward, Michael. *Inspiriting Influences: Tradition, Revision, and Afro-American Women's Novels.* New York: Columbia UP, 1989.

Badt, Karin Luisa. "The Roots of the Body in Toni Morrison: A *Mater* of 'Ancient Properties.'" *African American Review* 29.4 (1995): 567–77.

Baille, Justine. "Contesting Ideologies: Deconstructing Racism in African-American Fiction." *Women: A Cultural Review* 14.1 (2003): 20–36.

Bakerman, Jane S. "Failures of Love: Female Initiation in the Novels of Toni Morrison." *American Literature* 52.4 (1981): 542–63.

Ball, Karyn. "Introduction: Trauma and its Institutional Destinies." *Cultural Critique* 46 (Autumn 2000): 1–44.

Bate, Nancy Berkowitz. "Toni Morrison's *Beloved:* Psalm and Sacrament." Stave 26–70.

Benjamin, Jessica. *Psychoanalysis, Feminism, and the Problem of Domination.* New York: Pantheon, 1988.

Berger, James. *After the End: Representations of Post-Apocalypse.* Minneapolis: U of Minnesota P, 1999.

Bergner, Gwen. *Taboo Subjects: Race, Sex, and Psychoanalysis.* Minneapolis: U of Minnesota P, 2005.

Berry, Mary F., and John W. Blassingame. "Africa, Slavery, and the Roots of Contemporary Black Culture." *Chant of Saints: A Gathering of Afro-American Literature, Art, and Scholarship.* Ed. Michael S. Harper and Robert B. Stepto. Urbana: U of Illinois P, 1979. 241–56.

Billingslea-Brown, Alma Jean. *Crossing Borders through Folklore: African American Women's Fiction and Art.* Columbia: U of Missouri P, 1999.

Bjork, Patrick. *The Novels of Toni Morrison: The Search for Self and Place within the Community.* New York: Lang, 1992.

Boswell, Maia. "'Ladies,' 'Gentlemen,' and 'Colored': 'The Agency of (Lacan's Black) Letter' in the Outhouse." *Cultural Critique* 41 (Winter 1999): 108–38.

Boudreau, Brenda. "The Meaning of Selfhood in Toni Morrison's *Song of Solomon*." Carlacio 48–54.

Bourgois, Christian, ed. *Toni Morrison invitée au Louvre: Étranger chez soi.* Paris: Louvre, 2006.

Bouson, J. Brooks. *Quiet as It's Kept: Shame, Trauma, and Race in the Novels of Toni Morrison.* Albany: State U of New York P, 2000.

Bracher, Mark. *Lacan, Discourse, and Social Change: A Psychoanalytic Cultural Criticism.* Ithaca, NY: Cornell UP, 1993.

Branch, Eleanor. "Through the Maze of the Oedipal: Milkman's Search for Self in *Song of Solomon*." *Literature and Psychology* 41.1–2 (1995): 52–84.

Brenner, Charles. *An Elementary Textbook of Psychoanalysis.* New York: Doubleday, 1957.

Brenner, Gerry. "*Song of Solomon*: Rejecting Rank's Monomyth and Feminism." McKay 114–24.

Brogan, Kathleen. "American Stories of Cultural Haunting: Tales of Heirs and Ethnographers." *College English* 57.2 (1995): 149–65.

Brophy-Warren, Jamin. "A Writer's Vote: Toni Morrison on Her New Novel, Reading Her Critics and What Barack Obama's Win Means to Her." *Wall Street Journal Weekend Journal* 7 Nov. 2008: W5.

Brown, Joseph A. "To Cheer the Weary Traveler: Toni Morrison, William Faulkner, and History." *Mississippi Quarterly* 49.4 (1996): 709–26.

Brundage, W. Fitzhugh. *The Southern Past: A Clash of Race and Memory.* Cambridge, MA: Belknap–Harvard UP, 2005.

Burrows, Victoria. *Whiteness and Trauma: The Mother-Daughter Knot in the Fiction of Jean Rhys, Jamaica Kincaid and Toni Morrison.* New York: Palgrave, 2004.

Butler-Evans, Elliott. *Race, Gender, and Desire: Narrative Strategies in the Fiction of Toni Cade Bambara, Toni Morrison, and Alice Walker.* Philadelphia: Temple UP, 1989.

Byerman, Keith E. *Fingering the Jagged Grain: Tradition and Form in Recent Black Fiction.* Athens: U of Georgia P, 1985.

————. *Remembering the Past in Contemporary African American Fiction.* Chapel Hill: U of North Carolina P, 2005.

Carabi, Angels. "Interview with Toni Morrison on *Beloved.*" *Belles Lettres* 9.3 (1994): 38–48.

————. "Toni Morrison: The Novel Laureate Concludes Her Trilogy of Interviews with Angels Carabi by Musing on the Historical and Musical Background of Her Most Recent Novel *Jazz.*" *Belles Lettres* 10.2 (1995): 40–46.

Carden, Mary Paniccia. "Models of Memory and Romance: The Dual Endings of Toni Morrison's *Beloved.*" *Twentieth Century Literature* 45.4 (1999): 401–27.

Carlacio, Jami L., ed. *The Fiction of Toni Morrison: Reading and Writing on Race, Culture, and Identity.* Urbana, IL: NCTE, 2007.

Caruth, Cathy, ed. *Trauma: Explorations in Memory.* Baltimore: Johns Hopkins UP, 1980.

————. *Unclaimed Experience: Trauma, Narrative, and History.* Baltimore: Johns Hopkins UP, 1996.

Christian, Barbara. "'The Past Is Infinite': History and Myth in Toni Morrison's Trilogy." *Social Identities* 6.4 (2000): 411–28.

Christiansen, Annamarie. "Passing as the 'Tragic' Mulatto: Constructions of Hybridity in Toni Morrison's Novels." *Complicating Constructions: Race, Ethnicity, and Hybridity in American Texts.* Ed. David S. Goldstein and Audrey B. Thacker. Seattle: U of Washington P, 2007. 74–98.

Clark, Kenneth, and Mamie Clark. "Racial Identification and Preference in Negro Children." *Readings in Social Psychology.* Ed. Eleanor E. Macroby, Theodore M. Newcomb, and Eugene L. Hartley. London: Methuen, 1966. 169–78.

Clarke, Simon. *Social Theory, Psychoanalysis and Racism.* New York: Palgrave, 2003.

Clinton, Catherine. "'With a Whip in His Hand': Rape, Memory, and African-American Women." Fabre and O'Meally 205–17.

Collins, Patricia Hill. "Learning from the Outsider Within: The Sociological Significance of Black Feminist Thought." *Social Problems* 33.6 (1986) S14–S32.

Conner, Marc C., ed. *The Aesthetics of Toni Morrison: Speaking the Unspeakable.* Jackson: UP of Mississippi, 2000.

————. "From the Sublime to the Beautiful: The Aesthetic Progression of Toni Morrison." Conner 49–76.

————. "Wild Women and the Graceful Girls: Toni Morrison's Winter's Tale." *Nature, Woman, and the Art of Politics.* Ed. Eduardo A. Velasquez. New York: Rowman & Littlefield, 2000. 341–69.

Connerton, Paul. *How Societies Remember.* Cambridge: Cambridge UP, 1989.

Coonradt, Nicole M. "To Be Loved: Amy Denver and Human Need—Bridges to Understanding in Toni Morrison's *Beloved.*" *College Literature* 32.4 (2005): 168–83.

Cooper, Arnold M. "Toward a Limited Definition of Psychic Trauma." Rothstein 41–56.

Cormier-Hamilton, Patrice. "Black Naturalism and Toni Morrison: The Journey Away from Self-Love in *The Bluest Eye.*" *MELUS* 19.4 (1994): 109–27.

Cortina, Mauricio, and Giovanni Liotti. "Building on Attachment Theory: Toward a Mul-timotivational and Intersubjective Model of Human Nature." Annual meeting of the Rapaport-Klein Study Group. 11 June 2005.

Crombecque, Alain, ed. *Festival d'automne à Paris 14 septembre–19 décembre 2006*. 35th ed. Paris: Louvre, 2006.

Cummings, Kate. "Reclaiming the Mother('s) Tongue: *Beloved, Ceremony, Mothers and Shadows*." *College English* 52.5 (1990): 552–69.

Cutter, Martha J. "The Story Must Go On and On: The Fantastic, Narration, and Intertex-tuality in Toni Morrison's *Beloved* and *Jazz*." *African American Review* 34.1 (2000): 61–75.

Dalal, Farhad. *Race, Colour and the Processes of Racialization*. New York: Brunner-Rout-ledge, 2002.

Dalsgard, Katrine. "The One All-Black Town Worth the Pain: (African) American Excep-tionalism, Historical Narration, and the Critique of Nationhood in Toni Morrison's *Paradise*." *African American Review* 35.2 (2001): 233–48.

Daniels, Steven V. "Putting 'His Story Next to Hers': Choice, Agency, and the Structure of *Beloved*." *Texas Studies in Literature and Language* 44.4 (2002): 349–67.

Davidson, Rob. "Racial Stock and 8-Rocks: Communal Historiography in Toni Morri-son's *Paradise*." *Twentieth Century Literature* 47.3 (2001): 355–73.

Davis, Kimberly Chabot. "'Postmodern Blackness': Toni Morrison's *Beloved* and the End of History." *Twentieth Century Literature* 44.2 (1998): 242–60.

DeLancey, Dayle B. "Motherlove Is a Killer: *Sula, Beloved*, and the Deadly Trinity of Motherly Love." *Sage* 7.2 (Fall 1990): 15–18.

Demetrakopoulos, Stephanie. "Maternal Bonds as Devourers of Women's Individuation in Toni Morrison's *Beloved*." *African American Review* 26.1 (1992): 51–58.

Denard, Carolyn C. "Imagining a 'Third Thing': Morrison's View of Black Modernity." Fifth Biennial Conference of the Toni Morrison Society. Francis Marion Hotel, Charleston, SC. 27 July 2008.

———. "Interview with Toni Morrison." *Toni Morrison Society Newsletter* 6.2 (Fall 1999): 15, 4.

———, ed. *What Moves at the Margin: Selected Nonfiction of Toni Morrison*. Jackson: UP of Mississippi, 2008.

Douglas, Christopher. "What *The Bluest Eye* knows about Them: Culture, Race, Identity." *American Literature* 78.1 (2006): 141–68.

Doyle, Laura. "Bodies Inside/Out: Violation and Resistance from the Prison Cell to *The Bluest Eye*." *Feminist Interpretations of Maurice Merleau-Ponty*. Ed. Dorothea Olkowski and Gail Weiss. University Park: Pennsylvania State UP, 2006. 183–208.

Du Bois, W. E. B. *The Souls of Black Folk*. New York: Library of America, 1990.

Durrant, Sam. *Postcolonial Narrative and the Work of Mourning*. Albany: State U of New York P, 2004.

Duvall, John N. "Descent in the 'House of Chloe': Race, Rape, and Identity in Toni Morrison's *Tar Baby.*" *Contemporary Literature* 38.2 (1997): 325–49.

———. *The Identifying Fictions of Toni Morrison: Modernist Authenticity and Postmodern Blackness.* New York: Palgrave, 2000.

Eisen, Andrew R., and Charles E. Schaefer. *Separation Anxiety in Children and Adolescents: An Individualized Approach to Assessment and Treatment.* New York: Guilford, 2005.

Elia, Nada. *Trances, Dances, and Vociferations: Agency and Resistance in Africana Women's Narratives.* New York: Garland, 2001.

Elliott, Mary Jane Suero. "Postcolonial Experience in a Domestic Context: Commodified Subjectivity in Toni Morrison's *Beloved.*" *MELUS* 25.3–4 (2000): 181–202.

Erikson, Erik H. "The Problem of Ego Identity." *Journal of the American Psychoanalytic Association* 4 (1956): 56–121.

Erikson, Kai. "Notes on Trauma and Community." Caruth, *Trauma* 183–99.

Eyerman, Ron. "Cultural Trauma: Slavery and the Formation of African American Identity." Alexander et al. 60–111.

Fabre, Genevieve. "Genealogical Archeology or the Quest for Legacy in Toni Morrison's *Song of Solomon.*" McKay 105–14.

Fabre, Genevieve, and Robert O'Meally, eds. *History and Memory in African-American Culture.* Oxford: Oxford UP, 1994.

Fanon, Frantz. *Black Skin, White Masks.* Trans. Charles Lam Markmann. London: MacGibbon & Ker, 1968.

Felman, Shoshana, and Dori Laub. *Testimony: Crises of Witnessing in Literature, Psychoanalysis, and History.* New York: Routledge, 1992.

Ferguson, Rebecca Hope. *Rewriting Black Identities: Transition and Exchange in the Novels of Toni Morrison.* Brussels: Lang, 2007.

Finck, Sylviane. "Reading Trauma in Postmodern and Postcolonial Literature: Charlotte Delbo, Toni Morrison, and the Literary Imagination of the Aftermath." Diss. Louisiana State U and Agricultural & Mechanical College, 2006.

Fleischner, Jennifer. *Mastering Slavery: Memory, Family and Identity in Women's Slave Narratives.* New York: New York UP, 1996.

Flint, Holly. "Toni Morrison's *Paradise:* Black Cultural Citizenship in the American Empire." *American Literature* 78.3 (2006): 585–612.

Foster, Dennis A. "Trauma and Memory." *Contemporary Literature* 61.4 (2000): 740–47.

Fox-Genovese, Elizabeth. *Within the Plantation Household.* Chapel Hill: U of North Carolina P, 1988.

Franco, Dean. "What We Talk About When We Talk About *Beloved.*" *Modern Fiction Studies* 52.2 (2006): 415–39.

Friedlander, Saul, ed. *Probing the Limits of Representation: Nazism and the "Final Solution."* Cambridge, MA: Harvard UP, 1992.

Fultz, Lucille P. *Toni Morrison: Playing with Difference.* Urbana: U of Illinois P, 2003.

Furman, Jan. "Sethe's Re-memories: The Covert Return of What Is Best Forgotten." *Critical Essays on Toni Morrison's* Beloved. Ed. Barbara H. Solomon. New York: G. K. Hall, 1998. 261–71.

Furst, Sidney S. "Psychic Trauma and Its Reconstruction with Particular Reference to Post Childhood Trauma." Rothstein 29–39.

Galehouse, Maggie. "'New World Woman': Toni Morrison's *Sula.*" *PLL* 35.4 (1999): 339–62.

Gallego, Mar. "*Love* and the Survival of the Black Community." Tally, *Cambridge* 92–100.

Gillan, Jennifer. "Focusing on the Wrong Front: Historical Displacement, the Maginot Line, and *The Bluest Eye.*" *African American Review* 36.2 (2002): 283–98.

Gould, Rosalind. "Studies of Aggression in Early Childhood: Patterns of Attachment and Efficacy." *Psychoanalytic Inquiry* 2.1 (1982): 21–52.

Grant, Robert. "Absence into Presence: The Thematics of Memory and 'Missing' Subjects in Toni Morrison's *Sula.*" McKay 90–103.

Green, Marci, and Marc Scholes, eds. *Attachment and Human Survival.* London: Karnac, 2004.

Grewal, Gurleen. "Memory and the Matrix of History: The Poetics of Loss and Recovery in Joy Kogwa's *Obasan* and Toni Morrison's *Beloved.*" Singh, Skerrett, and Hogan, *Memory and Cultural Politics* 140–74.

Guerrero, Edward. "Tracking 'The Look' in the Novels of Toni Morrison." *Black American Literature Forum* 24.4 (1990): 763–73.

Gump, Janice. "Reality Matters: The Shadow of Trauma on African American Subjectivity." Celebration of J. D. Lichtenberg, Institute of Contemporary Psychotherapy and Psychoanalysis, Washington, DC. 11 Oct. 2000.

Guth, Deborah. "A Blessing and a Burden: The Relation to the Past in *Sula, Song of Solomon* and *Beloved.*" *Modern Fiction Studies* 39.4 (1993): 575–94.

Haaken, Janice. "The Recovery of Memory, Fantasy, and Desire: Feminist Approaches to Sexual Abuse and Psychic Trauma." *Signs* 21.4 (1996): 1069–94.

Hall, Cheryl. "Beyond the 'Literary Habit': Oral Tradition and Jazz in *Beloved.*" *MELUS* 19.1 (1994): 89–95.

Hall, Jacquelyn Dowd. *Revolt Against Chivalry: Jessie Daniel Ames and the Women's Campaign Against Lynching.* New York: Columbia UP, 1979.

Harding, Wendy, and Jacky Martin. *A World of Difference: An Inter-Cultural Study of Toni Morrison's Novels.* Westport, CT: Greenwood, 1994.

Hartman, Saidiya V. *Scenes of Subjection: Terror, Slavery, and Self-Making in Nineteenth-Century America.* New York: Oxford UP, 1997.

Hawthorne, Evelyn. "On Gaining the Double-Vision: *Tar Baby* as Diasporean Novel." *Black American Literature Forum* 22.1 (1988): 97–107.

Heinze, Denise. *The Dilemma of "Double-Consciousness": Toni Morrison's Novels.* Athens: U of Georgia P, 1993.

Henderson, Carol E. "Refiguring the Flesh: The Word, the Body, and the Rituals of Being in *Beloved* and *Go Tell It on The Mountain*." King and Scott 149–65.

Herman, Judith, MD. *Trauma and Recovery: The Aftermath of Violence—from Domestic Abuse to Political Terror.* New York: Basic Books, 1997.

Hesse, Erik, and Mary Main. "Second-Generation Effects of Unresolved Trauma in Non-maltreating Parents: Dissociated, Frightened, and Threatening Parental Behavior." *Psychoanalytic Inquiry* 19.4 (1999): 481–540.

Hesse, Erik, Mary Main, Kelley Yost Abrams, and Anne Rifkin. "Unresolved States Regarding Loss or Abuse Can Have 'Second-Generation' Effects: Disorganization, Role Inversion, and Frightening Ideation in the Offspring of Traumatized, Non-Maltreating Parents." Solomon and Siegel 57–106.

Hilfrich, Carola. "Anti-Exodus: Countermemory, Gender, Race, and Everyday Life in Toni Morrison's *Paradise*." *Modern Fiction Studies* 52.2 (2006): 322–49.

Hogue, Bev. "Naming the Bones: Bodies of Knowledge in Contemporary Fiction." *Modern Fiction Studies* 52.1 (2006): 122–42.

Holden-Kirwan, Jennifer L. "Looking Into the Self That Is No Self: An Examination of Subjectivity in *Beloved*." *African American Review* 32.3 (1998): 415–26.

Holloway, Karla F. C. "Revision and (Re)membrance: A Theory of Literary Structures in Literature by African-American Women Writers." *Black American Literature Forum* 24.4 (1990): 617–31.

hooks, bell. *Black Looks: Race and Representation.* London: Turnaround, 1992.

———. *Killing Rage.* New York: Holt, 1995.

Hubbard, Dolan. "In Quest of Authority: Toni Morrison's *Song of Solomon* and the Rhetoric of the Black Preacher." *CLA Journal* 35 (1992): 288–302.

Jackson, Chuck. "A 'Headless Display': *Sula*, Soldiers, and Lynching." *Modern Fiction Studies* 52.2 (2006): 374–92.

Jaffe, Daniel S. "Aggression: Instinct, Drive, Behavior." *Psychoanalytic Inquiry* 2.1 (1982): 77–94.

Jenkins, Candice M. "Pure Black: Class, Color, and Intraracial Politics in Toni Morrison's *Paradise*." *Modern Fiction Studies* 52.2 (2006): 270–96.

Jennings, La Vinia Delois. *Toni Morrison and the Idea of Africa.* Cambridge: Cambridge UP, 2008.

Jessee, Sharon. "'Tell me your earrings': Time and the Marvelous in Toni Morrison's *Beloved*." Singh, Skerrett, and Hogan, *Memory, Narrative, and Identity* 198–211.

Jesser, Nancy. "Violence, Home, and Community in Toni Morrison's *Beloved*." *African American Review* 33.2 (1999): 325–45.

Jimoh, A. Yemisi. *Spiritual, Blues, and Jazz People in African American Fiction.* Knoxville: U of Tennessee P, 2002.

Johnson, Michael K. "Teaching *Paradise*: Race, Justice, Violence, and the American West." Carlacio 166–76.

Jones, Carolyn M. "*Sula* and *Beloved:* Images of Cain in the Novels of Toni Morrison." *African American Review* 27.4 (1993): 615–27.

Jones, Gayl. *Liberating Voices: Oral Tradition in African American Literature.* Cambridge, MA: Harvard UP, 1991.

Jones, Jacqueline. *Labor of Love, Labor of Sorrow: Black Women, Work, and the Family from Slavery to the Present.* New York: Basic Books, 1985.

Jones, LeRoi. *Blues People: Negro Music in White America.* New York: Morrow, 1963.

King, Lovalerie, and Lynn Orilla Scott, eds. *James Baldwin and Toni Morrison: Comparative Critical and Theoretical Essays.* New York: Palgrave Macmillan, 2006.

King-Pedroso, Natalie. "P/plantation Politics in Toni Morrison's *Tar Baby.*" Carlacio 85–93.

Klotman, Phyllis R. "Dick-and-Jane and the Shirley Temple Sensibility in *The Bluest Eye.*" *Black American Literature Forum* 13.4 (1979): 123–25.

Kolmerten, Carol A., Stephen M. Ross, and Judith Bryant Wittenberg, eds. *Unflinching Gaze: Morrison and Faulkner Re-envisioned.* Jackson: UP of Mississippi, 1997.

Koolish, Lynda. "'To Be Loved and Cry Shame': A Psychological Reading of Toni Morrison's *Beloved.*" *MELUS* 26.4 (2001): 169–95.

Krumholz, Linda. "The Ghosts of Slavery: Historical Recovery in Toni Morrison's *Beloved.*" *African American Review* 26.3 (1992): 395–408.

Kuenz, Jane. "*The Bluest Eye:* Notes on History, Community, and Black Female Subjectivity." *African American Review* 7.3 (1993): 421–31.

Lacan, Jacques. *Écrits: A Selection.* Trans. Alan Sheridan. New York: Norton, 1977.

———. *Four Fundamental Concepts of Psycho-Analysis.* Ed. Jacques-Alain Miller. Trans. Alan Sheridan. New York: Norton, 1981.

———. *The Seminar of Jacques Lacan: Book II, The Ego in Freud's Theory and in the Technique of Psychoanalysis, 1954–1955.* Ed. Jacques-Alain Miller. Trans. Sylvana Tomaselli. New York: Norton, 1991.

LaCapra, Dominick. *Writing History, Writing Trauma.* Baltimore: Johns Hopkins UP, 2001.

Laub, Dori. "Bearing Witness or the Vicissitudes of Listening." Felman and Laub 57–74.

———. "An Event Without a Witness: Truth, Testimony and Survival." Felman and Laub 75–92.

Lee, Catherine Carr. "The South in Toni Morrison's *Song of Solomon:* Initiation, Healing, and Home." *Studies in Literary Imagination* 31.2 (1998): 109–23.

Lepow, Lauren. "Paradise Lost and Found: Dualism and Edenic Myth in Toni Morrison's *Tar Baby.*" *Contemporary Literature* 28.3 (1987): 363–77.

Leuzinger-Bohleber, Marianne, and Rolf Pfeifer. "Remembering a Depressive Primary Object: Memory in the Dialogue between Psychoanalysis and Cognitive Science." *International Journal of Psychoanalysis* 83.3 (2002): 3–33.

Lucas, Marion Brunson. *A History of Blacks in Kentucky.* Frankfort: Kentucky Historical Society, 2003.

MacArthur, Kathleen Laura. "The Things We Carry: Trauma and the Aesthetic in the Contemporary United States Novel." Diss. George Washington U, 2005.

Marks, Kathleen. *Toni Morrison's* Beloved *and the Apotropaic Imagination.* Columbia: U of Missouri P, 2002.

Marriott, David. "Bonding Over Phobia." *The Psychoanalysis of Race.* Ed. Christopher Lane. New York: Columbia UP, 1998. 417–30.

Mason, Theodore O. Jr. "The Novelist as Conservator: Stories and Comprehension in Toni Morrison's *Song of Solomon.*" *Contemporary Literature* 29.4 (1988): 564–81.

Mathieson, Barbara Offutt. "Memory and Mother Love: Toni Morrison's Dyad." Singh, Skerrett, and Hogan, *Memory, Narrative, and Identity* 212–32.

Matus, Jill. *Toni Morrison.* Manchester: Manchester UP, 1998.

Mayberry, Susan Neal. *Can't I Love What I Criticize? The Masculine and Morrison.* Athens: U of Georgia P, 2007.

———. "Something Other Than a Family Quarrel: The Beautiful Boys in Morrison's *Sula.*" *African American Review* 37.4 (2003): 517–33.

Mbalia, Doreatha Drummond. *Toni Morrison's Developing Class Consciousness.* London: Associated UP, 1991.

M'Baye, Babacar. "Resistance Against Racial, Sexual, and Social Oppression in *Go Tell It on the Mountain* and *Beloved.*" King and Scott 167–86.

McDougall, Joyce. "Parent Loss." Rothstein 135–51.

McDowell, Deborah E. "'The Self and the Other': Reading Toni Morrison's *Sula* and the Black Female Text." *Toni Morrison.* Ed. Harold Bloom. New York: Chelsea, 1990. 149–63.

McDowell, Deborah E., and Arnold Rampersad. Introduction. McDowell and Rampersad, *Slavery* vii–xiii.

———, eds. *Slavery and the Literary Imagination: Selected Papers from the English Institute, 1987.* Baltimore: Johns Hopkins UP, 1989.

McKay, Nellie Y., ed. *Critical Essays on Toni Morrison.* Boston: G. K. Hall, 1988.

McKee, Patricia. *Producing American Races: Henry James, William Faulkner, Toni Morrison.* Durham, NC: Duke UP, 1999.

McKittrick, Katherine. "'Black and 'Cause I'm Black I'm Blue': Transverse Racial Geographies in Toni Morrison's *The Bluest Eye.*" *Gender, Place, and Culture* 7.2 (2000): 125–42.

Medoro, Dana. "Justice and Citizenship in Toni Morrison's *Song of Solomon.*" *Canadian Review of American Studies* 32.1 (2002): 1–13.

Mermann-Jozwiak, Elisabeth. "Re-membering the Body: Body Politics in Toni Morrison's *The Bluest Eye.*" *LIT: Literature Interpretation Theory* 12.2 (2001): 189–203.

Michael, Magali Cornier. *New Visions of Community in Contemporary American Fiction: Tan, Kingsolver, Castillo, Morrison.* Iowa City: U of Iowa P, 2006.

———. "Re-Imagining Agency: Toni Morrison's *Paradise.*" *African American Review* 36.4 (2002): 643–61.

Middleton, Joyce Irene. "Orality, Literacy, and Memory in Toni Morrison's *Song of Solomon.*" *College English* 55.1 (1993): 64–75.

Mikkelsen, Nina. "Diamonds within Diamonds within Diamonds: Ethnic Literature and the Fractal Aesthetic." *MELUS* 27.2 (2002): 95–116.

Miller, Matthew L. "Literary Witnessing: Working through Trauma in Toni Morrison, Nuruddin Farah, Wilson Harris, and Chang-Rae Lee." Diss. U of South Carolina, 2005.

Mobley, Marilyn Sanders. "Call and Response: Voice, Community, and Dialogic Structures in Toni Morrison's *Song of Solomon.*" *New Essays on Song of Solomon.* Ed. Valerie Smith. Cambridge: Cambridge UP, 1995. 41–68.

———. *Folk Roots and Mythic Wings in Sarah Orne Jewett and Toni Morrison.* Baton Rouge: Louisiana State UP, 1991.

Mori, Aoi. *Toni Morrison and Womanist Discourse.* New York: Lang, 1999.

Morrison, Toni. *Beloved.* 1987. New York: Penguin, 1988.

———. *The Bluest Eye.* 1970. New York: Plume, 1994.

———. "'The Foreigner's Home': Introduction." Louvre Museum Auditorium, Paris, 6 Nov. 2006.

———. "'Harlem on My Mind': Contesting Memory—Meditations on Museums, Culture and Integration." Louvre Museum Auditorium, Paris, 15 Nov. 2006.

———. "Home." *The House That Race Built.* Ed. Wahneema Lubiano. New York: Vintage, 1998. 3–12.

———. *Jazz.* 1992. New York: Penguin, 1993.

———. *Lecture and Speech of Acceptance, Upon the Award of the Nobel Prize for Literature, Delivered in Stockholm on the Seventh of December, Nineteen Hundred and Ninety-three.* 1993. New York: Knopf, 2000.

———. *Love.* 2003. New York: Vintage International, 2005.

———. *A Mercy.* New York: Knopf, 2008.

———. *Paradise.* 1997. New York: Penguin, 1999.

———. *Playing in the Dark: Whiteness and the Literary Imagination.* 1992. New York: Vintage, 1993.

———. "Rootedness: The Ancestor as Foundation." *The Woman That I Am: The Literature and Culture of Contemporary Women of Color.* Ed. D. Soyini Madison. New York: St. Martin's, 1994. 492–97.

———. "The Site of Memory." *Inventing the Truth: The Art and Craft of Memoir.* Ed. William Zinsser. Boston: Houghton Mifflin, 1987. 103–24.

———. *Song of Solomon.* 1977. New York: Penguin, 1987.

———. *Sula.* 1973. New York: Penguin, 1982.

———. *Tar Baby.* 1981. New York: Penguin, 1982.

———. "Unspeakable Things Unspoken: The Afro-American Presence in American Literature." *Michigan Quarterly Review* 28 (1989): 1–34.

———. "Writing Lyrics." Louvre Museum Auditorium, Paris, 26 Nov. 2006.

Moses, Cat. "The Blues Aesthetic in Toni Morrison's *The Bluest Eye*." *African American Review* 33.4 (1999): 623–36.

Murray, Rolland. "The Long Strut: *Song of Solomon* and the Emancipatory Limits of the Black Patriarchy." *Callaloo* 22.1 (1999): 121–33.

Neumann, Erich. *Depth Psychology and a New Ethic*. Trans. Eugene Rolfe. Boston: Shambhala, 1990.

Nowlin, Michael. "Toni Morrison's *Jazz* and the Racial Dreams of the American Writer." *American Literature* 71.1 (1999): 151–74.

O'Reilly, Andrea. "In Search of My Mother's Garden I Found My Own: Mother-Love, Healing, and Identity in Toni Morrison's *Jazz*." *African American Review* 30.3 (1996): 367–79.

———. *Toni Morrison and Motherhood: A Politics of the Heart*. Albany: State U of New York P, 2004.

Osagie, Iyunolu. "Is Morrison Also Among the Prophets?: 'Psychoanalytic' Strategies in *Beloved*." *African American Review* 28.3 (1994): 423–40.

Otten, Terry. *The Crime of Innocence in the Fiction of Toni Morrison*. Columbia: U of Missouri P, 1989.

Page, Philip. *Dangerous Freedom: Fusion and Fragmentation in Toni Morrison's Novels*. Jackson: UP of Mississippi, 1995.

———. "Furrowing All the Brows: Interpretation and the Transcendent in Toni Morrison's *Paradise*." *African American Review* 35.4 (2001): 637–49.

Paquet, Sandra Pouchet. "The Ancestor as Foundation in *Their Eyes Were Watching God* and *Tar Baby*." *Callaloo* 13.3 (1990): 499–515.

Paquet-Deyris, Anne-Marie. "Toni Morrison's *Jazz* and the City." *African American Review* 35.2 (2001): 219–31.

Parker, Emma. "'Apple Pie' Ideology and the Politics of Appetite in the Novels of Toni Morrison." *Contemporary Literature* 39.4 (1998): 614–43.

———. "A New Hystery: History and Hysteria in Toni Morrison's *Beloved*." *Twentieth Century Literature* 47.1 (2001): 1–19.

Patell, Cyrus R. K. *Negative Liberties: Morrison, Pynchon, and the Problem of Liberal Ideology*. Durham, NC: Duke UP, 2001.

Pereira, Malin Walther. "Periodizing Toni Morrison's Work from *The Bluest Eye* to *Jazz*: The Importance of *Tar Baby*." *MELUS* 22.3 (1997): 71–82.

Pessoni, Michele. "'She was laughing at their god': Discovering the goddess within *Sula*." *African American Review* 29.3 (1995): 439–51.

Peterson, Nancy J. Beloved: *Character Studies*. London: Continuum, 2008.

Phillips, Michelle H. "Revising Revision: Methodologies of Love, Desire, and Resistance in *Beloved* and *If Beale Street Could Talk*." King and Scott 62–81.

Ramadanovic, Petar. *Forgetting Futures: On Memory, Trauma, and Identity*. Lanham, MD: Lexington, 2001.

Rampersad, Arnold. "Slavery and the Literary Imagination: Du Bois's *The Souls of Black Folk*." McDowell and Rampersad, *Slavery* 104–24.

Raynaud, Claudine. "*Beloved* or the Shifting Shapes of Memory." Tally, *Cambridge* 43–58.

Rayson, Ann. "Foreign Exotic or Domestic Drudge? The African American Women in *Quicksand* and *Tar Baby*." *MELUS* 23.2 (1998): 87–100.

Rigney, Barbara Hill. *The Voices of Toni Morrison*. Columbus: Ohio State UP, 1991.

Rody, Caroline. "Toni Morrison's *Beloved*: History, 'Rememory,' and a 'Clamor for a Kiss.'" *American Literary History* 7.1 (1995): 92–119.

Rokotnitz, Naomi. "Constructing Cognitive Scaffolding through Embodied Receptiveness: Toni Morrison's *The Bluest Eye*." *Style* 41.4 (2007): 385–408.

Rosenberg, Ruth. "Seeds in Hard Ground: Black Girlhood in *The Bluest Eye*." *Black American Literature Forum* 21.4 (1987): 435–45.

Rosenblatt, Paul C., and Beverly R. Wallace. *African American Grief*. New York: Routledge, 2005.

Rothberg, Michael. "Dead Letter Office: Conspiracy, Trauma, and *Song of Solomon*'s Posthumous Communication." *African American Review* 37.4 (2003): 501–16.

Rothstein, Arnold, MD, ed. *The Reconstruction of Trauma: Its Significance in Clinical Work*. Madison, CT: International Universities Press, 1986.

Rubenstein, Roberta. "History and Story, Sign and Design: Faulknerian and Postmodern Voices in *Jazz*." *Unflinching Gaze: Morrison and Faulkner Re-Envisioned*. Ed. Carol A. Kolmerten, Stephen M. Ross, and Judith Bryant Wittenberg. Jackson: UP of Mississippi, 1997. 152–64.

Rudwick, Elliott. *Race Riot at East St. Louis*. Chicago: U of Illinois P, 1982.

Ruisz, Melissa Ann. "Parting the Shadowy Veil: Trauma, Testimony, and Shadow in Toni Morrison's *Beloved*." MA thesis. U of Texas at El Paso, 2006.

Rushdy, Ashraf H. A. "Daughters Signifyin(g) History: The Example of Toni Morrison's *Beloved*." *American Literature* 64.3 (1992): 567–97.

———. "'Rememory': Primal Scenes and Constructions in Toni Morrison's Novels." *Contemporary Literature* 31.3 (1990): 300–323.

Ryan, Judylyn S. *Spirituality as Ideology in Black Women's Film and Literature*. Charlottesville: U of Virginia P, 2005.

Sabol, Jonathan Daniel. "Memory, History, and Identity: The Trauma Narrative in Contemporary North American and British Fiction." Diss. Fordham U, 2007.

Schore, Allan N. "Early Relational Trauma, Disorganized Attachment, and the Development of a Predisposition to Violence." Solomon and Siegel 107–67.

Schreiber, Evelyn Jaffe. *Subversive Voices: Eroticizing the Other in William Faulkner and Toni Morrison*. Knoxville: U of Tennessee P, 2002.

Schur, Richard L. "Locating *Paradise* in the Post–Civil Rights Era: Toni Morrison and Critical Race Theory." *Contemporary Literature* 45.2 (2004): 276–99.

Seshadri-Crooks, Kalpana. *Desiring Whiteness: A Lacanian Analysis of Race*. London: Routledge, 2000.

Shange, Ntozake. "Interview with Toni Morrison." *American Rag*, Nov. 1978, 48–52.

Siegel, Daniel J. "Attachment and Self-Understanding: Parenting with the Brain in Mind." Green and Scholes 21–35.

———. "An Interpersonal Neurobiology of Psychotherapy: The Developing Mind and the Resolution of Trauma." Solomon and Siegel 1–56.

Silverman, Kaja. *The Threshold of the Visible World.* New York: Routledge, 1996.

Simpson, Ritashona. *Black Looks and Black Acts: The Language of Toni Morrison in* The Bluest Eye *and* Beloved. New York: Lang, 2007.

Singh, Amritjit, Joseph T. Skerrett Jr., and Robert E. Hogan, eds. *Memory and Cultural Politics: New Approaches to American Ethnic Literatures.* Boston: Northeastern UP, 1996.

———. *Memory, Narrative, and Identity: New Essays in Ethnic American Literatures.* Boston: Northeastern UP, 1994.

Smith, Valerie. *Self Discovery and Authority in Afro-American Narrative.* Cambridge, MA: Harvard UP, 1987.

Solomon, Marion F., and Daniel J. Siegel, eds. *Healing Trauma: Attachment, Mind, Body, and Brain.* New York: Norton, 2003.

Stave, Shirley A., ed. *Toni Morrison and the Bible: Contested Intertextualities.* New York: Lang, 2006.

Stepto, Robert. "Intimate Things in Place: A Conversation with Toni Morrison." *Conversations with Toni Morrison.* Ed. Danille Taylor-Guthrie. Jackson: UP of Mississippi, 1994. 10–29.

Storhoff, Gary. "'Anaconda Love': Parental Enmeshment in Toni Morrison's *Song of Solomon.*" *Style* 31.2 (1997): 290–309.

Suranyi, Agnes. "*The Bluest Eye* and *Sula:* Black Female Experience from Childhood to Womanhood." Tally, *Cambridge* 11–25.

Tally, Justine, ed. *The Cambridge Companion to Toni Morrison.* Cambridge: Cambridge UP, 2007.

———. *The Story of* Jazz: *Toni Morrison's Dialogic Imagination.* Hamburg: Lit, 2001.

———. *Toni Morrison's (Hi)stories and Truths.* Hamburg: Lit, 1999.

Tate, Claudia. *Psychoanalysis and Black Novels: Desire and the Protocols of Race.* New York: Oxford UP, 1998.

Tettenhorn, Eva. "Empowering the Past: Mourning and Melancholia in Twentieth-Century African American Literature." Diss. State U of New York, 2002.

Thomas, Leester. "When Home Fails to Nurture the Self: Tragedy of Being Homeless at Home." *Western Journal of Black Studies* 21.1 (1997): 51–58.

Thompson, Bob. "Windows to the Soulful." *Washington Post* 4 Dec. 2008: C1, C4.

Timothy, Ellen L. "Individuation and the Paradox of Love: Toni Morrison's Pedagogy of Transformation and Healing." Diss. University of Washington, 2004.

Traylor, Eleanor W. "The Fabulous World of Toni Morrison: *Tar Baby.*" McKay 135–50.

Ubois, Lynette Marie. *"When the Old Time Go": Historical Trauma as Family Narrative in Faulkner, Rhys, Erdrich, and Morrison.* Diss. University of California, Berkeley, 2007.

Van der Kolk, Bessel A. "Trauma, Neuroscience, and the Etiology of Hysteria: An Exploration of the Relevance of Breuer and Freud's 1893 Article in Light of Modern Science." *Journal of the American Academy of Psychoanalysis* 28 (2000): 237–62.

Van der Kolk, Bessel A., and Onno Van der Hart. "The Intrusive Past: The Flexibility of Memory and the Engraving of Trauma." Caruth, *Trauma* 158–82.

Vickroy, Laurie. "The Politics of Abuse: The Traumatized Child in Toni Morrison and Marguerite Duras." *Mosaic: A Journal for the Interdisciplinary Study of Literature* 29.2 (1996): 91–109.

Volkan, Vamik. *Blind Trust: Large Groups and Their Leaders in Times of Crisis and Terror.* Charlottesville, VA: Pitchstone, 2004.

Wald, Priscilla. *Constituting Americans: Cultural Anxiety and Narrative Form.* Durham, NC: Duke UP, 1995.

Wall, Cheryl A. "Resounding *Souls:* Du Bois and the African American Literary Tradition." *Public Culture* 17.2 (2005): 217–34.

Walther, Malin LaVon. "Out of Sight: Toni Morrison's Revision of Beauty." *Black American Literature Forum* 24.4 (1990): 775–89.

Wardi, Anissa Janine. "A Laying On of Hands: Toni Morrison and the Materiality of Love." *MELUS* 30.3 (2005): 201–18.

Weinstein, Philip M. *What Else But Love?: The Ordeal of Race in Faulkner and Morrison.* New York: Columbia UP, 1996.

Werner, Craig. "The Briar Patch as Modernist Myth: Morrison, Barthes and Tar Baby As-Is." McKay 150–67.

Werrlein, Debra T. "Not So Fast, Dick and Jane: Reimagining Childhood and Nation in *The Bluest Eye.*" *MELUS* 30.4 (2005): 53–72.

Wilkerson, Margaret B. "The Dramatic Voice in Toni Morrison's Novels." McKay 179–90.

Williamson, Joel. *The Crucible of Race.* New York: Oxford UP, 1984.

Woodward, Joan. "Introduction to Attachment Theory." Green and Scholes 7–20.

Woodward, Kathleen. "Traumatic Shame: Toni Morrison, Televisual Culture, and the Cultural Politics of the Emotions." *Cultural Critique* 46 (2000): 210–40.

Wright, George C. *Racial Violence in Kentucky, 1865–1940.* Baton Rouge: Louisiana State UP, 1990.

Wyatt, Jean. *Risking Difference: Identification, Race, and Community in Contemporary Fiction and Feminism.* New York: State U of New York P, 2004.

Young, Allan. "Bodily Memory and Traumatic Memory." Antze and Lambek 89–102.

Yukins, Elizabeth. "Bastard Daughters and the Possession of History in *Corregidora* and *Paradise.*" *Signs* 28.1 (2002): 221–47.

Žižek, Slavoj. *For They Know Not What They Do: Enjoyment as a Political Factor.* London: Verso, 2002.

———. *The Sublime Object of Ideology.* London: Verso, 1995.

INDEX